TIPI

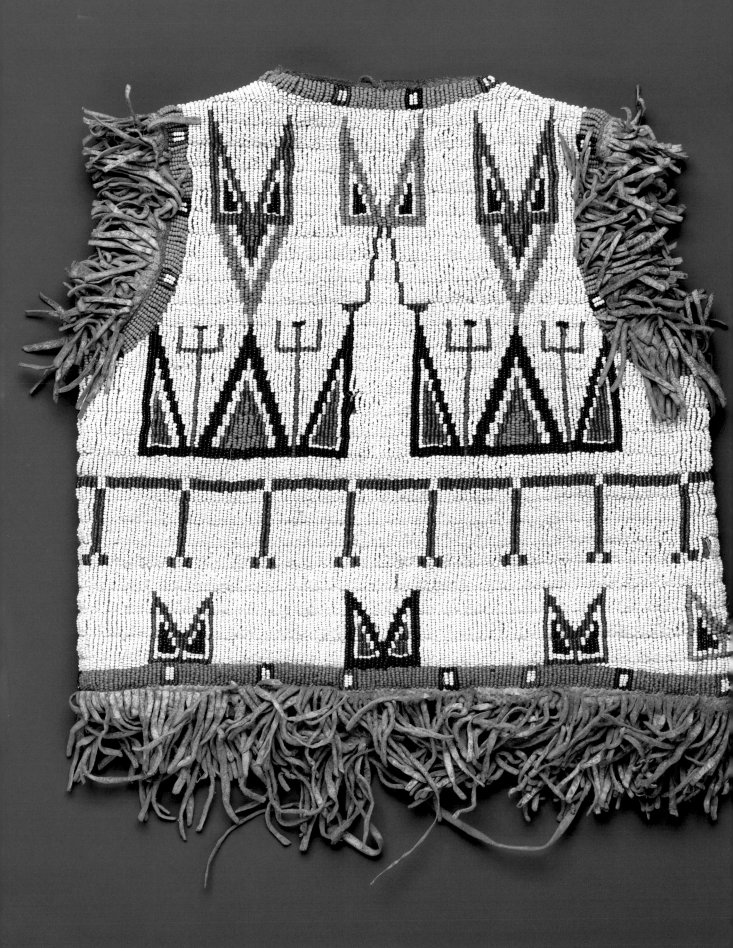

EDITED BY

NANCY B. ROSOFF

SUSAN KENNEDY ZELLER

TIPI

Heritage of the Great Plains

BROOKLYN MUSEUM

IN ASSOCIATION WITH

UNIVERSITY OF WASHINGTON PRESS SEATTLE AND LONDON

Published on the occasion of the exhibition *Tipi: Heritage of the Great Plains*, organized by the Brooklyn Museum.

Tipi: Heritage of the Great Plains is sponsored by American Express. Generous support is provided by the Barbara and Richard Debs Exhibition Fund, the National Endowment for the Humanities, the National Endowment for the Arts, and the Bay and Paul Foundations.

EXHIBITION ITINERARY

Brooklyn Museum
February 18–May 15, 2011

Autry National Center of the American West, Los Angeles
June 17–September 11, 2011

Minnesota History Center, Minnesota Historical Society, St. Paul
Spring 2012

LIBRARY OF CONGRESS CATALOGING-IN-PUBLICATION DATA

Tipi : heritage of the Great Plains /
edited by Nancy B. Rosoff, Susan Kennedy Zeller.
p. cm.
"Published on the occasion of the exhibition Tipi : Heritage of the Great Plains, organized by the Brooklyn Museum"—T.p. verso.
Includes bibliographical references and index.
ISBN 978-0-295-99077-4 (cloth : alk. paper)
ISBN 978-0-87273-166-0 (paper : alk. paper)
1. Tipis—Great Plains—Exhibitions. 2. Indians of North America—Dwellings—Great Plains—Exhibitions. 3. Indians of North America—Great Plains—Social life and customs—Exhibitions. 4. Great Plains—Social life and customs—Exhibitions. I. Rosoff, Nancy B. II. Kennedy Zeller, Susan. III. Brooklyn Museum.
E98.D9T57 2011
978.004'97—dc22
2010022208

Design by Ashley Saleeba
Printed in China
18 17 16 15 14 13 12 11   9 8 7 6 5 4 3 2 1

FOR THE BROOKLYN MUSEUM

James D. Leggio, Head of Publications and Editorial Services
Project Editor: Joanna Ekman
Copyeditor: Polly Cone
Indexer: Barbara E. Cohen
New photography of Brooklyn Museum objects by Sarah Kraemer and Christine Gant; digitization of historic images of Brooklyn Museum objects by Althea Morin, Digital Collections and Services, Brooklyn Museum

BROOKLYN MUSEUM

200 Eastern Parkway, Brooklyn, NY 11238-6052, U.S.A.
www.brooklynmuseum.org

UNIVERSITY OF WASHINGTON PRESS

P.O. Box 50095, Seattle, WA 98145, U.S.A.
www.washington.edu/uwpress

Cover: detail of fig. 36; back cover: detail of back of fig. 42; frontispiece: back of fig. 171; p. vi: detail of fig. 119; p. xvi: detail of fig. 23; p. 2: Tipis at sunset, Crow Fair, Montana, 2007 (Photo: Susan Kennedy Zeller); p. 36: detail of fig. 49; p. 38: detail of fig. 59; p. 56: Lower Brule Administration Building (Photo: Dan Feidt); p. 68: Crow Fair parade float, 2008 (Photo: Susan Kennedy Zeller); p. 76: detail of fig. 74; p. 98: detail of fig. 95; p. 106: Souvenir shop, Cherry Valley, New York, 2007 (Photo: Susan Kennedy Zeller); p. 116: detail of fig. 133; p. 118: detail of fig. 128; p. 140: detail of fig. 132; p. 144: detail of fig. 134; p. 164: detail of fig. 153; p. 168: detail of fig. 174; p. 213: detail of fig. 31; p. 214: detail of fig. 114; p. 221: fig. 177; p. 222: detail of fig. 124; p. 225: detail of fig. 57; p. 226: back of fig. 42; p. 228: fig. 126.

CONTENTS

FOREWORD

THIS BOOK AND THE EXHIBITION IT ACCOMPANIES OFFER NEW AND
informative perspectives about a familiar icon of the American cultural landscape.
The tipi is well known to many non-Native people but often through the lens of
Hollywood westerns and historical photographs that romanticized it as a symbol
of a bygone era. *Tipi: Heritage of the Great Plains* dispels stereotypes of the tipi as
a vestige of another time by presenting the architectural form as an aspect of a living
culture, deeply rooted in tradition. The book represents the first major contribution
to the general literature of tipis in more than fifty years, and the groundbreaking
exhibition is the first to take a comprehensive approach to understanding how the tipi
influenced the development of Plains culture and continues to shape contemporary
Plains identity and cultural traditions.

The exhibition was inspired by the Brooklyn Museum's extraordinary holdings
of Plains material, which were acquired primarily in the first decades of the twentieth
century during a vigorous era of collection building. Among the exceptional works
are those of the Nathan Sturges Jarvis collection, which was assembled by Jarvis when
he was a surgeon at Fort Snelling, Minnesota, in the 1830s. Other outstanding works
include the Osage collection, acquired in 1911 by the Museum's first Curator of Ethnology, Stewart Culin (served 1903–29); and a rare tipi liner from earlier Reservation
times painted with autobiographical war exploits by the Húnkpapa Lakota leader
Rain-in-the-Face (circa 1835–1905).

Tipi: Heritage of the Great Plains is the product of careful and extensive planning by the exhibition's curators, Nancy B. Rosoff, Andrew W. Mellon Curator, Arts of the Americas, and Susan Kennedy Zeller, Associate Curator of Native American Art, who developed the exhibition themes and strategies in consultation with a diverse team of Native and non-Native consultants. The curators each contributed an illuminating essay to this volume, in which six scholarly essays are complemented by personal narratives of tipi life, history, and art written by Native Plains people from diverse backgrounds—tribal elders, military veterans, artists, and an architect. We are profoundly grateful to all of the catalogue authors: Heywood and Mary Lou Big Day (Crow), elders and cultural specialists; Christina E. Burke, Curator of Native American and Non-Western Art, Philbrook Museum of Art, Tulsa, Oklahoma; Teri Greeves (Kiowa), artist; Barbara A. Hail, Curator Emerita, Haffenreffer Museum of Anthropology, Brown University, Providence, Rhode Island; Emma I. Hansen (Pawnee), Senior Curator, Plains Indian Museum, Buffalo Bill Historical Center, Cody, Wyoming; Michael P. Jordan, Curatorial Assistant, Sam Noble Oklahoma Museum of Natural History, Norman; Dixon Palmer (Kiowa), Charter Member of the Black Leggings Warrior Society; Lyndreth Palmer (Kiowa), Commander of the Black Leggings Warrior Society; Harvey Pratt (Southern Cheyenne/Arapaho), artist; Dennis Sun Rhodes (Arapaho), architect and President of the Great Horse Group, Minneapolis (formerly AmerINDIAN Architecture); Bently Spang (Northern Cheyenne), artist, curator, and educator; and Daniel C. Swan, Associate Curator of Ethnology, Sam Noble Oklahoma Museum of Natural History, and Associate Professor of Anthropology, University of Oklahoma, Norman.

The Brooklyn Museum is pleased to offer *Tipi: Heritage of the Great Plains* to a broad American audience through a tour to two other distinguished venues. I extend my thanks to my colleagues John Gray, President and CEO of the Autry National Center of the American West, Los Angeles; and Daniel Spock, Director, Minnesota History Center, Minnesota Historical Society, St. Paul, for presenting this landmark exhibition in their communities.

Generous awards from the National Endowment for the Humanities for planning and implementation in large part made this exhibition a reality. We are also most grateful to the National Endowment for the Arts and the Bay and Paul Foundations for supporting object conservation; to American Express for its corporate leadership, which made the exhibition possible; and to the Barbara and Richard Debs Exhibition Fund for its generous support.

For the ongoing support of the Museum's Trustees, we extend special gratitude to Norman M. Feinberg, Chairman, and every member of our Board. Without the confidence and active engagement of our Trustees, it would not be possible to initiate and maintain the high level of exhibition, education, and publication programming exemplified by *Tipi: Heritage of the Great Plains.*

ARNOLD L. LEHMAN
DIRECTOR, BROOKLYN MUSEUM

PREFACE AND ACKNOWLEDGMENTS

THE IDEA BEHIND *TIPI: HERITAGE OF THE GREAT PLAINS* WAS FIRST hatched in 2005, in conversations with the artist and museum and exhibitions specialist Tim Ramsey (Choctaw/Southern Cheyenne). We envisioned the tipi as an animating focal point for a major exhibition exploring the arts and culture of Plains peoples, and featuring the Brooklyn Museum's strong but little-known collection of Plains material.

Brooklyn's Plains collection consists of some seven hundred objects, which mostly entered the Museum during the twentieth century through both purchases and gifts. The holdings include a broad range of objects associated with Plains tribes such as storage bags, cradleboards, clothing, weapons, tools, and painted parfleches, all of which are representative of nineteenth- and twentieth-century lifestyles. The artistry of numerous tribes is represented, primarily Crow, Kiowa, Lakota and Dakota, Shoshone, Blackfeet, and Northern and Southern Cheyenne. Before 2005 only minor research and few consultations with Native peoples had been conducted in connection with this material. As a result, many works were not identified by tribe or artist beyond a general "Plains" designation. Most had not been on view since the early 1960s.

The exceptions were two groups of objects that have been well documented and published. The Nathan Sturges Jarvis collection, which was assembled by Jarvis when he was a surgeon at Fort Snelling, Minnesota, between 1833 and 1836, consists of 157 rare and very early examples of men's and women's clothing, pipes, clubs, and cradleboards, primarily from Yankton, Yanktonai, and Métis tribes. Selections from this important collection have been displayed in the Hall of the Americas and other permanent galleries over the years. The Osage collection, acquired in the field in 1911 by Stewart Culin, the Museum's first Curator of Ethnology, consists of approximately eighty-five objects, twenty-four of which were included in the 1991 exhibition (and accompanying catalogue) *Objects of Myth and Memory: American Indian Art at the Brooklyn Museum.*

Tipi: Heritage of the Great Plains provided an opportunity to survey and catalogue the Museum's entire Plains collection. We invited two Plains scholars to come to the Museum to assist with the cataloguing. We are very grateful to Barbara Hail, Curator Emerita, Haffenreffer Museum of Anthropology, Brown University, and Emma Hansen, Senior Curator, Plains Indian Museum, Buffalo Bill Historical Center, for taking time out of their busy schedules to come to New York for a week to accomplish this task.

As part of the exhibition-planning process, we also engaged Caren S. Oberg, a consultant in museum audience research and evaluation, to conduct and analyze focus groups and visitor surveys to determine the level of visitor interest in and knowledge of the tipi and Plains culture. These evaluations revealed a popular misconception of the tipi as a historic relic that relates exclusively to past traditions and ways of life. Objects made from manufactured materials such as canvas and metals or artworks that reflected American patriotism and Christian beliefs were regarded as somehow less authentic than those made of natural materials or related to Native spiritual beliefs. These insights and others gleaned during the evaluation process informed the development of the exhibition's thematic sections and interpretive strategies, in which we foregrounded the relationship between past and present in tipi culture and Plains life. We decided to present the early use of European trade goods such as glass beads, various types of metals, and cotton, silk, and wool fabric as an extension of how Native people have always adopted new materials to create innovative art forms—a creative tradition that continues today.

To ensure an accurate and sensitive representation of the tipi and associated objects important to Plains peoples, we organized two exhibition-planning meetings in 2007 with a diverse team of consultants, including Native American scholars, artists, and tribal members. During these meetings, funded by a National Endowment for the Humanities Public Programs Planning Grant, the team initially reviewed and discussed more than two hundred fifty objects selected for the exhibition; refined and developed the exhibition themes; identified interpretive strategies; and determined how historic and contemporary works would be presented. This process was critical to making sure that we complied with the guidelines of the Native American Graves Protection and Repatriation Act (NAGPRA) and displayed culturally appropriate objects in a respectful way. To guarantee that the themes, interpretive strategies, and design reflected the recommendations of the consultants, we brought the group together six months later to respond to the exhibition plan. Throughout the planning and implementation process, we continued to communicate with our team of consultants. We would like to express our deep gratitude to the following for serving on the exhibition planning team: Gerard Baker (Mandan Hidatsa), Park Superintendent, Mount Rushmore National Memorial, Keystone, South Dakota; Mary Lou and Heywood Big Day (Crow), elders and cultural specialists; Christina E. Burke, Curator of Native American and Non-Western Art, Philbrook Museum of Art, Tulsa, Oklahoma; Teri Greeves (Kiowa), artist; Barbara Hail; the late Don Moccasin (Rosebud Lakota), Cultural Documentarian for the Sićangu Heritage Center, Sinte Gleska University, Rosebud Indian Reservation, South Dakota; Iris Heavy Runner Pretty Paint (Blackfeet), Co-Director of Research Opportunities in Science for Native Americans, University of Montana, Missoula; Tim Ramsey; Bently Spang (Northern Cheyenne), artist, curator, and educator; and Daniel C. Swan, Associate Curator of Ethnology, Sam Noble Oklahoma Museum of Natural History, and Associate Professor of Anthropology, University of Oklahoma, Norman. In preparation for the exhibition, we also organized a one-day consultation in 2007 to examine and discuss the Museum's Rain-in-the-Face Tipi Liner with scholars of ledger art from the disciplines of art history and anthropology, tribal members including a descendant of the Húnkpapa Lakota leader, a contemporary Lakota artist who makes painted tipis and tipi liners, and the textile conservator who cleaned the liner. We thank the following members of this advisory group for giving generously of their time and expertise: Janet Catherine Berlo, Professor of Art History at the University of Rochester; Christina E. Burke; Christine Giuntini, Textile Conservator, The Metropolitan Museum of Art, New York; Marcella LeBeau, the great-granddaughter of Chief Rain-in-the Face, and her daughter Diane Booth; Tim Mentz from the Tribal Historic Preservation Office, Standing Rock Sioux Tribe; and Donald B. Tenoso (Húnkpapa Lakota), artist and Research Associate at the National Museum of Natural History, Smithsonian Institution, Washington, D.C. We would also like to thank Ellen Pearlstein, Associate Professor, Information Studies and UCLA/Getty Program in the Conservation of Ethnographic and Archaeological Materials, and Bruce Tabb, Special Collections Librarian, University of Oregon Libraries, Eugene, for their assistance with additional Rain-in-the-Face research.

We extend our heartfelt thanks to those people who offered their warm hospitality to us when we traveled in the Plains. The entire Big Day family, especially Heywood, Mary Lou, and their son Derek, graciously hosted us at Crow Fair, where we participated in the raising and disassembling of their tipi camp and, best of all, stayed in one of the family's tipis. This wonderful experience convinced us of the value of having a tipi in the exhibition that all visitors could enter. Other generous hosts who shared their homes and traditions with us were Gerard and Mary Kay Baker at Mount Rushmore, Margaret MacKichan and Don Moccasin at Sinte Gleska, Vanessa and Carl Jennings in Anadarko, and the Nahwooksy family in Lawton.

Many individuals and institutions assisted in the preparation of the exhibition and accompanying publication. We are deeply grateful to the lenders and their staff: at the American Museum of Natural History, New York: Peter M. Whiteley, Curator, North American Ethnology; Laila Williamson, Senior Scientific Assistant, North and South American Ethnology; and Kristen Mable, Registrar for Archives and Loans/

Anthropology; at the Buffalo Bill Historical Center: Emma Hansen; Rebecca West, Curatorial Assistant, Plains Indian Museum; Elizabeth Holmes, Registrar; and Mary Robinson, Housel Director, McCracken Research Library; at the Denver Art Museum: Nancy Blomberg, Curator, Native Arts Department; Jennifer Pray, Curatorial Assistant; and Lori Iliff, Associate Director, Exhibitions & Collections Services/Registrar; at the Fenimore Art Museum, New York State Historical Association, Cooperstown, New York: Eva Fognell, Curator, Thaw Collection of American Indian Art; at The Field Museum, Chicago: Jonathan Haas, MacArthur Curator, Anthropology of the Americas; Gordon Ambrosino, Collections Manager, Department of Anthropology; Patricia Lord, Assistant Registrar, Department of Anthropology; and Jerice Barrios, Rights and Reproductions Coordinator; at the Haffenreffer Museum of Anthropology, Brown University: Thierry Gentis, Associate Curator; and Barbara A. Hail; at the Milwaukee Public Museum: Dawn Scher Thomae, Collections Manager/Associate Curator, Anthropology Section; Christine Del Re, Senior Conservator; Claudia Jacobson, Registrar; and Susan Otto, Photography Department; at the Montana Historical Society, Helena: George Oberst, Curator of History and Ethnology; and Patty Dean, Curator of History; at the Montclair Art Museum, Montclair, New Jersey: Twig Johnson, Senior Curator of Native American Collection; at the National Museum of the American Indian, Smithsonian Institution, Washington, D.C.: Ann McMullen, Curator; Cécile Ganteaume, Associate Curator; Patricia L. Nietfeld, Supervisory Collections Manager; Linda J. Greatorex, Assistant Collections Manager; Thomas E. Evans, Museum Technician; Rajshree Solanki, Registration Loan Specialist; and Lou Stancari, Photo Archives; at the Natural History Museum of Los Angeles County, Los Angeles: Margaret Hardin, Acting Deputy Director of Research and Collections, Division Chief for History and Anthropology, Anthropology Curator; and Chris Coleman, Collections Manager; and at the Peabody Museum of Archaeology and Ethnology, Harvard University, Cambridge, Massachusetts: Castle McLaughlin, Associate Curator of North American Ethnography; Susan Haskell, Curatorial Associate; Simone Barnes, Assistant Curator; and Genevieve Fisher, Registrar.

We would like to thank the following individuals for additional collections research: at the Denver Museum of Nature & Science: Chip Colwell-Chanthaphonh, Curator of Anthropology & NAGPRA Officer; Isabel Tovar, Collections Manager, Anthropology Department; René Payne, Photo Archivist, Bailey Library & Archives; and Joyce Herold, Curator Emerita, Anthropology Department; at the National Museum of Natural History, Smithsonian Institution, Washington, D.C.: JoAllyn Archambault, Head, American Indian Program, Department of Anthropology; Candace Greene, Ethnologist, Collections and Archives Program, Department of Anthropology; Felicia Pickering, Museum Specialist, Ethnology; and Susan Crawford, Collections Registrar; at New-York Historical Society: Miranda Schwartz, Reference Librarian; and Marilyn Kushner, Curator and Head, Department of Prints; and at Peabody Essex Museum, Salem, Massachusetts: Karen Kramer Russell, Associate Curator of Native American Art.

The talented artists who generously agreed to lend works to the exhibition deserve special mention: Marcus Amerman (Choctaw Nation of Oklahoma), Carol Emarthle-Douglas (Northern Arapaho/Seminole), Linda Haukaas (Sićaŋǧu Lakota), Vanessa Jennings (Kiowa), Kevin Pourier (Oglala Lakota), and Harvey Pratt (Southern Cheyenne/Arapaho). We would also like to take this opportunity to recognize the artists who created the two tipis commissioned for the exhibition: Lyle Heavy Runner (Blackfeet), who painted the Blackfeet tipi, in consultation with the late Ricy Crawford and his wife, Naomi, who sewed the canvas cover; and Ken Woody (Mohawk), who made the Lakota-style buffalo-hide tipi.

At the Brooklyn Museum, we would particularly like to thank Arnold L. Lehman, Director; Judith Frankfurt, Deputy Director for Administration; Charles Desmarais, Deputy Director for Art; and Kevin Stayton, Chief Curator, for their support of this project and their advice in bringing it to fruition. Judith Paska, former Vice Director for Development, and her able staff, past and present, especially Rob Krulak, Lidy Chu, and Leslie Brauman, worked tirelessly to secure funding for this very ambitious project. Judy Kim, former Head of the Exhibitions Division, and Megan Doyle Carmody, former Exhibitions Manager, facilitated the administrative aspects of the project. Ken Moser, Vice Director for Collections and Carol Lee Shen Chief Conservator, and Lisa Bruno, Tina March, and Jakki Godfrey of his staff did a superb job of cleaning and conserving objects for this publication and exhibition. Matthew Yokobosky, Chief Designer, embraced working with a diverse group of consultants and devised an inspired exhibition installation; Walter Andersons and his highly capable staff of art handlers executed the plan to perfection, learning to erect tipis with determination and skill. Registrars Elizabeth Reynolds, Katie Welty, and Deana Setzke coordinated a large number of loans and planned the exhibition tour with impressive care. Deborah Wythe coordinated the work of talented staff photographers Sarah Kraemer and Christine Gant, and that of photo researchers Katherine Hausenbauer and Alana Corbett, who did an outstanding job in acquiring and preparing all the visual materials for this book. Sallie Stutz, Vice Director for Merchandising, and Sally Williams, Public Information Officer, and their staffs made sure that the exhibition and publication reached the widest audience. Radiah Harper, Vice Director for Education and Program Development, and her staff, especially Alexa Fairchild, Traslin Ong, and Allison Day, developed an exciting array of school and family programs, and assisted with the focus group evaluations. Alisa Martin, Marketing and Visitor Services Manager, and her staff coordinated the visitor surveys. Web components were designed by Shelley Bernstein, Chief of the Technology Department, and her staff.

The production of this book was expertly supervised by James Leggio, Head of Publications and Editorial Services. We owe an enormous debt of gratitude to Joanna Ekman, Senior Editor, who guided the contributions of twelve different authors with her extraordinary insight and organization. At University of Washington Press, we thank Pat Soden, Jacqueline Ettinger, and Kerrie Maynes for their support and enthusiasm, and Ashley Saleeba for her superb design.

Many other current and former Brooklyn Museum colleagues provided assistance and support during the project, especially Teresa Carbone, Georgia de Havenon, Judith Dolkart, Barry Harwood, Ellen Kuenzel, Deirdre Lawrence, and Terri O'Hara. We could not have accomplished this project without the tactical management of Rima Ibrahim, our outstanding Curatorial Assistant of the Arts of the Americas and Europe.

Over the course of this six-year project, we received assistance from many interns: Miranda Appelbaum, Angela Gaspar, Rachel Gershman, Laura Herring, Robin Levine, Jill Luedke, David Quinn, Kevin Savell, and Lauren Smith. We especially acknowledge the contributions over two years of Chase Cohen, Intern/Research Associate extraordinaire, who provided invaluable research and coordinated the section devoted to tipi-inspired contemporary architecture.

Sadly, we lost two dear friends and colleagues during the planning of the exhibition, and we regret that they could not see the results of their efforts. Fred Nahwooksy invited us in 2005 to participate in an oral-history workshop with Comanche and Kiowa elders and artists that he had organized at the Comanche Cultural Center in Lawton, Oklahoma. We were able to record several stories about tipis and meet artists whose work relates to the tipi theme. Fred's generosity, ideas, and contacts were extremely helpful throughout the project. Don Moccasin was a valued member of our exhibition-planning team. His wisdom about Lakota language, culture, and tipi etiquette was instrumental in the development of the exhibition's content. Both he and Fred will be greatly missed.

Finally, we are grateful to our families and friends, who put up with our crazy schedules, late hours, and many trips away from home.

NANCY B. ROSOFF
SUSAN KENNEDY ZELLER

(opposite)
Map of the Great Plains with present locations of tribes

TIPI

TIPI

HERITAGE OF THE GREAT PLAINS

NANCY B. ROSOFF

ALTHOUGH THE TIPI IS OFTEN ASSOCIATED IN THE POPULAR IMAGINA-
tion with all Native American tribes, this iconic architectural form is, in fact, specific
to the Native peoples of the Great Plains region of North America. The tipi, also
referred to as a lodge, represents the heart of Plains culture. It facilitated each tribe's
nomadic way of life and was the center of social, religious, and creative traditions.
Today, Plains people live in modern homes, but the tipi remains an enduring architectural form, emblematic of Plains tribal identity and used by many for celebratory and
ceremonial occasions. As the Blackfeet educator Iris Pretty Paint has observed, "What
distinguishes Plains identity from other tribes is that the Plains culture was created
as tribes came into a specific lifestyle. The Plains identity comes from the land, the
languages, and respecting our ways of knowing. You had to have certain things to sur-
vive and the tipi was a profound and critical component of Plains culture because it
enabled us to be who we are."[1] This volume and the exhibition it accompanies examine
the central role of the tipi for Plains people from the 1800s to the present and explore
the ongoing vitality of this architectural tradition.

NATIVE PEOPLES OF THE GREAT PLAINS

The Great Plains of North America is a vast area that covers approximately a half-
billion acres, from the foothills of the Rocky Mountains in the west to the Mississippi

Fig. 1. Wind Cave National Park, South Dakota, August 2006 (Photo: Michael Forsberg)

River in the east. The north–south boundaries extend from Canada's Saskatchewan River to the Rio Grande River in northern Mexico. This extensive landscape, which includes flat and rolling grasslands, river valleys, mountains, and intermountain basins, is divided into three main regions: the Northern, Central, and Southern Plains (fig. 1). More than thirty Plains tribes live in these regions: the Blackfeet, Crow, Shoshone, and Northern Cheyenne in the north; the Arapaho and the Sioux Nation[2] in the Central Plains; and the Pawnee, Osage, Kiowa, Southern Cheyenne, Comanche, and Plains Apache in the south. Native people adapted to the severe climate of long, bitterly cold winters and brutally hot summers by adopting a nomadic way of life, which was sustained by abundant herds of buffalo, and supplemented by pronghorn, deer, elk, and wild plants. Family groups of varying sizes moved camp according to the seasons and the location of grazing herds that thrived in the tall grass of the prairies. The tipi—from the Santee (Dakota) word meaning "dwelling"[3]—was the ideal portable home for this way of life.

When bands moved camp, tipis and household items were transported on a travois, a wooden platform that was attached to two tipi poles. Before they were replaced by horses in the eighteenth century, dogs were used to drag the travois (fig. 2); consequently, tipis were relatively small (about ten feet wide and high). As the use of horses became widespread, tipis became larger (ten to twenty-five feet wide and high). This nomadic lifestyle of Plains culture came to an end after Native people were forced onto reservations beginning in the mid-nineteenth century.

Plains history is usually divided into three periods: Pre-Reservation (before 1860); Early Reservation (1860–91); and Late Reservation (1891 to the present). During the Pre-Reservation era, Native people moved freely around the Plains, hunting the plentiful buffalo, gathering native plants, and living in portable buffalo-hide lodges. Intertribal warfare was pervasive and was reflected in the preponderance of highly decorated weaponry (figs. 3–5, and see essays by Kennedy Zeller and by Swan and Jordan in this volume), but this was also a period during which trade and artistic expression flourished.

The Reservation period initiated the disintegration of the traditional Plains way of life. In order to remove Native people from lands desired by a rapidly growing settler population, the federal government confined American Indians to reservations administered by non-Native superintendents and agents of the Bureau of Indian Affairs. Although the reservations were established by treaty for the exclusive use of particular tribes, white settlers continued to occupy Native lands in violation of these agreements. For example, when gold was discovered in the Black Hills of South Dakota in the early 1870s, white miners under U.S. Army protection flooded the area, which was part of the Great Sioux Nation Reservation established by the Fort Laramie Treaty of 1868. Facilitated by the arrival of the railroad lines Atchison, Topeka and Santa Fe (which extended from Kansas to Colorado in 1873) and Great Northern Railroad (which crossed the Dakotas from the Great Lakes in 1889), these illegal incursions provoked decades of armed conflict between Plains tribes and federal troops. Compounding the collapse of Pre-Reservation life was the ongoing decimation of the Native population by diseases of European origin such as smallpox;[4] the

Fig. 2. Blackfeet couple and dog travois in front of a tipi, Canada, 1892. National Museum of the American Indian, Smithsonian Institution, Washington, D.C., P22452

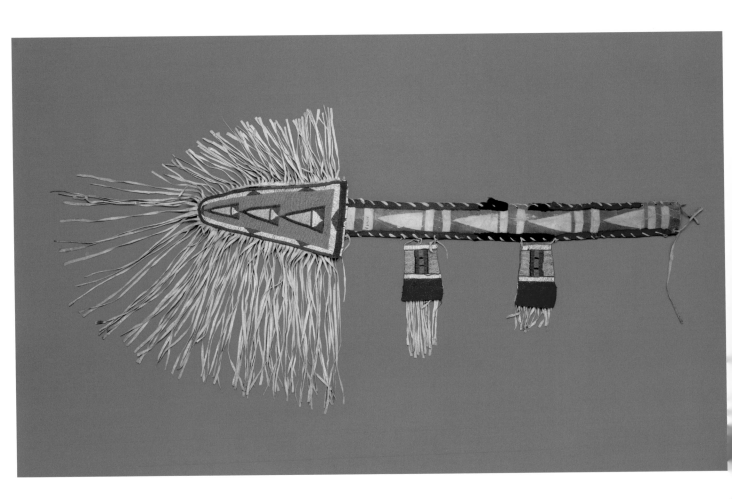

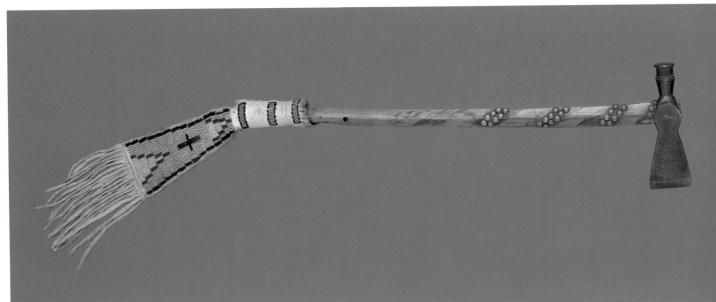

wholesale slaughter of the buffalo in the 1880s by professional hunters; and the banning of Native religious, ceremonial, and social organizations by the Department of the Interior, which issued a Code of Indian Offenses in 1883 and imprisoned violators. The near-extinction of the buffalo deprived Plains people of their traditional source of food and material for clothing and shelter. Out of necessity, canvas came to replace hide as the material for tipi covers and was one of the goods distributed to Native people as part of the terms of formal treaties between the U.S. government and the tribes of the Southern and Central Plains in 1867–68.[5] The tipi was later replaced by one-room log cabins, often government-built and imposed on Plains people by missionaries and federal agents, who awarded special privileges and rations to those who lived in houses (see Hansen and Sun Rhodes essays in this volume). Despite forced acculturation, many Native people continued to erect family tipis near their government-built houses (fig. 6).

TIPI CONSTRUCTION, FUNCTION, AND HISTORY

Constructed of locally available materials (timber and hides) and easily erected and taken down, the Plains tipi was a masterpiece of structural design (fig. 7). The framework provided stability against strong winds, and the taut cover kept out snow and rain. The interior liner, which hung along the lower half of the cover, deflected drafts and water condensation, provided privacy, and helped ventilate the smoke from the central fire. Flaps (also referred to as ears or wings) on either side of the smoke hole were also manipulated to release smoke. Rainwater ran down to the ground along straight tipi poles that had been cleaned of bark and smoothed. Hide covers were initially held down by sod blocks or large stones that were rolled off when the camp was moved; these weights were eventually replaced by sharpened wooden pegs that were inserted through holes in the base of the cover and hammered into the ground.[6]

No. 245. Modern Indian Home. Photo. By J. A. Anderson.

Shoshoni. 2.

To erect a tipi, a hide or canvas cover is stretched over a pole framework to form a slightly tilted cone (measuring ten to twenty-five feet in diameter at the base), which slants toward the back, away from the doorway. Tipi doorways usually face east in order to greet the rising sun. Depending on the tribe, the pole framework is built over a three- or four-pole foundation (figs. 8a, b; see also Hansen essay in this volume). The number of poles varies according to tipi size, tribal preference, and access to timber, which is scarce in the Southern Plains and more abundant in the north. Lodgepole pine trees (so named for their use) are preferred for tipi poles, followed by red cedar. Some tribes, such as the Blackfeet, Crow, and Sioux of the Northern and Central Plains, lived in close proximity to excellent stands of lodgepole pine and always had ample supplies for use and trade. Southern Plains tribes such as the Kiowa, Comanche, and Apache, on the other hand, had to travel great distances to the foothills of the Colorado Rockies or to the Black Hills of South Dakota in order to cut down poles or to trade for them. For these southern tribes, tipi poles were highly valued. Among the Plains Apache, for example, five poles were worth one horse.[7]

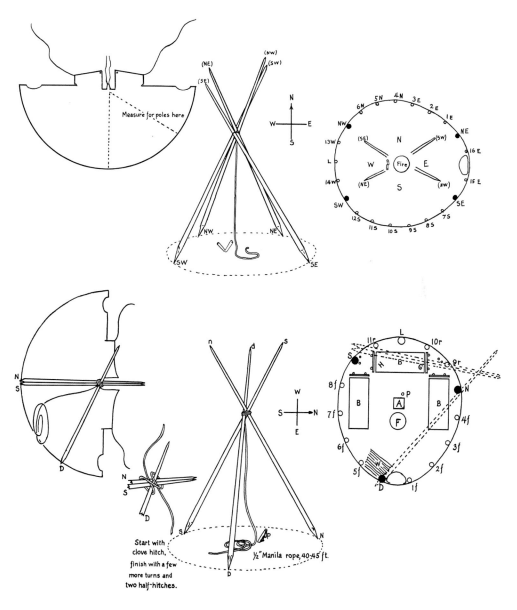

Fig. 9. Peyote tipi of the Native American Church, home of Mrs. Isabel Lopez, Oilton, Texas, 1995 (Photo: Daniel C. Swan)

(opposite, above)
Fig. 10. Lew W. Brace (Kiowa, dates unknown). Peyote Box, 1941. Anadarko, Oklahoma. Wood, pigment, brass, green felt lining, 7⅛ × 19½ × 7 in. (17.9 × 49.5 × 17.6 cm). Denver Art Museum, Anonymous gift, 1948.361

(opposite, below)
Fig. 11. Osage artist. Peyote Rattle, late 19th or early 20th century. Pawhuska, Oklahoma. Gourd, glass beads, metal, feathers, brass, sinew, nut or seed, cork, 27 9/16 × 2¾ in. (70 × 7 cm). Brooklyn Museum, Museum Expedition 1911, Museum Collection Fund, 11.694.9059

Tipis were first and foremost homes and the center of family life[8] (see Burke essay in this volume), but Plains people also constructed tipis for numerous other uses. Special tipis were erected as medicine lodges used to store sacred objects, seclusion areas for menstruating women, and toys for children's play. Today an all-white canvas lodge is preferred for the night-long ceremonies of the Native American Church, founded in the 1890s (fig. 9). In these services, also called meetings, singing is accompanied by drumming and the shaking of rattles, and peyote is consumed as a sacrament or healing medicine; many of the ritual objects used in the ceremony are decorated with tipi images (figs. 10–12).[9] The warrior societies of some tribes had their own tipis; the revival of the Kiowa Black Leggings Warrior Society and the creation of its ceremonial painted lodge are discussed in the Palmer and Palmer interview and the essay by Swan and Jordan in this volume.

Fig. 12. Fox artist. Peyote Cup, circa 1900–1920. Iowa. German silver, 3⅛ × 3 in. (7.9 × 7.6 cm). National Museum of the American Indian, Smithsonian Institution, Washington, D.C., 24/7485

Fig. 13. Large group of Dakota Sioux men sitting inside a double tipi, Standing Rock Agency, North Dakota, circa 1880–89. Photograph by David Frances Barry (1854–1934). Denver Public Library, Western History Collection, David Frances Barry/B-740

The double tipi, another lodge with a special function, was used for large gatherings such as treaty signings, gifting ceremonies, and coming-of-age celebrations (fig. 13). Generally erected only for the duration of an event, the double tipi consisted of a tall center pole set in the ground with other poles that were laid against it in a

Fig. 14. Tipi ring at Site 48CA4023 in northeastern Wyoming, 2001 (Photo: John Greer, Greer Services, Casper, Wyoming)

Fig. 15. Deeply Incised Tipi, Red Canyon site, Wind River Basin, Wyoming, 1996 (Photo: Julie E. Francis)

semicircle. Multiple tipi covers were attached to the pole framework, leaving a wide, east-facing opening.[10]

Although there is no definitive date for the beginning of tipi use, some scholars have interpreted the numerous circles of stones found throughout the Northern Plains and dating to about three or four thousand years ago as the bases for tipis. Referred to as tipi rings, the stone circles are between eleven and twenty-four feet in diameter and may have weighed down the bottom edges of hide tipi covers (fig. 14).[11] It is thought that groups tended to return seasonally to the same areas and that the stone rings were left behind and reused. After European steel-blade axes and knives were introduced in the seventeenth century, it became easier for Plains people to use sharpened wooden pegs to hold down the covers.[12] Other archaeological evidence, dating from about the early sixteenth century, includes the many tipi images in petroglyphs and pictographs found throughout the basins of the Bighorn and Wind rivers in Montana and Wyoming. Incised tipi images (fig. 15) are more common than painted ones; the latter are apparently of later date, to judge from the lack of erosion and brightness of pigments seen in many such pictographs.[13]

The tipi has held a fascination for non-Natives since the sixteenth century, when European explorers recorded their observations of the conical tents. Pedro de Castañeda de Nájera, who traveled with Francisco Vásquez de Coronado in 1540–42, made note of encounters with a people (possibly Apache) living near the Keres Pueblo in northern New Mexico who had hide tents and used dogs to carry tipi covers and drag poles for their encampments.[14] The explorer Don Juan de Oñate (1550?–1630) provided the first record of painted tipis in the journals of his travels in the upper Rio Grande valley in 1598–99, noting that he saw a camp with "fifty tents made of tanned hides, very bright red and white in color and bell shaped, with flaps and openings, and built so skillfully as those of Italy and are so large that in most ordinary ones four different mattresses and beds were easily accommodated."[15] Oñate also mentioned that the tents were transported on the backs of dogs.

In the nineteenth century, artists' sketches as well as written accounts of expeditions almost always included representations and descriptions of tipis. The American naturalist artist Titian Ramsay Peale (1799–1885), a member of the 1819 expedition led by Stephen H. Long to the Rocky Mountains, sketched the first known picture by a

Fig. 16. George Catlin (American, 1796–1872). *Ft. Snelling at the Mouth of the St. Peters River 7 Miles Below the Falls of St. Anthony, Upper Mississippi,* 1852. Oil on canvas, 11 × 14 in. (27.9 × 35.6 cm). Gilcrease Museum, Tulsa, Oklahoma, 0126.2119

white artist of buffalo-hide tipis.[16] The Swiss artist Karl Bodmer (1809–1893) depicted many Plains tipi camps in 1833–34 while accompanying the expedition sponsored by Prince Maximilian of Wied.[17] The artist and collector George Catlin (1796–1872) painted many portraits and scenes of Plains life. A showman as well as an artist, Catlin recognized the value of displaying artifacts, including a buffalo-hide tipi, in his exhibitions.[18] He observed the tipi camp below Fort Snelling, Minnesota, in 1833 (fig. 16), the same year that Nathan Sturges Jarvis was stationed there as an army surgeon. During his tour of duty Jarvis acquired an important Plains collection that would ultimately enter the collection of the Brooklyn Museum (see figs. 5, 17, 30–32, 121–23, 125, 133, 135).[19]

DEVELOPMENT OF THE TIPI AND TIPI ARTS

The evolution of the tipi and tipi arts must be seen in relation to three central elements of the Plains culture and way of life. The buffalo, the staple food of Plains people and their most important natural resource, played a large role in ritual and belief. The horse, crucial to hunting and warfare, had special significance in Plains society. Finally, a long history of trade, both intertribal and with non-Natives, was not only fundamental to the Native economy but also introduced new materials, which stimulated artistic innovation.

The Buffalo

Plains life revolved around the buffalo, the largest land mammal in North America.[20] Although the term *buffalo* is widely used, the accurate name for the animal is American bison, or *Bison americanus*. Seventeenth-century English settlers observed buffalo herds as far east as the Potomac River,[21] but the Great Plains were the animals' true home, with population estimates ranging from ten to thirty million at the beginning of the nineteenth century.[22] The meat of the buffalo was the principal food of Plains people. Many tribes acknowledged its importance in their Native languages: the Blackfeet called bison meat *natapi waksin* ("real food"), and all other food *istapi waksin* ("nothing food").[23] The meat was dried to preserve it for later consumption and was also pounded with fat and fruit such as chokecherries to make a high-calorie food known as pemmican. Plains people used more than a hundred parts of the buffalo for various purposes: the guts for containers, dung for fuel, bones for tools and implements, and sinew for cordage. In addition, fur-covered bison hides were employed as rugs, blankets, and robes and, when cleaned of fur and tanned, provided the perfect material for tipi covers, clothing (fig. 17), and containers (see fig. 50).[24]

The buffalo was honored and revered in everyday life as well as in religious ceremonies and rituals throughout the Plains region, and as a result, the animal's image appears on a variety of objects such as clothing, bags and pouches (fig. 18), shields, and drums. According to the creation stories of many tribes such as the Crow, Cree, and Arapaho, the buffalo existed before human beings, who were created because animals, especially the buffalo, would sustain them.[25] In the stories of other tribes,

Fig. 17. Yanktonai artist. Moccasins, early 19th century. Collected by Dr. Nathan Sturges Jarvis, Sr., Fort Snelling, Minnesota. Buffalo hide, beads, bird quills, porcupine quills, tin, deer hair, sinew, pigment, 11 × 5 in. (27.9 × 12.7 cm). Brooklyn Museum, Henry L. Batterman Fund and the Frank Sherman Benson Fund, 50.67.23a, b

human beings were created from the bison, as in the Lakota oral tradition, where humans arose from a blood clot suffered by the animal.[26]

Various ceremonies of Plains tribes were dedicated to the buffalo. The Mandan Okipa and the Hidatsa Red Stick ceremonies were performed to honor and express gratitude to the animals and call them to a village.[27] The Lakota Buffalo Ceremony, or Buffalo Sing, held after a girl's first menses, ensured that she would possess the virtues most desired of a Lakota woman (chastity, fecundity, industry, and hospitality) by receiving the assistance of the animal's spirit.[28] The buffalo was one of the many spirits honored during the annual Sun Dance, a sacred four-day ceremony held every summer that included a painted buffalo-skull altar, the wearing of sacred buffalo robes, and the consuming of buffalo tongues and backfat.[29] The members of the Lakota medicine society called the Buffalo Dreamers received visions and were believed to

have the ability to assume the animal's form in order to harness its power for healing purposes (see fig. 82). A Sioux breechcloth decorated with a quilled image of a buffalo head may have been worn during one of these dances (fig. 19). Members of certain warrior societies dressed and danced as buffalo and considered themselves to have the strength of the animal as well as the wisdom to guide and protect their people.[30]

Since the nineteenth century, both Native and non-Native people have worked to bring the buffalo back from near-extinction. Today many Plains people are taking an active role in restoring herds by entering into alliances with conservation biologists, ecosystem scientists, and advocates of range restoration.[31] The resurgence of buffalo herds on the Plains is restoring cultural pride, promoting economic sustainability, and inspiring artistic creativity, exemplified by the inlaid buffalo-horn spoons by the Oglala Lakota artist Kevin Pourier (fig. 20).

Fig. 19. Sioux artist.
Breechcloth, first half
20th century. Central or
Northern Plains. Flannel,
dyed porcupine quills,
metal, glass beads, yarn,
57 × 12¼ in. (145 × 31 cm).
Brooklyn Museum, Henry
L. Batterman Fund, 46.78.2

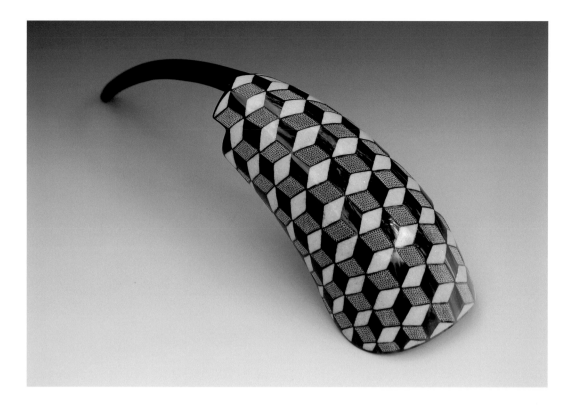

Fig. 20. Kevin Pourier
(Oglala Lakota, b. 1968).
Escher-ish Horn Spoon,
2009. Buffalo horn,
mother-of-pearl, 17 ×
3½ in. (43.2 × 8.9 cm).
Collection of the artist
(Photo: Kevin Pourier)

The Horse

The horse revolutionized Plains culture. Having become extinct in the Americas some ten thousand years ago, the animal was reintroduced in North America by Spanish explorers in the sixteenth century. After the Pueblo Uprising of 1680 drove Spanish missionaries and colonists from the Southwest, the horses they left behind were rapidly distributed throughout the region. Tribes living in the northwestern Plains acquired horses through long-established trading networks and intertribal horse raiding before the first white explorers arrived in the area. By the end of the eighteenth century, the horse had spread throughout the Great Plains.[32] This development allowed Plains people to travel greater distances, easing the westward migration of several tribes such as the Sioux, Cheyenne, and Crow, who originally lived in the Great Lakes region. The horse enabled Native people to hunt buffalo, conduct long-distance trade, and wage war more efficiently and made it possible to carry larger tipis and more belongings (fig. 21). Women devoted more hours to artistic production, for which there was increased demand since horses allowed people to transport more possessions. Horseback riding required specialized equipment such as saddles, saddle blankets, quirts, bridles, and saddlebags, which were often elaborately decorated (figs. 22–24).[33]

Like the buffalo, the horse became fully integrated into Plains culture and was associated with important values of bravery, wealth, and generosity. Horse ownership became a mark of status and economic wealth. Among the Blackfeet, men who owned many fine horses lived in the largest and best-furnished tipis and wore the highest-quality clothing. These wealthy men increased their prestige and status in

5825. The Trail Makers—Blackfeet Indians—Glacier National Park, Montana.
On Main Line Great Northern Railway
See America First

© 1912 BY ROLAND W. REED.

the tribe by making gifts of food and horses and by lending horses to those in need for buffalo hunting and moving camp.[34] Horses were sometimes obtained through trade, but most often by raiding enemy camps, and horse stealing became a tangible measure of a warrior's bravery. Young men risked their lives to sneak into an enemy's village and steal horses near the owner's tipi (fig. 25). Horse stealing was a coup—a great warrior achievement that was highly respected by family and friends.[35] A successful horse thief had the right to boast about his exploit and might record it on his shirt (see fig. 133) or on his tipi liner (see Kennedy Zeller essay in this volume).[36] Acts of bravery were traditionally followed by acts of generosity, and a warrior would often give a stolen horse to a widow or other unfortunate member of the village.[37]

Plains men trained their horses for buffalo hunting and warfare and developed special relationships with them so that the horses became extensions of their owners. Among the Teton Sioux, horses that served their owners well in battle by carrying them to safety were honored with songs and ornaments such as an eagle feather tied to the mane or tail, a strip of red cloth fastened around the neck, and designs painted on the body.[38] Highly esteemed horses were adorned with exquisite ornaments such as beaded masks (fig. 26), and they were paraded through camp before the men left for battle and upon their successful return and in other public celebrations.[39]

Many Plains tribes viewed the horse as sacred. The Blackfeet, for example, integrated the horse so completely into their religious beliefs that the animal was viewed

(above)
Fig. 21. Blackfeet men and women on horseback with the women pulling travois, Glacier National Park, Montana, 1912. Photograph by Roland Reed (1864–1934). Denver Public Library, Western History Collection, X-33137

(opposite)
Fig. 22. Cree artist. Pad Saddle, first half 19th century. Northern Plains. Hide, beads, pigment, stroud wool cloth, deer or buffalo hair, old hide parfleche, metal, canvas, 19 1/8 × 13 3/8 in. (48.5 × 34 cm). Brooklyn Museum, Henry L. Batterman Fund, 46.78.7

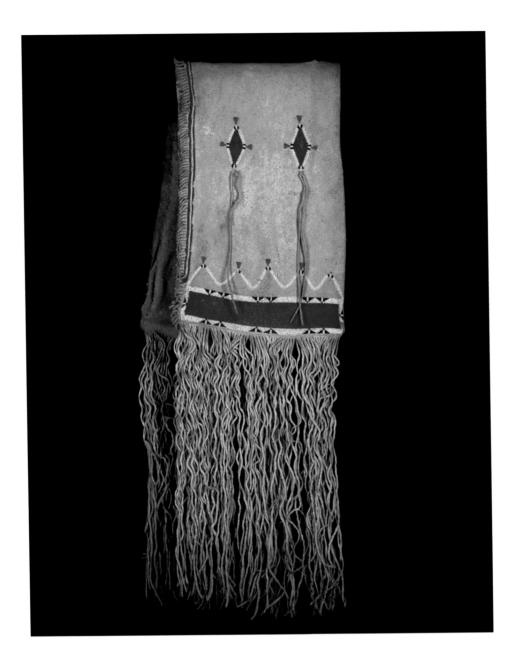

Fig. 23. Osage artist. Saddlebag, late 19th or early 20th century. Pawhuska, Oklahoma. Buffalo hide, cloth, beads, 41¾ × 11¹³⁄₁₆ in. (106 × 30 cm). Brooklyn Museum, Museum Expedition 1911, Museum Collection Fund, 11.694.9009

Fig. 24. Crow artist. Saddle and Stirrups, circa 1890–1900. Flathead Indian Reservation, Montana. Wood, rawhide, sinew, leather, beads, cotton, wool, canvas, commercial leather; saddle 17 × 20 × 26 in. (43.2 × 50.8 × 66 cm), stirrups 11 × 6 × 9½ in. (27.9 × 15.2 × 24.1 cm). Buffalo Bill Historical Center, Cody, Wyoming, Simplot Collection, Gift of J. R. Simplot, NA.403.178.1 and NA.403.178.2

Fig. 25. His Fight (Húnkpapa Sioux, dates unknown). *Man Stealing Horses*, 1884. Ink on paperboard, 6⅛ × 11½ in. (15.5 × 29.2 cm). National Museum of the American Indian, Smithsonian Institution, Washington, D.C., 20/1633

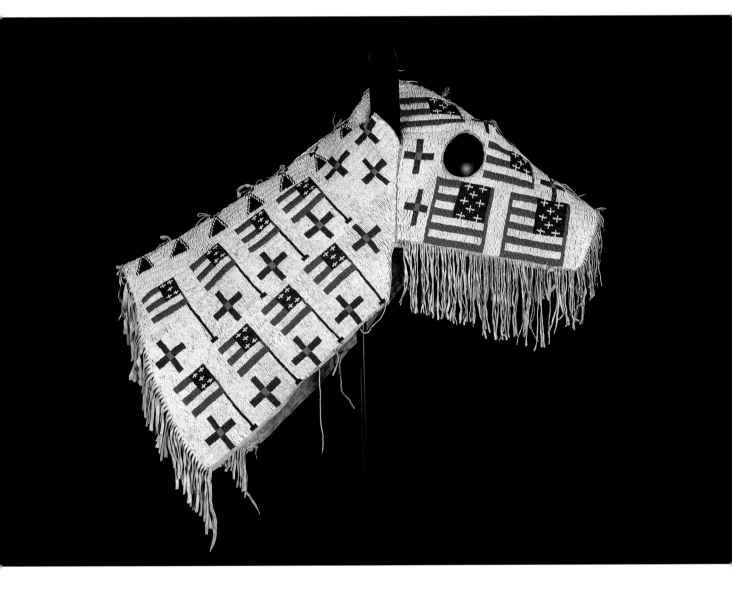

Fig. 26. Teton Sioux artist. Horse Mask, circa 1900. North or South Dakota. Cowskin, deerskin fringe, glass seed beads, 37 × 28½ in. (94 × 72.4 cm). Thaw Collection, Fenimore Art Museum, Cooperstown, New York, T0070 (Photo: John Bigelow Taylor)

as a gift from the sky or water spirits.⁴⁰ Horses were believed to have spiritual powers, which were conveyed to men in dreams and visions. These visions brought men the healing powers of horse medicine and ensured success in capturing and training horses, hunting, and warfare.⁴¹ Plains people acknowledged their relationship to the horse through images depicted on clothing (fig. 27), tipi liners (see figs. 74, 87), and other objects. Today, horses continue to play an important practical role in ranching and herding, but for Plains people they also represent pride in their cultural heritage, as reflected in contemporary works of art such as the carved horse effigy stick by the Húnkpapa Lakota artist Butch Thunder Hawk (fig. 28) and in cultural events such as the daily parades of regalia-draped horses that occur every morning at Crow Fair, an annual three-day August celebration on the Crow Reservation in Montana (see Big Day interview in this volume).

Trade and Innovation

Intertribal exchange networks, which introduced new materials into Native people's lives and influenced the objects they produced, were established thousands of years before the arrival of the white man on the North American continent.⁴² Prior to European contact, trade networks spanned the Plains region and extended into the Southwest, Plateau, Gulf Coast, and Eastern Woodlands regions.⁴³ Much of this trade was centered on agricultural villages along the upper Missouri River of the Mandan-Hidatsa and Arikara, who traded surplus agricultural products for dried meat, buffalo

Fig. 29. Yankton or Yanktonai artist. Pemmican Bag, circa 1883. Standing Rock Agency, North Dakota. Hide, quills, beads, metal, horsehair, 9⅝ × 8³⁄₁₆ × 4 in. (24.4 × 20.8 × 10.2 cm). Peabody Museum of Archaeology and Ethnology, Harvard University, Cambridge, Massachusetts, 30-69-10/K22 (Photo: © 2010 Presidents and Fellows of Harvard College)

robes, hides, and hide garments decorated with quillwork.[44] The sites of pre-eighteenth-century Plains farming villages have also yielded trade items such as obsidian, probably quarried in western Wyoming, and red pipestone from Minnesota.[45] Marine shells from the Pacific coast, especially dentalium shells from Vancouver Island, were highly coveted by Plains people and were used in making ornaments and decorating clothing (see fig. 128).

The diffusion of European trade goods in the Great Plains during the seventeenth, eighteenth, and nineteenth centuries followed established intertribal exchange networks. Groups in the Northern Plains had access to horses from the Southwest

Fig. 30. Eastern Sioux artist. Knife and Sheath, early 19th century. Collected by Dr. Nathan Sturges Jarvis, Sr., Fort Snelling, Minnesota. Steel, bone, hide, quills, copper, cloth; knife in sheath 13 × 6 in. (33 × 15.2 cm). Brooklyn Museum, Henry L. Batterman Fund and the Frank Sherman Benson Fund, 50.67.59a, b

Fig. 31. Eastern Sioux artist. Knife Sheath, early 19th century. Collected by Dr. Nathan Sturges Jarvis, Sr., Fort Snelling, Minnesota. Rawhide, buckskin, porcupine quills, tin, sinew, thread, 9½ × 3¼ in. (24.1 × 8.3 cm). Brooklyn Museum, Henry L. Batterman Fund and the Frank Sherman Benson Fund, 50.67.41

and European products from the Northeast, which were transported by Apache, Ute, Kiowa, Comanche, and Cheyenne traders who took goods to and from the mercantile centers.[46] The goods were then exchanged with interior tribes by Crow and Blackfeet traders.[47] European trade goods included colored glass beads; woolen cloth; metal tools and weapons such as arrowheads, knives, and axes; guns and ammunition; copper; tin cans; brass kettles; and commercial paints.[48]

The introduction of new materials through trade led to innovations in artistic production. A Sioux quilled and beaded hide bag, for example, incorporates a metal chain-link handle (fig. 29). Sheaths for Eastern Sioux hide knives dating to about 1830 are decorated with quillwork and small metal cones (figs. 30, 31). Usually made from cans, metal cones produced a tinkling sound reminiscent of the small carved deer hooves that were sewn onto garments and attached to objects. Silk ribbons were attached to a variety of traditional garments and accessories such as an elk-antler roach spreader used to spread out a bundle of red-dyed animal hair for a man's headdress (fig. 32). A bear-claw necklace with a 1789 Washington Peace Medal illustrates the incorporation of a new status object into a traditional Crow man's necklace, as well as the use of multicolored glass beads, the trade material that had the greatest impact on Native artistic production (figs. 33, 34).[49]

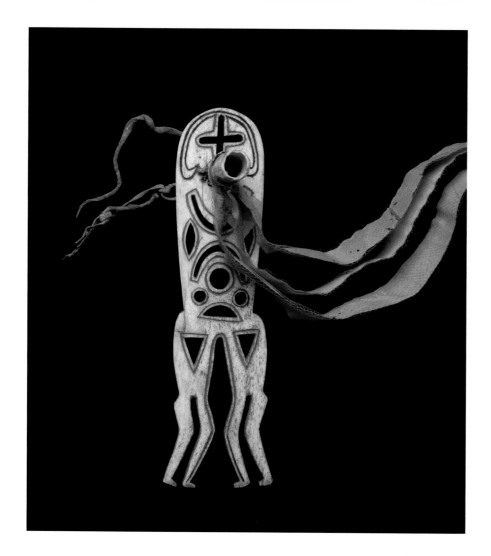

Fig. 32. Sioux artist. Roach Spreader, early 19th century. Collected by Dr. Nathan Sturges Jarvis, Sr., Fort Snelling, Minnesota. Elk antler, canine femur, hide, pigment, silk ribbon, 6¼ × 1½ in. (15.9 × 3.8 cm). Brooklyn Museum, Henry L. Batterman Fund and the Frank Sherman Benson Fund, 50.67.163

Fig. 33. Crow artist. Necklace, 1850–1900. Northern Plains. Glass and brass beads, bear claws, silver George Washington Peace Medal (dated 1789), rawhide, circumference 25¾ in. (65.4 cm). Montclair Art Museum, Montclair, New Jersey, Gift of Earle W. Sargent, Richard M. Sargent, and William P. Sargent, Jr., S1971.150

Fig. 34. Jefferson Peace Medal, 1801. United States. Silver, diam. 4 in. (10.2 cm). Brooklyn Museum, Gift of F. Ethel Wickham in memory of her father, W. Hull Wickham, 49.135.4

Glass was unknown in North America before the seventeenth century and beads were introduced into the western Great Lakes region about 1675 by French fur traders.[50] The white, blue, and black beads were called pony beads because they were transported by traders on ponies.[51] During the eighteenth century French, English, Russian, and Spanish traders brought beads to Native tribes living west of the Missouri River.[52] Pony beads, which were used sparingly to outline areas and edges, were quickly replaced by smaller glass beads, called seed beads, beginning about 1840, because they were an inexpensive alternative available in large quantities and many colors.[53] Seed beads were widely sought after by Plains women and they eventually replaced the more time-consuming quill embroidery (see Hail essay in this volume), enabling women to cover entire surfaces of clothing, bags, and cradles with colorful and intricate beaded designs (fig. 35; see fig. 163).

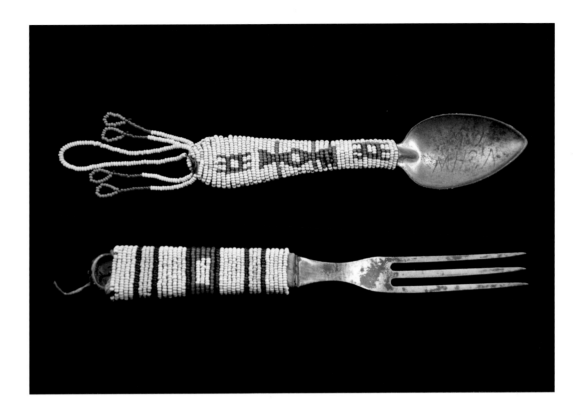

Another widespread trade item, canvas cloth, replaced buffalo hide as the material for lodge covers and liners. The use of canvas resulted in lighter and larger tipis in the nineteenth century. New trade markets and materials also gave rise to new art forms made for non-Native consumers, as exemplified by the large painted-hide wall hanging by the Shoshone artist Cadzi Cody, also known as Cotsiogo (fig. 36). In this work Cotsiogo painted a Sun Dance, a ceremony that drew a tourist audience. The hanging includes an American eagle in place of a buffalo head at the apex of the dance poles. The hide also depicts a variety of scenes of daily life in a tipi camp: a celebratory Wolf Dance, a buffalo hunt, women butchering buffalo, and warriors on horseback returning to camp. Cotsiogo created this nostalgic work at a time when the Shoshone had been removed from their established lifestyle and relocated to the Wind River Reservation in Wyoming; like many other Plains people in these circumstances, the artist turned to the tourist economy as a means of support.

Plains women incorporated ready-made trade items such as silverware into their households for reasons of efficiency, but they often decorated them in a Plains style to make them their own (fig. 37). A leather doctor's bag is another example of a ready-made item that has been given a decidedly Sioux makeover (fig. 38); it is unknown whether this bag was made for sale or for use by the Cheyenne River Sioux woman who beaded it.

Today, Plains artists continue to create innovative art forms, many crossing traditional artistic gender roles. Some Plains men such as the award-winning Oglala Lakota artist Todd Yellow Cloud Augusta have taken up beadwork (see fig. 166). Contemporary female artists incorporate figurative designs on bags and clothing, working in a pictographic style that was used exclusively by men until Plains women first

Fig. 38. Cheyenne River Sioux artist. Bag, circa 1900. Cheyenne River Reservation, South Dakota. Commercial leather, buffalo hide, beads, pigment, and metal, 7¼ × 11 × 5¼ in. (18.4 × 27.9 × 13.3 cm). Denver Art Museum, 1966.242

Fig. 39. Linda Haukaas (Sićanǧu Lakota, b. 1957). *Protecting Our Families*, 2009. Ink and colored pencil on late 1800s ledger paper, 11 × 17 in. (27.9 × 43.2 cm). The British Museum, Presented in part by Estelle and Morton Sosland (Photo: Stephen Lang)

adopted it in the early twentieth century. The Sićanǧu Lakota artist Linda Haukaas embraces the male ledger-art tradition in her work (fig. 39). Other contemporary artists interpret traditional Plains objects in new and surprising media; Marcus Amerman's (Choctaw) warrior shields are created from fused glass (fig. 40), and Bently Spang (Northern Cheyenne) makes his warrior shirts from family photographs (fig. 41). A beaded tipi sculpture made by the Kiowa artist Teri Greeves exemplifies

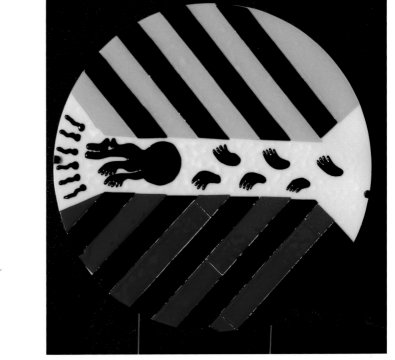

Fig. 40. Marcus Amerman (Choctaw Nation of Oklahoma, b. 1959). *Shield #2*, 2008. Fused glass, 22 × 22 × ½ in. (55.9 × 55.9 × 1.3 cm). Collection of the artist (Photo: Marcus Amerman)

Fig. 41. Bently Spang (Northern Cheyenne, b. 1960). *Modern Warrior Series: War Shirt #3*, *The Great Divide*, 2006. Photographic film, photographs, sinew, velvet, found objects, 41 × 60 × 11¼ in. (104.1 × 152.4 × 28.6 cm). Montclair Art Museum, Montclair, New Jersey, Museum Purchase; Gifts made in honor of Elaine and Hal Sterling, and Acquisitions Fund, 2006.9 (Photo: Peter Jacobs)

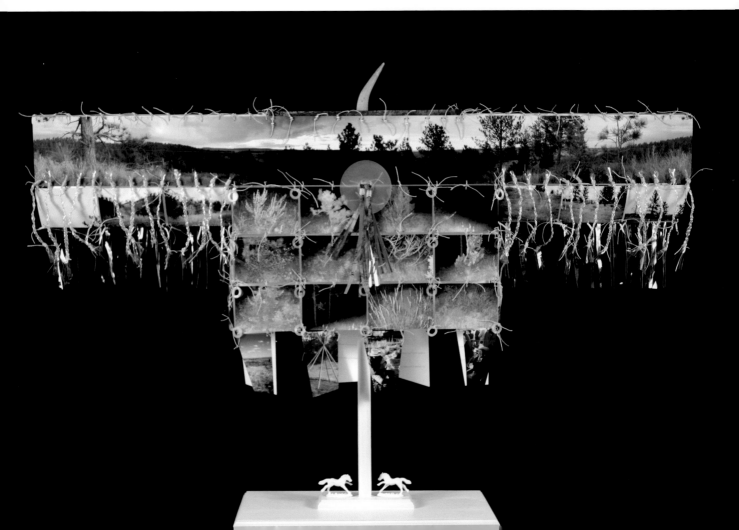

the great talent and creativity of Plains artists today (fig. 42). Specially commissioned for the Brooklyn Museum's exhibition *Tipi: Heritage of the Great Plains*, the sculpture combines a traditional medium—beadwork—with contemporary subject matter—Kiowa life in the twenty-first century.

TIPIS TODAY

Plains culture, like that of any society, is constantly evolving as new materials and technologies are developed, introduced, and adopted. In the context of the severe hardships Native people have endured throughout the history of white occupation and control, cultural continuity and innovation have particular significance. Today, Plains tribes are sovereign nations, but many still struggle with the legacy of white domination: poverty, unemployment, health problems, and lack of education. Cultural practices and artistic expressions, flourishing both on and off the reservations, are the glue that keeps tribal identity strong and vital. Emma Hansen notes that the Plains ancestral traditions are "continuous threads that have been passed down through generations":

This does not mean that Native people are frozen in the nostalgic past, but rather that they revere and honor the accomplishments of their elders and those who came before them while living as vital members of their own communities. They respect and celebrate the tribal heritages, histories, and traditions that have provided a sense of cohesion and identities for their people, but they also actively innovate and create their own futures on reservations and in small towns and cities throughout North America.[54]

The living history and tradition of the tipi are everywhere evident at the annual Crow Fair celebration in Montana (see Hansen essay in this volume). Walking around the fair campground in August 2007, one could see traditional tipis furnished with rugs and air mattresses; hangers draped with ceremonial regalia, jeans, and T-shirts; and powwow drummers sitting on lawn chairs. Outdoor kitchens were equipped with propane stoves and coolers full of food. Each tipi camp was surrounded by cars and trucks. Youths on horseback proudly rode around the campground. Young people strolled in powwow regalia, wearing sunglasses and baseball caps, and dancers donned traditional dress, checking their makeup in car side-view mirrors. For its participants in the twenty-first century, Crow Fair exists in the past, present, and future, without distinctions of time or judgments of authenticity.

PART 1 / THE QUINTESSENTIAL AMERICAN ARCHITECTURAL FORM

THE ART OF TIPI LIVING

EMMA I. HANSEN

ON A COOL AUGUST EVENING IN MONTANA, THE MUTED SOUNDS OF Crow Fair can be heard through the canvas tipi walls. The voices of the announcers, sounds of the drums, and singing continue into the night as the powwow dance competitions, intertribal dancing, and ceremonial adoptions of new tribal members take place. Some family members and friends have left the dance grounds to return to camp, where they gather under arbors to visit or relax in their tipis, and voices and laughter can be heard from neighboring camps. For the Apsáalooke—or Crow, as they are popularly identified today—Crow Fair is a reunion for tribal members and a time to commemorate their ancestors' lives as Plains buffalo hunters and to reintroduce this heritage to younger generations. Crow speakers refer to this celebration—consisting of a powwow, parades, a rodeo, and an exhibition of tribal arts—as *uhba'asaxpiluua* (meaning "where they make the noise"), a term for any dance, celebration, or social gathering.[1] To the Crow and thousands of Native people from many tribes as well as international visitors, this event is characterized by the encampment of an estimated fifteen hundred tipis distributed in family compounds throughout the grounds located along the banks of the Little Bighorn River at Crow Agency, Montana—a tribal community often identified as the "Tepee Capital of the World" because of the Crow Fair (fig. 43). Such tipi encampments take place throughout the Great Plains at other large intertribal celebrations such as the annual North American

Fig. 43. Crow Fair Camp, Crow Agency, Montana, 2007 (Photo: Susan Kennedy Zeller)

Indian Days at Browning, Montana, and in more intimate ceremonial contexts such as the Sun Dance and Native American Church meetings.

For contemporary Plains Native people, tipis—or lodges, as they are sometimes called—are more than nostalgic reminders of eighteenth- and nineteenth-century life. Tipis serve as powerful symbols of a unique and creative existence of tribal peoples on the Great Plains before Euro-American colonization, Native depopulation, and confinement to reservations—at a time when buffalo, deer, and elk were abundant, and the people had the freedom to move seasonally in search of game to hunt or native plants to gather. As a functional and universal dwelling style on the Plains, the tipi has a cultural significance among Plains tribes that is deeply rooted in diverse and fundamental tribal values, histories, and assumptions.

TIPI TRADITIONS

Among Plains Native people, everything related to the tipi belonged to women's areas of authority and responsibility. In addition to setting up their lodges and dismantling and packing them on travois when their bands moved to different locations, women were in charge of acquiring the wood for poles and preparing them for use, creating the tipi covers, maintaining the lodges, and providing the decorative elements and furnishings for the use of the family.

The Crow refer to the tipi as *ashé*, meaning "home," or *ashtáale*, meaning "real home."[2] As they moved into reservation log homes and, later, brick houses, they began to use the term *ashtáale* specifically to refer to the more traditional tipi

housing.[3] Crow oral traditions featuring exploits of Yellow Leggings (Issaatshíilish)
illustrate the origin and cultural significance of the tipi itself, as well as its tribally specific structure composed of a framework of twenty-one poles, including a base of four
poles. Yellow Leggings brought the tipi to the Crow, who, according to oral traditions,
had previously made their homes in the shelter of caves or rock overhangs. Yellow
Leggings also introduced to the Crow people the symbolism of the tipi's various elements as well as the respect, values, and protocols associated with it.[4]

Like the Crow, Blackfeet and Shoshone people construct their lodges on a base
of four poles. Others, such as the Arapaho, Lakota, Cheyenne, and Kiowa, use a
three-pole base with varying numbers of additional poles. For women, who had the
primary responsibility for creating and maintaining tipis, the acquisition and preparation of adequate numbers of strong, heavy poles required careful planning and assistance (fig. 44). Carl Sweezy, a renowned Southern Arapaho artist who was born in
about 1881, remembered that the women of his youth took great pride in constructing
and maintaining their tipis:

Fig. 45. Pawnee family in tipi, Oklahoma, circa 1885. Photograph by William S. Prettyman (1858–1932). Western History Collections, University of Oklahoma Libraries, Norman, Cunningham-Prettyman Collection, #143

The important thing, besides the know-how, was the lodge poles. These must be long and straight and slender, and for a good family lodge, there must be from sixteen to twenty of them. They must be of some wood like cedar that would not rot when they were exposed to rain and snow. Such poles were not easy to find on the Plains, and the women took great care in them.[5]

During the fall months, Blackfeet women cut new tipi poles of lodgepole pine. After locating, cutting, and bringing the poles into camp, a woman often enlisted the help of young men by preparing berry soup and inviting them to a feast in exchange for help with peeling the bark from the poles.[6] Although tipis and the labor associated with them were considered to be in the sphere of women's responsibilities, male relatives often assisted with this arduous but necessary work.

The Pawnee lived most of the year in earth lodges in villages situated along the banks of the Platte River and its tributaries so that the women could tend their gardens of corn, beans, squash, and melons, but during the winter and summer buffalo hunts, the bands lived in two types of hide-covered lodges. During the winter hunt, they lived in the standard conical hide tipi (*káracapí*) supported by a frame of thirteen poles with a three-pole foundation (fig. 45). With the fire burning in the middle of the lodge, the tipi provided protection from the cold, but it could be too warm for summer months. During the summer hunt, Pawnee women used the hide tipi cover over a framework of poles and lightweight elm or willow saplings to construct an open-faced shelter with a curved roof. They located a long rectangular fireplace just outside the shelter to the north of the entrance. This type of construction simplified preparation for the yearly migration and the travel itself, since the lightweight saplings were more easily fashioned and transported than heavier tipi poles.[7]

For the Pawnee constructing the hide cover for a tipi was a major undertaking that had to be planned at least two years in advance in order to accumulate at least eight buffalo hides as well as the sinew to sew them together.[8] An experienced lodge maker would supervise the somewhat complex work of fitting the hides together, with four or five other women doing the actual sewing over about four days. For this assistance the lodge owner compensated all the women with gifts of dried buffalo meat, clothing, or trade goods and provided them with meals for the duration of the work.[9]

Men sometimes painted scenes recording their accomplishments in hunting and warfare on tipi covers, which, together with the oral recitation of these deeds, served as a means of documenting individual biographies as well as tribal histories (fig. 46). They also painted images of creatures they had seen in visions or dreams and regarded as sources of their own supernatural powers. Following the directions they had received in their visions, men often called upon other men who were skilled artists to paint the outlines of the figures, which were later filled in by assistants. Although the distinctive designs of such paintings are often owned by individuals and families who uniquely understand their full symbolism, there are some tribal conventions. An example is the band along the bottom of Blackfeet lodge covers that is often painted in red and represents the earth, with unpainted circles symbolizing fallen stars. On many covers, a row of rounded shapes along the top of the lower band represents foothills; a row of pointed forms symbolizes the mountains. The tops of such tipi covers, painted in black, represent the night, with unpainted circles within this area indicating constellations such as the Pleiades or Big Dipper. The cross at the back of the cover near the top is said to symbolize the morning star or butterfly, which is believed to bring powerful dreams to the lodge owner.[10]

Arapaho, Cheyenne, and Lakota women often decorated their tipi covers with circular hide ornaments covered in beadwork or porcupine quillwork and pendants of small dewclaws wrapped in quillwork.[11] Other tribes such as the Crow preferred that their tipi covers remain undecorated (fig. 47).

Creating and maintaining a fine lodge required collaboration and shared responsibilities, so that women's industriousness and creativity were held in high esteem. Living in a tipi involved other shared cultural values for women such as generosity, hospitality, and humility. The Crow woman Pretty Shield (fig. 48) recalled a woman she knew when she was a child in the mid-nineteenth century who possessed all these traits as well as a beautifully maintained tipi:

Its poles were taller, its lodge-skin whiter and cleaner, its lining, beautifully painted, reaching all around it. Its back-rests, three of them, were made with head-and-tail robes; and always Kills-good burned a little sweet-grass, or sweet-sage, so that her lodge smelled nice. . . . Yes, and the shoulder-blades of buffalo that Kills-good used for dishes were bleached snow white, and always she placed a little square of rawhide under each of them when she gave meat to anybody. . . .

How I loved to watch Kills-good pack her things to move camp. The painting on her parfleches was brighter, her bags whiter, than those of any other Crow woman; and, ah, she had so many pretty things. Besides, I thought her favorite horse, a proud pinto, was far and away the best horse in the Crow tribe. And yet Kills-good was not proud. Instead, she was kindly and so soft-spoken that all the people loved her.[12]

Pretty Shield's granddaughter Alma Hogan Snell also spoke of the role of women as lodge keepers:

The lodge keepers were actually the backbone. Like my grandma always said, "If a man stayed in a lodge by himself, it was no good." It just wasn't a home until there was a lodge keeper there. So many things they had to do. Yet, they found time to make beauty of it.[13]

According to her granddaughter, Pretty Shield was "a good lodge maker."[14] Although buffalo-hide lodges had long disappeared and been replaced by canvas ones, Pretty Shield told her granddaughter about the care with which she had prepared, pieced together, and sewn buffalo hides for a tipi. Snell related how the old buffalo-hide lodges had particular spiritual significance for the Crow:

The lodges would be a sanctuary. It actually is a place of refuge. It protects you. It means so much more. I think it means more than a house, actually. It has the animal structure to it, the buffalo animal structure to it that protects us even from other animals that could invade the lodge. You could wrap up in a buffalo robe and stay still. The smell of the buffalo is so over-whelming and yet the hide is so tough. My grandmother says it protected them from many things, the buffalo.[15]

Fig. 49. Kanza (Kaw)
artist. Parfleche, early
20th century. Pawhuska,
Oklahoma. Rawhide,
pigment, 25½ × 11¾
in. (64.8 × 29.8 cm).
Brooklyn Museum,
Museum Expedition 1911,
Museum Collection Fund,
11.694.9042

Fig. 50. Arapaho artist. Parfleche, circa 1850. Wyoming. Buffalo rawhide, pigment, 29 × 16¾ in. (73.7 × 42.5 cm). Milwaukee Public Museum, E327 (Photo: Joanne Peterson)

Women furnished their tipis with functional yet often finely decorated parfleches and boxes made of rawhide and painted in geometric designs (figs. 49–51); soft, tanned buffalo robes; backrests made of slender peeled willow sticks laced together with sinew and sometimes trimmed with red or blue trade cloth embellished with beadwork or porcupine quillwork (see fig. 108); bowls made from rawhide or carved from wood (fig. 52); carved wooden or horn spoons (figs. 53, 54); and bags made from tanned hide and decorated in porcupine quillwork, beadwork, or natural pigments (figs. 55–58). To these furnishings Pawnee women added large mats woven of bulrush for the floor coverings and wooden mortars and pestles used for grinding corn. The Pawnee used clay pottery until the early 1800s, when they began to acquire brass kettles and buckets and metal pans.[16] Like other Plains peoples, they also added metal knives, wool blankets, and other tools to more traditional household items. (See Hail essay in this volume.)

Fig. 51. Sioux artist. Storage Box, circa 1890. Northern Plains. Rawhide, pigments, tanned deer hide, wool cloth, 7½ × 17 × 8¼ in. (19.1 × 43.2 × 21 cm). Buffalo Bill Historical Center, Cody, Wyoming, Chandler-Pohrt Collection, Gift of Mr. William D. Weiss, NA.106.262

Fig. 52. Siksika (Blackfeet) artist. Bowl, circa 1865. Blackfeet camp, United States or Canada. Wood, copper, lead-fill repair, 6¹³⁄₁₆ × 12⁷⁄₈ × 16³⁄₁₆ in. (17.3 × 32.8 × 41.1 cm). Peabody Museum of Archaeology and Ethnology, Harvard University, Cambridge, Massachusetts, 28-16-10/98291 (Photo: © Presidents and Fellows of Harvard College)

Fig. 53. Lakota artist. Spoon, 19th century. Northern Plains. Mountain sheep horn, porcupine quills, metal, and horsehair, l. 10 in. (25.4 cm). Brooklyn Museum, Brooklyn Museum Collection, X1126.22

Fig. 54. Sioux artist. Spoon, circa 1890. Northern Plains. Cow horn, porcupine quills, tin cones, horsehair, l. 10¼ in. (26 cm). Buffalo Bill Historical Center, Cody, Wyoming, Chandler-Pohrt Collection, Gift of Mr. William D. Weiss, NA.106.182

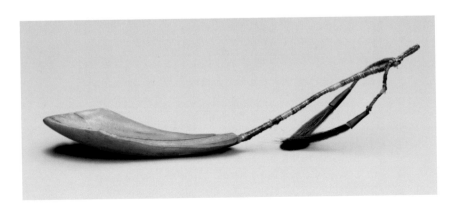

Fig. 55. Sioux artist. Storage Bag, circa 1880. Northern Plains. Tanned deer hide, porcupine quills, glass beads, feathers, horsehair, tin cones, 14½ × 19½ in. (36.8 × 49.5 cm). Buffalo Bill Historical Center, Cody, Wyoming, In memory of Frank O. Horton and Henrietta S. Horton, NA.106.630

Fig. 56. Cheyenne artist. Storage Bag, circa 1870. Northern Plains. Tanned buffalo hide, glass beads, tin cones, horsehair, 11 × 25 in. (27.9 × 63.5 cm). Buffalo Bill Historical Center, Cody, Wyoming, Gift of Mr. Robert Garland, NA.106.14b

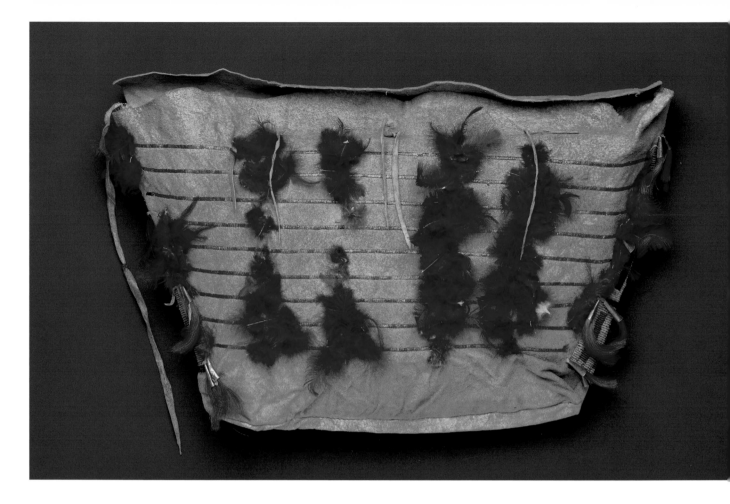

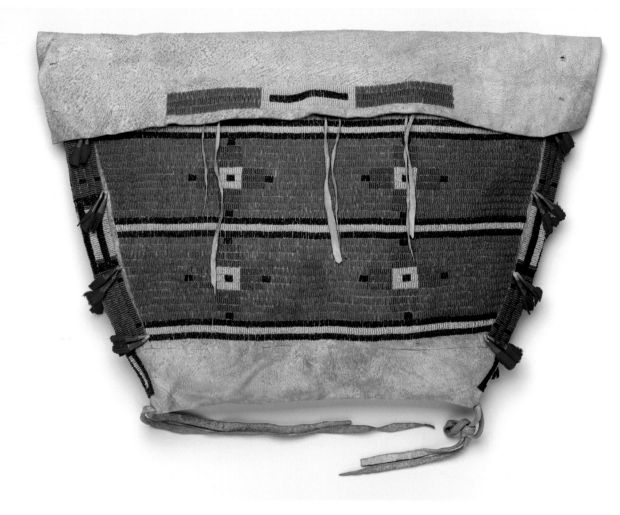

Tipi furnishings as well as personal items were transportable, functional, and practical, yet they were also carved, painted, quilled, beaded, and otherwise embellished to reflect distinctive cultural traditions. Because the beautifully decorated parfleches and other bags, buffalo robes, backrests, and other household items as well as the tipi itself were designed to be packed and transported by dogs and horses and on travois when bands moved camp, some scholars have characterized Plains material culture as possessing "an aesthetic of mobility."[17]

Although all women were expected to have skills in hide tanning and other basic arts, some women who were particularly talented in a specific decorative medium were called upon to produce specialized items with gifts provided in payment. Cheyenne, Arapaho, and Lakota women who excelled in beadwork or porcupine quillwork belonged to special societies or guilds whose membership was limited to women of high moral character (see Hail essay in this volume). Only women of these societies had the right to make the decorations for sacred tipis or tipi liners. A tipi liner, made of tanned hide, or later canvas or muslin, and tied to poles along the interior of a tipi, created an air space that reduced heat loss during the winter and kept the lodge cool during the summer. Men sometimes painted scenes of their hunting or warfare exploits on tipi liners as they did on lodge covers (see Kennedy Zeller essay in this volume). Women painted geometric designs on liners or decorated them with porcupine quillwork or beadwork.

Peaceful and efficient living in a tipi required organization and a definite arrangement of furnishings with specific places for family members where they habitually sat, ate, worked, and slept (fig. 59). Buffalo robes for bedding at night were folded during the day and placed around the perimeter of the tipi away from the entrance. In Arapaho tipis, as in those of other tribes, the eastern part of the tipi near the entrance belonged to the women, who worked and stored their cooking equipment in this area. Men had the western side opposite the door at the rear of the lodge. Here, on poles or tripods, men hung their necessities of hunting and warfare—shields and bow cases and quivers (fig. 60)—and their sacred bundles containing medicines and other materials that provided power and protection. The fireplace was placed directly under the opening at the top of the tipi.[18]

Tipi protocol was based on the cultural values of respect, generosity, and hospitality. Crow children learned to respect the sacredness of men's weapons and bundles at the rear of the tipi and to understand that they should not disturb them.[19] According to Pretty Shield, honored visitors were invited inside to sit in the rear of the tipi, where they were offered water and food.

When old people were the visitors they were given dried tenderloin from which all sinew had been stripped. This fine meat was first dried, and then pounded up and mixed with bone-marrow. It was served to men in bowls made of box-elder wood. . . . Old women got theirs on squares of rawhide.[20]

In this way, Crow people demonstrated respect for their elders, who provided leadership as well as advice and guidance on daily living and sacred matters.

Fig. 59. Interior of a Crow tipi, Crow Agency, Montana, 1907. Photograph by Richard Albert Throssel (1882–1933). American Heritage Center, University of Wyoming, Laramie

Fig. 60. Yankton artist. Bow, Bow Case, and Quiver, early 19th century. Collected by Dr. Nathan Sturges Jarvis, Sr., Fort Snelling, Minnesota. Wood, elk horn, thread, horsehair, stroud cloth, sinew, metal, pigment, buffalo hide, mallard scalps, remnants of feathers; l. of bow 44 in. (111.8 cm); bow case and quiver with arrows 5¾ × 41 in. (14.6 × 104.1 cm). Brooklyn Museum, Henry L. Batterman Fund and the Frank Sherman Benson Fund, 50.67.27a, b

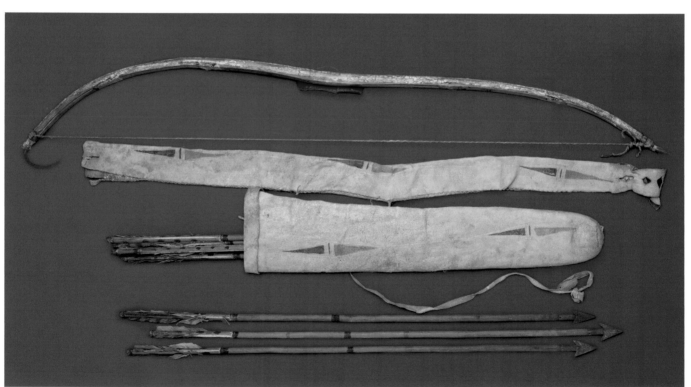

The first thing I remember about my childhood is the tipi where my family lived. It was one of many that belonged to our band or village, and was always somewhere not far from the Agency. . . . We were within sound of the big bell that hung above the stable at the Agency and was rung at seven in the morning and at noon and at six in the evening to tell the employees there when to go to work and when to stop. On good days, too, we could hear the bugle calls from Fort Reno, a mile and a half away from the Agency on the high land across the Canadian River. For us in our villages, these bells and bugle calls served as clocks when we needed to take notice of time in the white man's way.[21]

In the above passage, Carl Sweezy related how his family experienced the changes and transitions of the new life on the Cheyenne and Arapaho Reservation in Indian Territory in the late nineteenth century. During his early childhood, the family still moved seasonally within the reservation lands, living in villages that were located in sheltered areas near the river for protection from the cold during the winter and on cooler, higher ground during the summer. As they did in Pre-Reservation times, the Arapaho moved their entire villages to hunt game for meat and hides for trade — deer and small game, since buffalo were no longer available — and to camp in areas with good supplies of wood, water, and fresh pasture for the horses. According to Sweezy, although the buildings of the Cheyenne and Arapaho Agency at Darlington and Fort Reno had been established on the reservation by this time, there were still few fences and farms to limit tribal members' movements.

To us who were young, its streams and thickets and prairies seemed to stretch to the end of the world, but when we listened to the talk of the old men and women we knew they considered the Reservation small and the white settlements too close to us.[22]

When the agent Brinton Darlington established the Upper Arkansas Agency in 1870 to administer Southern Cheyenne and Arapaho affairs, he had called all the traditional leaders together to encourage them to abandon their tipis for government-built houses and to begin new lives as farmers. The Arapaho were slow to make these drastic changes, as Sweezy recounted:

But, this meant a great change, and one we could not make in a hurry. We liked our tipis, with all of our things around us in a circle. I have heard white people talk, of late, about the modern circular house, with arrangements for heat and plumbing in the center, new as tomorrow, they say. Well, ours were circular, with a central fire, but I never heard an Arapaho boast that the idea was a new one.[23]

Some of the Southern Arapaho leaders, like Little Raven, who eventually accepted a government house built at Cantonment and plowed and planted some of the land around it, continued to maintain tipis along with their houses (see fig. 6).[24]

According to the Dakota scholar Ella Deloria, the Early Reservation log houses were "small, one room affairs, low and dark, and dank, because of the dirt floors [fig. 61]. Compared with the well-constructed tipis with their manageable wind flaps for ample ventilating, the cabins were hot and stuffy. Germs lurked everywhere, causing general sickness, and the death rate increased."[25] After 1887, when the federal government divided reservation lands into allotments that were assigned to individual families under the Dawes Act, tribal members were able to build larger and better-constructed houses and began to adapt some elements of tipi living to their new environment (see Sun Rhodes essay in this volume).[26] Dakota people made large wall coverings of muslin reminiscent of the earlier tipi linings and called by the same term—*ozan*—to protect the log houses from drafts and dirt. Men painted pictographs of warfare, hunting, and camp and courtship scenes on the coverings, which were sometimes purchased for museum collections.[27]

Encouraged by missionaries on the reservations, women made patchwork quilts as substitutes for buffalo robes to be used in their log houses or for ceremonial gift giving to honor and thank individuals through the distribution of material goods. Women also made parfleches, although out of cowhide, for the same purposes. Among the Lakota, women's quilting groups organized and continued some of the traditions of the earlier porcupine quillwork societies, with status attached to those who excelled in this art (see fig. 129).[28]

The Lakota artist and scholar Arthur Amiotte has said that the log house "represents more than just a house where people lived. It was an entire experiment wherein Lakota people, who had previously lived in tipis, were now making the transition to living an agrarian lifestyle."[29] Although Plains Native people have made this and many more difficult transitions since the late nineteenth century, they have not forgotten their tribal origins and the ongoing significance of many cultural traditions, including the powerful symbol of the tipi.

The "Bed Room" of American Horse.

No. 1363.

Fig. 61. American Horse's
bedroom, Pine Ridge
Reservation, South Dakota,
1891. Photograph by C. G.
Morledge (1865–1948).
Denver Public Library,
Western History
Collection, X-31435

THE ARAPAHO TIPI

DENNIS SUN RHODES

LESSONS OF THE TIPI THAT I LEARNED FROM MY GREAT-GRANDMOTHER, Nellie Three Bulls Sun Rhodes, and the rich culture of my Arapaho people have been central to my practice as an architect over the past thirty years. Long before my professional training, I began to see how architecture can affect how we view ourselves and how it could be used to celebrate Native culture for tribes around the country. In my work for American Indian people, I have tried to honor the fire and water, as well as the seven directions of the natural world (east, west, south, north, sky, earth, and one's soul) and the symbolic essence of earth's creatures.

I grew up on the Wind River Indian Reservation in Wyoming. It is a beautiful high-prairie landscape with the Wind River Mountains to the west, the Owl Creek Mountains to the north, and the grand expanse of the prairie to the south and east. The winters are mild, with great summers for horseback riding.

We lived four and a half miles east of Ethete along the Little Wind River. About twenty-seven miles east of Ethete near Riverton, this river joins the Big Wind River, and the old people say that during the spring runoff, the river would howl as it made its way through the Wind River Canyon in the northeastern section of the reservation. It could be heard for many miles around, acquiring the name for the landscape in and around it, the Big Wind River valley.

I was a curious child with lots of energy who loved to draw on any surface — on the ground or on paper of any sort. I caught the attention of an older man, George

Panther Quiver, who was training for the honorary role of drum keeper for the western edge of the reservation. He lived on the road going to the small town of Lander. He and his family made stops at my great-grandmother's home when they came to the valley along the Little Wind River to visit during the summertime. My great-grandmother, whom I called Grandma Nellie, would always cook up a big meal. George and his sons and my great-granduncle, Robert Sun Rhodes, would sing songs into the night. They would usually stay overnight, and Grandma would make room in her one-room log cabin for the elders. The young ones would sleep outdoors in a shade structure built of tree boughs and branches during the summertime. What wonderful times those visits brought to our home.

GRANDMA NELLIE'S TIPI STORY

I learned the Arapaho language at home. Grandma Nellie also taught me English. She went to school through the seventh grade at the Fort Washakie Government School in the late 1800s. People would come to her home and speak English to her, and she would answer in Arapaho because she did not like the way English sounded. In addition to an understanding of both languages, Grandma Nellie gave me a love of learning. Some of the most important of these lessons were about the tipi, which is called *neyeihe'*, meaning "my lodge" or "my home" in the Arapaho language.

Grandma Nellie told me she was still living her life as if she were in the tipi. The space in her cabin had to be used for many purposes to fit the seasons and the time of day, just as it had in the tipi. Her cabin was built about fifteen years before I was born. They say she had saved enough money to pay the carpenter $500, and with family support she bought the materials to build the log cabin. The logs came from the Little Wind River, and the clay to fill the spaces between the logs came from the white hills across the river. All Grandma Nellie had to do was add water and the clay held together. She would replace the clay every once in a while.

Her one-room log home faced the south because it was warmer there and she could see the road. A window to the east took the place of the tipi's east-facing door. There was also a window to the south, but there were no openings to the north or west because in the summer the hot afternoon sun came from the west, and in the winter a cold wind came from the north. Grandma Nellie would take out the stove in the summertime and bring it back indoors when it got cold in the fall, just as she had done with the fire in her tipi. Summer cooking was done outdoors.

Grandma had a shade structure with mats to sleep on so the teenage relatives could live outside in the hot weather. She placed beds inside the cabin on the west, north, and east sides for sleeping, in keeping with the way that her family had lived and slept in the tipi. She made us get up early in the morning so that she could make the space look like a living room during the day. When the stove was brought back inside and placed in the center of the cabin, it became the focal point of the home, generating plenty of heat during the winter months. We were taught to always turn left when we entered the cabin, just as my great-grandmother had done in the tipi. There was room to walk around the back of the stove to pay respect to the fire for

Figs. 62a, b. Nellie Three Bulls Sun Rhodes's cabin, Wind River Indian Reservation, Wyoming, early 1950s, and diagram of its layout (Photo and diagram: Dennis Sun Rhodes)

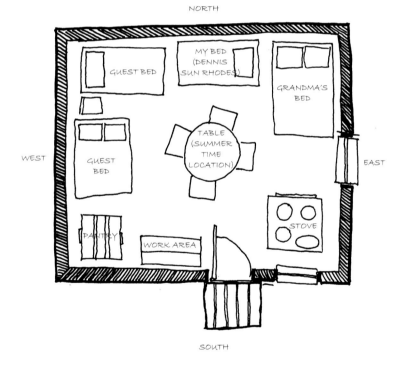

giving us warmth in the wintertime and providing a place for us to cook our food (figs. 62a, b). During the 1950s, a medicine bundle was hung on the northwest wall. Later, when Grandma Nellie had more visitors, she put the medicine bundle away in a large suitcase under her bed and brought it out only when it was needed. She was a specialist in doctoring women during pregnancy.

Life in that cabin with Grandma Nellie taught me many lessons. We were told to be quiet when we came in and to be quiet when our elders spoke. We learned by listening to what was talked about. We learned to look away when Grandma or young girls changed their clothes. This taught us to be respectful of one another and to know our place in this modern lodge and the world at large.

MODERN TIPI CULTURE AT HOME

My first experience with the tipi occurred during a visit to George Quiver's homestead when I was five years old. George was amused at my ability to speak the Arapaho language—rare for someone my age. He kept me talking while watching me build things out of the earth using sticks and stones. He asked me if I would like to see a structure that the Arapaho lived in when they first moved to the reservation. I did, and I told him so. "Oh, you want to see what I have out back," he said. He took me out to a tree near an old irrigation ditch. Nestled within the tree's branches were poles maybe thirty feet long. He told me that the Arapaho home was called a tipi. He said that the tipi lodge is put up in what we used to call "the wartime way" because it could be taken down quickly when soldiers were coming during the Indian Wars of the 1860s and 1870s.

He took three poles and made a tripod—one pole in the southwest, another to the northwest, and the door pole to the southeast. Besides the three poles for the tripod, he used a total of eighteen other poles (see fig. 63). There was a special way that you laid the poles onto the tripod. He continued with five poles on the northeast side of the door pole. The poles had to be held up as the rope was brought around to secure them in place. Then six more poles were placed onto the southeast side of the tipi, and again the poles were held in place as the rope was brought around to hold them. The last five poles—the lodge pole, which had the tipi skin attached, and two on either side of it—were then put in place. Then the canvas covering was wrapped around the poles and secured. Finally two longer poles were attached to the tipi's "ears," flaps at the top that were adjusted to keep the smoke out or to work with the wind to vent the fire. One pull on the rope, and the tipi came down.

Not too long after our visit with George Quiver, I asked Grandma Nellie about the tipi for the second time, and she said she grew up in a tipi and that when she married her husband, Sun Roads, they got their own tipi to live in. (Our family name was changed to Sun Rhodes by the Indian agent on the reservation after a fire destroyed the tribal records in the 1920s.) She told me our people used poles that had to be car-

Fig. 63. Arrangement of Arapaho tipi poles before the lodge pole (with canvas cover attached) and the two ear-flap poles are added (Photo: Dennis Sun Rhodes)

ried by horse-drawn travois and that the poles became shorter as they were dragged over the prairie. She said that once a year the women of the tribe would go into the forest to get the lodge poles. After they found a good stand of poles, they would cut and process them right away and then let them dry for a couple of days before putting them on the horse-drawn travois to be taken back to the village site (fig. 64). They were set up with the entry facing the rising sun in the east. (The same protocol was observed when villages gathered together for a Sun Dance Ceremony because the camp was organized in a horseshoe shape with an east-facing opening.) Because the tipi was mobile, the women could put together an entire village in a few hours.

THE ESSENCE OF THE TIPI TODAY

Things began to change over to the modern way of life for the Arapaho people and for the rest of Indian country in the late 1960s, when the federal government started to make houses for American Indians. They built little boxes that were made up of a nest of small spaces inside small spaces. Each functional space was too small, and there was no connection to the land. Even the one-room log cabin had a tipi's connection to the prairie landscape. The government made us live in these houses without any regard for what this would do to our cultural life. In fact, most Native people now accept this type of a house and call it home, but my childhood experience with our

Fig. 64. Pretty Enemy beside horse dragging tipi poles in Bighorn Mountains, Crow Reservation, Montana, early 1900s. Photograph by William H. Rau (1855–1920). McCracken Library Collection, Buffalo Bill Historical Center, Cody, Wyoming, LS.95.213

tribal culture and specifically with the tipi led me in a different direction. With the encouragement of Grandma Nellie, I left the reservation for architecture school at Montana State University in Bozeman. I started looking for another way of making buildings for American Indian people, and I am still engaged in this endeavor more than thirty years later. The tipi design has influenced many of my architectural projects, some of which are described below.

The Elmer Running House

Elmer Running was a shaman of the Oglala Sioux tribe who lived on the Rosebud Indian Reservation in South Dakota. We knew each other for twenty years, and I designed a home and ritual environment for him—which we were planning to build when we secured the funding. But sadly, Running died in the late summer of 2009. Running lived in the federal-housing box-style home, which he had set up to suit his needs, although its architectural limitations meant that he could not accommodate his lifestyle within one building. He had created separate outbuildings for both storage and additional bedrooms, and his ritual space was also outdoors. In the redesign of Running's home, I incorporated all critical components inside, following tipi protocols. The essential elements are an east-facing doorway, a ritual space for ceremonies, and a feast area for gatherings with appropriate accommodation for the attendees. Each space flows into the next, as in the tipi. The layout of this modern home fits the schematic that I drew years before to illustrate how the Plains American Indian home could develop from a traditional tipi form to incorporate the conveniences of modern times (fig. 65). The top of this diagram shows a traditional tipi arrangement. The middle section illustrates the critical components that needed to be incorporated into the new design; and the bottom part reflects modifications of the important elements for a contemporary lifestyle. To enter this home, echoing tipi protocol, you approach the house from the east. Upon crossing the threshold, you turn and walk to the left, reflecting the way the sun crosses the sky. The south side of the house immediately to the left of the doorway is the place for women and contains the kitchen. The west, the place of honor for Running as headman of the home, is where he would conduct ceremonies in the circular space using coals from the fire pit. The ritual feast area is in the center, just as it is in the tipi. Following tipi protocols, your path continues in a clockwise direction toward an extension of the men's area on the north side, where there are bedrooms. Next to the entrance is another bedroom, which corresponds to the place in the tipi of the "old man" or the "old woman," who is the keeper of the door and the fire. The outside of the redesigned home would still be used for tool storage, as well as for gardens and water collection. I am bemused that Elmer's lifestyle anticipated the green architecture that is a hot subject today.

Division of Indian Work

In 1993 the Division of Indian Work (DIW), a large social-service agency in Minneapolis, gave me the opportunity to design a four-story multi-use office building to

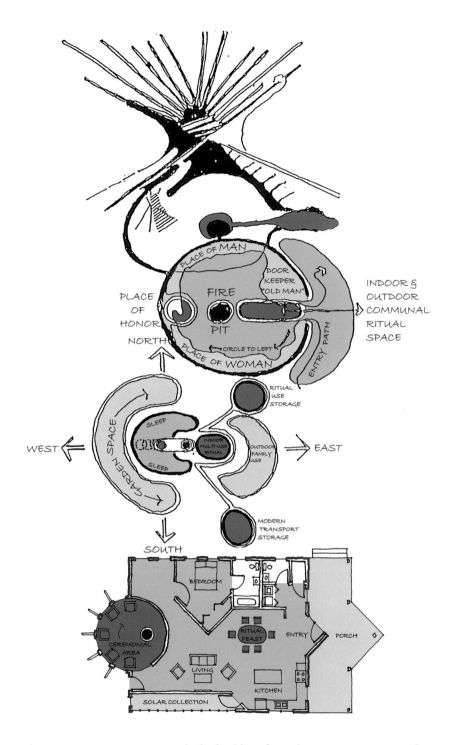

house their operations. You approach the building from the west to see a special symbolic entryway dedicated to the moon, a woman's symbol (fig. 66). That is appropriate
because for more than fifty years women have been at the helm of the DIW, doing
good work for American Indians. You walk through the building to the lower level,
which opens onto a meeting space bathed in natural light with a central fireplace
(fig. 67). The elders are able to walk around the fire as they did in the old days in the
tipi. They get hot cedar coals and other elements they use in their doctoring ceremonies from the hearth. The room opens to a garden landscaped with native plants.

Fig. 66. Division of Indian Work, Minneapolis, 1993 (Photo: Don Wong)

Fig. 67. Lower-level meeting space, Division of Indian Work, Minneapolis, 1993 (Photo: Don Wong)

Wakpa Sica Reconciliation Place

In 1998 I began a design for the Wakpa Sica Reconciliation Place, which stands adjacent to the site of historic Fort Pierre Chouteau, the largest fur-trading post in the West during the early 1800s (fig. 68). The center, located across the river from Pierre, South Dakota, is dedicated to better understanding between the Sioux nations and descendants of the white settlers. It includes a museum, gift shop, offices, and meeting space, and a Sioux Nation Judicial Center will follow in a later phase. The facility also includes outdoor space for ceremonial activities and interpretive trails. The first phase of the project, completed in 2003, was the Wolakota, or welcome center.

The Wakpa Sica complex takes its form from the tipi village that existed on the prairie at the old fort. On one side is a building housing both the Sioux Nation cultural museum (to the north) and the future judicial center (to the south). To the west of the building, completing the village circle, are seven large tipi structures representing the seven Sioux nations.

The building as a whole forms a symbolic eagle. In the center of the structure, the space below the eagle's beak serves as the welcome center to the complex. The cultural museum and the judicial center make up the wings of the building/eagle.

Lower Brule Tribal Headquarters

I was asked to design the tribal government center for the Lower Brule tribe in South Dakota in 1999. One hour south of Wakpa Sica, on the west bank of the Missouri River, the structure is sited on a bluff overlooking the Missouri and provides modern,

Fig. 68. Rendering of the Wakpa Sica Reconciliation Place, Lower Brule Sioux Reservation, South Dakota, 1998 (Drawing: Dennis Sun Rhodes)

efficient office space for tribal operations (fig. 69). A large tipi-shaped space with a beautiful view of the river through a large window on the eastern side of the structure serves as the place of honor where the elected council meets (fig. 70). A painted semicircular design on the southwest side of the building represents a spread-out tipi cover.

OUR CULTURE LIVES ON

For more than thirty years I have worked with American Indian people around the country, combining the best of modern architecture with building traditions from many different cultures. These cultures are rooted in the deep past but are alive, growing, and changing. My goal is to help realize through my architecture positive creative visions that carry these cultures into the future.

Fig. 69. Lower Brule
Administration Building,
Lower Brule Sioux
Reservation, South Dakota,
1999 (Photo: Dennis Sun
Rhodes)

Fig. 70. Council Chambers,
Lower Brule Administration
Building, Lower Brule Sioux
Reservation, South Dakota,
1999 (Photo: Dennis Sun
Rhodes)

ASHTÁAHILE (CROW TIPIS)

Interview conducted by Susan Kennedy Zeller with Heywood and Mary Lou Big Day, Crow Indian Reservation, Pryor, Montana, July 15, 2008. The Big Days are both tribal elders whose first language is Crow; she is a doll maker, and he is a tribal culture keeper (fig. 71).

SKZ: Why do the Crow have a four-pole-frame tipi?

HBD: The meaning of [the four-pole frame] is the four winds or directions. The four poles of the frame are set up, and then ten more poles are added in between [the canvas cover is tied to one of the ten poles and then lifted into place and wrapped around the poles], plus there's two poles on the outside for the flaps. So there is a total of sixteen poles or eighteen [for a bigger tipi]. In the old days as they got more horses they added another two poles and turned it into a twenty-pole tipi for a large family, and all the way up to size twenty-four. Before [they had] canvas, they used buffalo skins, and they scraped them and turned them into a tipi . . . and the tipis all face to the east.

SKZ: Why do tipis face east?

HBD: When the women are having babies in the tipi, they position themselves so that the baby's head will be east. And as the children grow up, they start walking toward the east, and a lot of the mornings when they [the Crow] break up the camp, they set out to the east. They kind of make a circle like the sun that will go [from the east] toward the south and then head to the west, and that's how [they] followed the buffalo.

Fig. 71. Heywood and Mary Lou Big Day wearing their traditional regalia, circa 2008

SKZ: What about different parts of the tipi?

HBD: I'm going to talk about the collar [lacing] pins. Now the collar pins are the little bitty stakes [that lace the front of the tipi together]. I believe they call [the tree they are made from] a red birch—it has little red speckles. There's a lot of them [red birch trees] over here in Montana. The collar pins belong to the women, and the women put them in and take them out. The collar pin is also a good weapon. Before the [wood] stakes we used rocks to hold down the [tipi] cover and there [would be] tipi rings [of stones, so] other tribes would know where the Crow camps were. After so many years the Crow got wise and they used [wooden] stakes that they could pull up and pack, and pretend that there was no camp. Once they pulled the stakes out, like you see [after] Crow Fair, there's no [sign of a] camp.

Some of the women would carve these stakes. They'd go out to the hills or out to the mountains if they had lost their loved ones to their enemies. For revenge, they would put a mark on a stake [to invoke bad spirits against the enemy].

Also, the women have to have a good luck charm. Let me tell you a story about the red birch. There was a man who had been gone in the enemy territory for so long—about two months (they usually were gone for about a month or three weeks), but he wasn't coming back for another month or month and a half. And [his] wife was beginning to worry about him, and one night she was praying along the creek bank and saw a red birch collar pin. She picked it up and slept with it. At the same time her husband was down at the creek someplace else and was leaning against a red birch as he was sleeping. The man dreamt and saw his wife. He saw his children and his wife who was carrying a red birch [pin] and saw that the woman was worried. She also had a dream and saw her husband and saw that he was [alive and] lying by a red birch. That's their communication—through the red birch. And that's why the red birch is really centric to the women.

MLBD: The buckskin banner on the tip of the tipi pole is [also] a woman's decoration for the tipi. We have one that belonged to Heywood's mother, but they go fragile, and we don't put it up.

HBD: They take some buckskin [to make the banner] from the coyote, timber wolf, elk, or buffalo. There's six animals that they make the buckskin from, and they slice it into strips. My mother had thirteen banners—thirteen is meant for thirteen months [yearly periods of the moon]. The [banners] offer prayers for good spirits and show it is a good tipi.

SKZ: Mary Lou, when was the first time you remember you were ever in a tipi?
MLBD: Well, the first time I lived in a tipi was when me and Heywood got married. When we get married, the family usually puts tipis up for us in Crow ways. When we have daughter-in-laws, we give them gifts and we give them a tipi so that's their shelter, that's a woman's shelter. We give them a tipi, the liner, and the rug. We did [that] for my daughter-in-laws. That's what I had too—they gave me a tipi, and so we started off with a tipi for a lot of years. We used it for Crow Fair and Sun Dance.

The women clean the tipis as soon as they get up and see that the lining and everything are there. We had beds, a mattress. Today [people use] a canvas floor, a mattress and box spring, and sheets and blankets. They furnished differently in the old days—a buffalo robe [was used as bedding], and you kept two buffalo robes plus trinkets and food like dried meat and dried berries in a bag like an envelope [a parfleche]. Well, they made dried chokecherries in the old days. I remember when Heywood and I were married his mother was still making dried chokecherries.

SKZ: Do the children learn about tipis?
MLBD: Yes, what we did, the first time it was just Heywood and I. He would cut the tipi poles, and [our] boys were just our great-grandchildren's age then and they were playing around. And I would drag [the poles] to the road and start peeling, and all the boys would do is play. But we did it with them until they grew older, and now they know how, and they do it with their wives like we did. And they are teaching their

boys and girls too. But now, I don't know about our great-grandchildren—I don't see my grandkids teaching the great-grandchildren, so I don't know if we are going to lose that [tradition] or not, but the boys are still doing it.

SKZ: Crow tipis today, why are they all white?

HBD: In the old days the [Crow] had their own ways of painting them, each family had their color, but not anymore. We do have painting and also beadwork. They do beadwork right in the middle of the back. It was like right up through your backbone there was a strip of beadwork. Tribes used to paint a buffalo, bear, mountain lion, coyote, [or] timber wolf on their tipis. Now starting in the 1930s [or] 1940s, you don't see it anymore—before that you used to see a lot of [painted tipis] in the horse and the bear tribes. We found out that a lot of the people who have [a] horse or other animal or even landscape designs on [their] tipi as good luck charms do not respect that there are rules for using these designs and some "thou shalt nots." It is wrong to paint a design that doesn't belong to your family. The older people are not telling the kids the rules and that's why the [traditional] designs are gone now.

SKZ: What are doorway songs?

HBD: The doorway song was sung the night before the breakup of the camp. When they broke up the camp and they went to another area, they would sing in the doorway three times: the night before they broke up the camp, and the first two nights of new camp. What it meant is they wanted the good spirits to come over, so there would be no accidents and nothing would happen [on the way to] the next stop, and the camp would have good water and be near the buffalo. Once the men and the [male] teenagers sang, the people in the tipi would give them something [to eat] like dried meat or fruit or berries, and they would eat it right away. [Or] sometimes it's men and women who sing. Men are lead singers, women are backup singers. [*Heywood begins to sing a doorway song.*] That's the song that I heard the first time, back in the early forties during World War II. I liked it and I kept it in my mind, and I still remember that song. That's a doorway song.

SKZ: Can you tell me about some Crow Fair memories and changes today (fig. 72)?

MLBD: The one I first remember? Well, I was pretty young. I was probably eight. We were allowed to have fun, and there were less tipis then.

Now I'm a woman, and I have daughter-in-laws and now granddaughter-in-laws. You see, I had Heywood and the boys [my sons] for a lot of years and I'm used to having Heywood and the boys put the tipi up and being the only woman in the family, and now the daughter-in-laws [take part] (fig. 73).

HBD: I must've been about five or something. We used to camp close to a knoll—there was a road that went right in there. The rodeo area was up on the knoll, and my dad got a bucking horse and [the Native cowboys] had to sit on it. [Everybody bet on either the horse or the cowboy.] If the cowboy can sit on the horse, he wins. If the horse bucks him off, the horse wins. That's how it works.

Fig. 72. Regalia parade, Crow Fair, Harding, Montana, August 2008 (Photo: Susan Kennedy Zeller)

Back in the beginning, Crow Fair was an agricultural fair. During World War I, the boss farmer [government agent] would come along to see the oats and the barley and the calves and the chickens, sheep and horses. So once a year it took us two days to get down there [to Crow Fair]. We rode down and camped over in between the Bighorn River and Pryor, and the next day we got out [our] plants and agricultural [products] and we paraded and showed them off as if to say "this is what I have and grow, and this is what I raised (animals)." So the boss farmer didn't have to come around to us and could put in a full report.

HBD: Monday they break up the camp, and in the old days, like I was telling you, there was singing the night before, so they could have good spirits and a good journey. They have a parade dance Monday morning and go from tipi camp to tipi camp. It's a [way to say] "thank you, each and every one of you, it was a very good Crow Fair, glad you came over and we saw each other, and we will meet each other next year," and they make a vow to meet them. For the parade they get four pipe carriers [honorary ceremonial positions held by men] — veterans from each district, like Loyola, Crow Agency, St. Xavier, or Pryor. The veterans [tell] their stories, [like] "I went overseas right in the battle where the bullets were flying back and forth, and I'm safe and I came back over here and I [hope] that we see each other next year." So that's the whole philosophy of the parade dance.

SKZ: How is the tipi important to the Crow family and culture?

HBD: On my part—if I don't have the frame of the poles, I won't have any tipis. In other words, if I don't [provide the] backbone, we don't have nothing. I'm the frame, and when I go over the hill and I'm not coming back, then somebody has to look after everything. So that's my whole idea, that I teach my boys so they know how to show my daughter-in-laws. I don't care what kind of a nationality they are, I don't care. If they want to learn, they could learn. If you find someone and you want to go into the family, you choose. You choose to be in the family, so a lot of my daughter-in-laws choose to be in the Big Day family. So I have to teach them, and they have to listen to me. So if you are one of my daughter-in-laws, you choose to be part of an Indian family, you choose. And I hold you into my family, and I have to teach you. I even teach the boys. If we don't have the frame of the poles, then we won't have any shelter, and the women have to provide the covers so we can be warm. I'm the backbone, so I'm the cultural [keeper], and [Mary Lou is] the tipi. The mother is the tipi [she owns the tipi and nurtures the family], and—there's no doubt about it—[the father is] the backbone.

Fig. 73. Big Day family
tipi camp at Crow Fair,
Harding, Montana, 2007
(Photo: Susan Kennedy
Zeller)

THE RAIN-IN-THE-FACE TIPI LINER

SUSAN KENNEDY ZELLER

IN 1889, IN A TIPI CAMP LOCATED FORTY MILES FROM THE STANDING Rock Agency on the Lakota Reservation, North Dakota, the artist Edwin Willard Deming spent many days watching the Húnkpapa Lakota warrior Rain-in-the-Face paint his war exploits on his muslin tipi liner (fig. 74). Although he spoke no English at that time, Rain-in-the-Face (Ité Omágažu; circa 1835–1905) narrated the battle histories of the scenes he was depicting. Deming, on assignment for *Outing* magazine, was on his first visit to Indian Territory, but he had studied sign language and had learned as many spoken Lakota words as he could.[1] Somehow the two artists, mature Lakota warrior and promising young non-Native painter, were able to communicate (figs. 75, 76). Deming made a drawing of Rain-in-the-Face, which the warrior inscribed with his name glyph (now unlocated; fig. 77), and Rain-in-the Face gave the tipi liner to Deming.[2] Deming treasured this gift and the inscribed portrait and would not part with either in his lifetime.[3]

Rain-in-the-Face's painted liner was displayed at the Brooklyn Museum in 1922 as part of an exhibition of Deming's paintings and sculptures, alongside his Native American collection, and the Museum acquired the liner from Deming's widow in 1943. A rare example from earlier Reservation times (1880–1920), the liner is especially important because we are sure of its provenance and, moreover, because it was produced by the artist-warrior to reflect his personal choices of significant events rather than commissioned for a non-Native patron. This rich document allows us to

explore Lakota pictographic warrior painting as a powerful and beautiful form of tipi art and as a vehicle for reinforcing spiritual and social values.

Although little is known about Rain-in-the-Face's domestic life, his role as a warrior has been recounted by many writers, who give conflicting versions of his accomplishments in battle.[4] Deming's original diaries are lost, and only partial typewritten transcriptions have been found.[5] Since conclusive written descriptions of the images on this liner are unavailable, other interpretive means have been used to decode them. One source is pictographic art—other tipi liners, ledger drawings (works in journal books and on paper), and winter counts (calendars). Additional written sources are the memoir of De Cost Smith (1864–1939), the artist who accompanied Deming and coauthored the articles for *Outing*; an interview with Rain-in-the-Face just prior to his death, on September 14, 1905, by the writer and medical doctor Charles Eastman (Lakota); published accounts of Lakota battles

Fig. 74. Rain-in-the-Face (Húnkpapa Lakota, circa 1835–1905). Tipi Liner, 1889. Standing Rock Reservation, North Dakota. Cotton, pigment, crayon, pencil, 67¹¹⁄₁₆ × 201¹⁵⁄₁₆ in. (172 × 513 cm). Brooklyn Museum, Frank L. Babbott Fund, 43.221.1

that occurred from 1850 to 1876; the records of Standing Rock Reservation; and the remembrances of James McLaughlin, the Standing Rock government agent.[6] In addition, the Brooklyn Museum held a special consultation in 2007 with scholars and descendants of Rain-in-the-Face to discuss this liner and its interpretation.

STANDING ROCK RESERVATION

Even after the Lakota were forced onto reservations in the 1870s, tipis remained an important part of their lifestyle through the 1890s.[7] Some Húnkpapa Lakota lived at or near the agency compound at Standing Rock, the reservation established in 1869 on the western bank of the Missouri River near Fort Yates. Most Lakota, however, lived much farther out in the territory and would come into the center only for rations, trade, and special events. During his monthlong stay on the Lakota

Fig. 75. Rain-in-the-Face, undated. Photograph by Laton Alton Huffman (1854–1931). National Archives at College Park, Maryland

Fig. 76. Edwin Willard Deming in front of tipi, 1889. Knight Library, University of Oregon, Eugene

Fig. 77. Edwin Willard
Deming (American,
1860–1942). *Rain-in-the-
Face*. Drawing. Location
unknown (Photo from
The Craftsman 10 [1906],
courtesy Offices of United
Crafts, Eastwood, New
York)

reservation, Deming had the opportunity to observe this way of life firsthand. He witnessed numerous Lakota returning home from the agency as he traveled to the warrior Flying-by's camp. The Lakota traveled in wagons with their lodge (tipi) poles tied on top of household goods and sticking out at all angles. Some people used horse-drawn travois carrying smaller loads, and the men often rode their horses alongside them. Flying-by's tipi camp consisted of twenty-five tipis and several log houses located on a flat piece of land by the Grand River. Rain-in-the-Face had his tipi and brush sweat lodge set up a hundred yards away (fig. 78). After staying in this camp a short time, Deming was invited to attend a dance, and everyone in the area packed up their tipis and moved about ten miles away. Deming reported seeing roughly a thousand tipis set up around a special dance lodge. This structure was made as a permanent log shelter but had a shape that was tipi-inspired. The twelve-sided lodge was about sixty feet in diameter with walls ten to twelve feet high. The roof was formed from poles and brush tapering to an open peak in the center so that a fire could be built inside. This dance lasted a few days and then the entire band moved back to its own camp.[8]

Every two weeks all the Lakota struck their tipi camps and traveled to the Standing Rock Agency to join the entire Húnkpapa Lakota band. Because the few buffalo herds that remained in the region had been pushed north and that area was now off limits as a hunting ground, government treaties prescribed bimonthly cattle butcherings to distribute beef to each registered Lakota. The Lakota used these rationing events as social occasions, similar to the annual summer gatherings of tipi camps before the Natives were removed to reservations. Flying-by set up his band about

753. View of Indian camp, Pine Ridge Agency, S. D., Jan. 17th, 1891

Fig. 78. Rain-in-the-Face tipi camp and brush sweat lodge, Standing Rock Reservation, North Dakota, 1889. Photograph by Edwin Willard Deming (1860–1942). New-York Historical Society

Fig. 79. View of Indian camp (Lakota tipi camp), Pine Ridge Agency, South Dakota, January 17, 1891. Yale Collection of Western Americana, Beinecke Rare Book and Manuscript Library

three miles south of the agency amid 4,200 other tipis.⁹ Deming observed that "for miles and miles in all directions could be seen teepees and wicky ups or brush-lodges, while small bands of Indian ponies, guarded by boys, were scattered over the plain as far as the eye could reach."¹⁰ An 1891 photograph of a Lakota tipi gathering at a nearby agency gives a sense of the spectacle Deming would have seen (fig. 79).

THE RAIN-IN-THE-FACE TIPI LINER AND LAKOTA LIFE AND CULTURE

Tipi liners are large hangings that were made from buffalo hides before 1850 and from canvas or (as in the case of the Rain-in-the-Face liner) cotton muslin in later years.

The liner is suspended along the lower half of the interior tipi walls and serves to deflect drafts and rainwater and to provide privacy for those inside (see fig. 59). Liners also function aesthetically to beautify the lodge. In the past they were sometimes embellished by women with porcupine quillwork, beadwork, or geometric paintings (see Hail essay in this volume) or by men with pictographic paintings of their warrior exploits.

The Rain-in-the-Face tipi liner is made from two pieces of cotton muslin, each thirty-five inches wide, sewn together along the long edge. The muslin is of the type that was distributed under the terms of the Treaty of 1868, which dictated that certain domestic goods were to be rationed to the Lakota each year by the federal government.[11] Even after the 1868 treaty was broken by the government in 1876, the practice of allocating these goods, clothing materials, and beef to Native Americans continued under other settlement acts through the 1880s.

The paintings on the Rain-in-the-Face liner are located along the entire upper half and depict vignettes of horse stealing, individual war encounters, counting coup (touching the enemy with a special coup stick, lance, club, or rifle and then getting away safely), and taking prisoners. Most of the depictions show Lakota fighting Crow, their traditional enemies. There is evidence of federal army weaponry and battle gear among the equipment used by the combatants, especially the Crow, who often served as scouts for the army; some of the Lakota also use guns, presumably captured in battle. Rain-in-the-Face first outlined the figures in pencil and then filled them in with a combination of pigment and crayons without gradation or shading. The color choices may have been completely arbitrary, dependent on the availability of supplies, or the hues may have been deliberately selected to accurately represent horses, clothing, or accoutrements.[12] The paintings have no indication of setting such as a ground line or landscape elements. As a result, the figures lack solid form but have great energy and animation, seeming to race across the length of the liner from right to left. This two-dimensionality is often seen in warrior art produced between 1850 and 1900.[13]

According to one theory, this flat style of painting, despite its repetitive themes, became a codified way to identify combatants by dress and weaponry.[14] The paintings are representational in the sense that they are based on pictographic signs used and understood by Native peoples all over the Plains; a warrior depicted with two feathers in his hair, for example, is understood to represent a man who has completed two successful war exploits. Similar pictographs were used for centuries in rock art, love letters, directions to campsites, warnings of danger to tipi camps, heraldic paintings on special tipi covers, warrior shirts, robes, ledger drawings, and winter counts. Many of these pictographs were recorded by non-Native artists visiting the Plains area. In the 1830s George Catlin (1796–1872) depicted several warriors wearing their pictographic shirts.[15] The Swiss artist Karl Bodmer (1809–1893) not only portrayed the Mandan warrior Mato-Tope wearing his pictographic garb but also shared his own art supplies with the warrior. Mato-Tope produced his own pictographic drawings, now in the Joslyn Art Museum, Omaha, from this encounter.[16] Garrick Mallery, in his 1888–89 work for the Smithsonian Institution, recorded numerous pictographs, extending the compilation work done by the eighteenth-century schoolteacher Henry Schoolcraft.[17]

Although there are minor variations, the various pictographs maintain greater overall stylistic consistency than other Plains art forms (such as the geometric designs used by women), perhaps because tipi-liner art is associated with the reinforcement and continuity of spiritual power.

The subject matter painted on tipi liners reflects the prominent role of warfare in the Lakota religion. According to Lakota oral tradition, White Buffalo Calf Woman brought the sacred pipe to the Lakota and gave them instructions on how to live their lives. Part of these laws dictated that all people who were their allies were always to be treated as friends, and all people who were enemies were always to be treated as foes.[18] For instance, the Cheyenne were considered friends, referred to as Cheyenne Lakota (or Lakhôta, from *lakhôta*, meaning "allies"), and they fought alongside the Lakota. It was not unusual for the Cheyenne and Lakota to intermarry; the Crow and Gros Ventre were considered traditional *thóka* (enemies). Thus White Buffalo Calf Woman dictated that warfare was a sacred duty of Lakota men.[19] Although tipi liners are not sacred objects themselves, they did serve as mnemonic devices for displaying warriors' personal histories, narrating their stories, and singing the associated warrior songs. If these activities were done in a public setting, it was believed, a warrior's spiritual power was enhanced.[20] Since the successful warrior depended on these powers for protection, guidance, and wisdom, the public acknowledgment of war deeds gave the warrior strength and honor. Painted liners could also be hung in the larger tipis of military societies and portray several different society members' deeds.[21] Such military associations unified warriors, and the recitation of the warriors' stories portrayed gave spiritual strength to the entire camp[22] (see Swan and Jordan essay in this volume).

Warfare was essential to the Lakota not only for protection and spiritual enrichment but for the acquisition of spoils—primarily horses, the most prized article of exchange and gift giving. The demonstration of generosity through bestowing gifts and sharing with others was indispensable to the establishing, maintaining, and solidifying of relationships. The tipi liner, with its vignettes portraying war deeds such as horse raids, was not merely a bragging device: it could function as a formalized method of training young warriors to take up their adult roles in the society.[23] It reinforced other ways of maintaining the tradition: warriors were pointed out to young boys as exemplars of how to win respect, and teenagers were encouraged to join war parties to begin acquiring such honors and gaining spiritual power.[24] Thus, tipi-liner pictographs presented powerful cultural values in an easily understood art form that integrated the spiritual and the secular.[25]

ISSUES OF INTERPRETING THE RAIN-IN-THE-FACE TIPI LINER AND PLAINS PICTOGRAPHIC ART

In September 2007 a consultant group consisting of descendants of Rain-in-the-Face, the Lakota NAGPRA (Native American Graves Protection and Repatriation Act) cultural adviser for Standing Rock, an Oglala Lakota artist and researcher, and non-Native ledger-art and winter-count scholars met with the Brooklyn Museum curators to review the Rain-in-the-Face tipi liner (fig. 80).[26] The meeting yielded valuable

Fig. 80. Consultants around Rain-in-the-Face's tipi liner, Brooklyn Museum, September 17, 2007 (Photo: Brooklyn Museum, Arts of the Americas)

information, with consensus on some ideas and a diversity of opinion concerning others. Much of the group's discussion, characterized by a generous sharing of knowledge, was exploratory in its questions and tentative in its conclusions, and additional consultations are planned.

One of the most difficult aspects of interpretation concerns the sequence of events on the liner. In contrast to the non-Native sense of time as a fixed and linear progression, the Native viewpoint conceives of time as a continuous circle of past and present and emphasizes the resonance of historic and contemporary events, both ceremonial and secular. A tipi liner reflects this view: where the account begins and ends depends less on chronology than on the meaning of the events to the individual warrior-artist. Thus, empty spaces like those that occur in the Rain-in-the-Face liner's composition have been read in terms of the warrior's vantage point and interpreted as indicating that time has passed or that events took place a certain distance away from each other (though we cannot date or locate each scene without knowing which specific battle is depicted in the work).[27] Moreover, the warrior-artist could choose how he wanted to narrate the events depicted in his oral recitation: when the liner was taken down it could be folded or rolled in any manner to emphasize a particular vignette or create a different beginning. Frances Densmore, a music ethnologist who worked with the Sioux, reported that Swift Dog, her Húnkpapa Lakota informant, narrated and sang the story of his tipi liner to her when the liner was not hanging.[28]

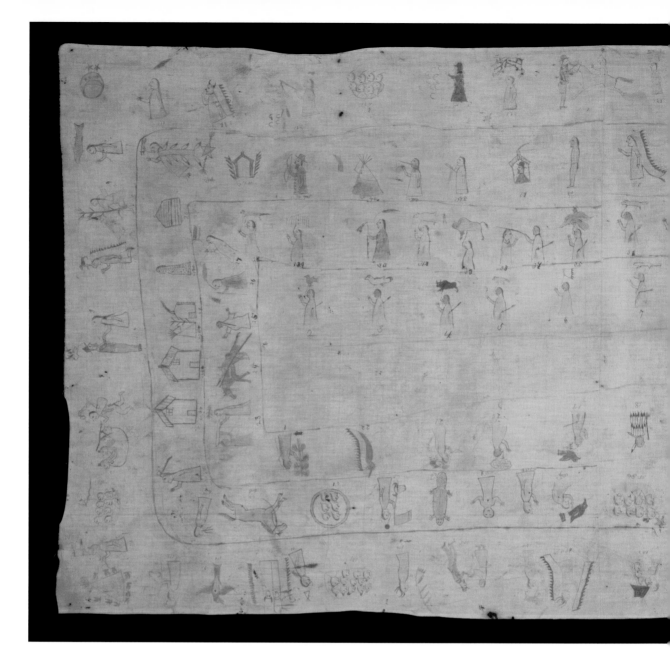

The centrality of the artist's personality—in this case, Rain-in-the-Face's—distinguishes tipi liners from other pictographic forms such as winter counts and ledger drawings. For a winter count, a historian is chosen to depict, each year, one notable event that affected the entire tribe. One pictograph, or occasionally two, stands for the history of many people. These representations are organized in a chronological progression even if the calendar is composed in a circle (fig. 81). The same winter count generally has more than one artist, since the calendars are maintained for several generations and, moreover, sometimes copies are made in order for another artist to continue the depictions.[29]

Ledger drawings display a wide range of subjects and compositions, but like the winter counts and in marked contrast to most tipi liners, they are often not self-referential (though they might depict individuals). Drawings of the Lakota warrior Black Hawk, for example, show a sequence of ceremonial actions (fig. 82).[30] Ledger

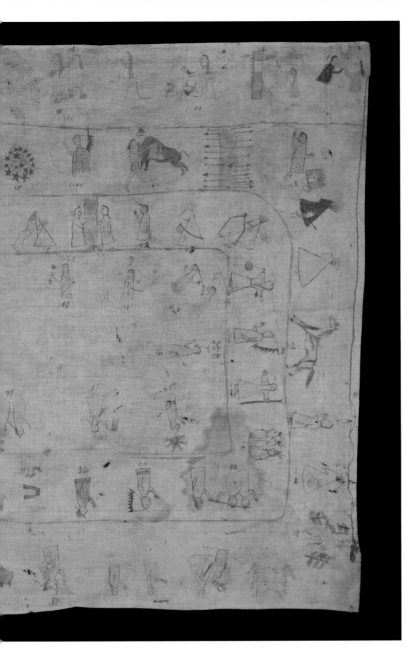

Fig. 81. Lakota artists. Rosebud Reservation Winter Count, 1752–1887. Muslin, ink, colored pencil, 35 × 69½ in. (89 × 176 cm). National Anthropological Archives, Smithsonian Institution, Washington, D.C., 2001–10

Fig. 82. Black Hawk (Lakota [Sans Arcs Sioux], circa 1832–1890). *Black Hawk's Ceremony*, double-page spread from a ledger book. Colored pencil and ink on paper, 10¼ × 16½ in. (26 × 41.9 cm). Fenimore Art Museum, Cooperstown, New York, Thaw Collection, Gift of Eugene V. and Clare E. Thaw (Photo: John Bigelow Taylor, N.Y.C.)

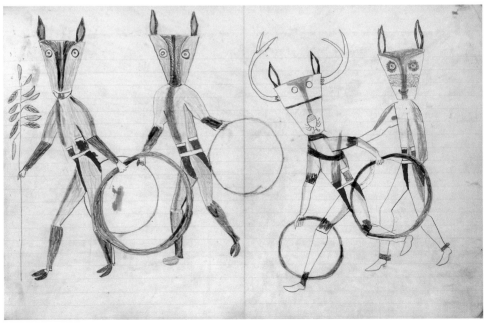

artists also depicted group events such as dances, large battles, tipi camp life, buffalo hunts, and the signing of peace treaties; the ledger book owned by the Oglala Lakota warrior Red Hawk includes two fine drawings showing, respectively, a trade scene between a Crow and a Lakota warrior and a peace meeting (figs. 83, 84). Some ledger drawings, commissioned by U.S. Army soldiers from scouts of friendly tribes, evoked memories of traditional life, but others reflected contemporary events: the Native Americans sent to Florida as prisoners of war in the late nineteenth century drew images of their train journey to Florida and their incarceration.[31] A ledger artist need not have participated in the event he depicted. Amos Bad Heart Bull (Oglala Lakota) created numerous drawings of the 1876 Battle of Little Bighorn representing his interpretation of events, although he did not take part in the conflict, in which the Lakota and Cheyenne defeated General George Custer's cavalry (fig. 85).

In contrast to these other pictographic forms, tipi-liner warrior art almost always refers to the self. The Rain-in-the-Face liner is composed of drawings that represent either singular episodes in the artist's life such as a particular horse raid or a series of his personal combats during a greater battle engagement. We know that Rain-in-the-Face participated in the two major defeats of the U.S. Army by the Plains Natives—the Fetterman Fight in 1866, when the Lakota were victorious against Captain William Fetterman's troops near Fort Phil Kearny, and the Battle of Little Bighorn in 1876, but as yet it has not been possible to determine conclusively whether actions

Fig. 83. Pte Wakannajiu (Holy Standing Buffalo) (Oglala Sioux, dates unknown). *Trading Gun for Pistol*, from the Red Hawk Ledger Book, circa 1890. Crayon and ink on paper, 7½ × 12¼ in. (19.1 × 31.1 cm). Milwaukee Public Museum, E2063-238

Fig. 84. Pte Wakannajiu (Holy Standing Buffalo) (Oglala Sioux, dates unknown). *Council of Peace*, from the Red Hawk Ledger Book, circa 1890. Crayon and ink on paper, 7½ × 12¼ in. (19.1 × 31.1 cm). Milwaukee Public Museum, E2063–2254

Fig. 85. Amos Bad Heart Bull (Oglala Lakota, 1869–1931). *Battle of Little Big Horn*, circa 1890. Ink, pencil, and watercolor on paper, 7 × 12 in. (17.8 × 30.5 cm). Drawing no longer extant (Photo from Helen Blish, *A Pictographic History of the Oglala Sioux* [Lincoln: University of Nebraska Press, 1967])

from these large battles are depicted on the liner. Rain-in-the-Face was a mature warrior when Deming saw him paint this war sheet, so he had forty years of exploits from which to choose. What is likely is that all the scenes represent experiences that the proud Rain-in-the-Face considered essential to his individuality.

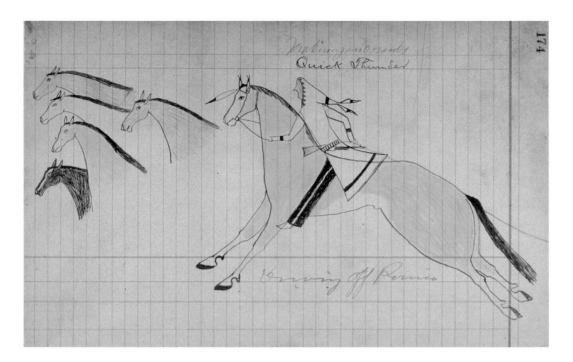

Fig. 86. Quick Thunder
(Wakinyano ranko) (Oglala
Sioux, dates unknown).
Running Off Ponys, from the
Red Hawk Ledger Book,
circa 1890. Crayon and
ink on paper, 7½ × 12¼ in.
(19.1 × 31.1 cm). Milwaukee
Public Museum, E2063–174

Fig. 87. Detail of Rain-
in-the-Face's tipi liner
depicting horse stealing

Tipi-liner art does have some characteristics in common with other forms of
Plains pictographic art. All painters readily adopted new materials, including inks,
pencils, commercial paints, muslin, and papers. Often the partial figure stands for
the whole, a metonymic device, such as depicting several horses' heads to indicate
more than one horse or part of a warrior to indicate the whole (figs. 86, 87). Other
shared conventions include the technique of flat planes and the absence of landscape
elements, the emphasis on details such as horses' hooves and weaponry, the use of
headdresses, clothing, shields, and other elements to identify figures with actual individuals, and the inclusion of proper regalia for each depicted event. Lakota art nor-
mally represents figures in left profile,[32] in part because this view allowed the artist to
show identity signifiers such as bows, guns, and lances, generally held on the left side

in battle. The shield was also held on the left and swung around as needed for protection.[33] The profile view may also have been chosen for compositional clarity.

AN ANALYSIS OF THE RAIN-IN-THE-FACE TIPI LINER

Several of the approximately twenty-one vignettes depicted on the Rain-in-the-Face liner have been selected for analysis below.[34] These particular scenes have been chosen because they not only represent many classic subjects of pictographs such as horse raids, taking coup, and fighting but also illustrate events that appear to be more singularly associated with Rain-in-the-Face. The analyses synthesize information gleaned from the team of consultants, from primary sources such as the memoirs of De Cost Smith and James McLaughlin, and from scholarly studies by Marsha Bol, Janet Berlo, Helen Blish, Frank McCoy, and others.

SCENE 1: Top, right (fig. 87). This horse-stealing scene depicts one man, wearing a hooded black capote (cloak) with red stripes made from a Hudson's Bay blanket, herding nine horses. His beaded-legging design varies, with patterns of x's on the outside and omega-like forms on the inside. He carries a Winchester rifle. The running horses are vividly drawn, with several partial horses overlapping and tucked behind the front one, as seen in ledger art (see fig. 86). Only one horse has actually been lassoed. The horse markings are distinctive and might indicate particular horses.

SCENE 2: Top, second from right (fig. 88). In this conflict between four warriors, three protagonists are the attackers. Two are indicated by partial heads and torsos, and a third is shown in the act of falling from his horse. The animal has been shot and is stumbling as blood streams from its side and its nose. The saddle on the horse is a U.S. Army McClellan model. All three attackers have red forehead paint and are wearing the hair topknots that identify them as Montana Crow. They shoot rifles at the man standing on the ground, who returns their fire, represented as bursts from the guns. This central standing character, who might be Rain-in-the-Face, has dismounted from his saddled red horse and staked it and turns back to battle the three attackers. The scene possibly represents an aborted ambush, horse raid, or other mission: the central character is bare-chested, stripped for warfare, with his blanket wrapped around his waist and secured by a cartridge belt, while the Crow are wearing their capotes, as if ambushed and giving chase.

SCENE 3: Top, third from right (fig. 89). This battle rescue scene shows two figures riding on the same horse while one riderless horse gallops in front. The mounted horse has his tail decorated for war with a red tie and feather. Its front rider is male with a red-painted forehead, one black feather in his hair in front, and two white feathers with black tips in his hair at the back.[35] (Eagle feathers were awarded for each successful mission.) The male rider carries a shield decorated with a bird in the center and one (eagle?) feather dangling on either side. The ends of a long, fringed, decorated sash peep out from under the shield, as well as a fringed quiver case with

Fig. 88. Detail of Rain-in-the-Face's tipi liner depicting battle between one Lakota warrior, possibly Rain-in-the-Face, and three Crow warriors

Fig. 89. Detail of Rain-in-the-Face's tipi liner depicting a Lakota warrior, possibly Rain-in-the-Face, rescuing a woman

a diamond pattern. The man carries a bow in his left hand. His leggings have a blue triangular pattern on a yellow background. The second rider, much smaller, holds onto the front rider by the shoulders and appears to be female. She has a red crescent of face paint and two long braids. Her dress is blue with a skirt that flips back, and she wears solid-color leggings. The scene can be identified with some certainty as depicting a rescue rather than a capture, since the female would be sitting in front of the man if she were his hostage. This scene may relate to an incident known from Standing Rock oral history—that of Rain-in-the-Face saving the daughter of the Upper Yanktonai subchief Black Prairie Dog. This rescue took place during the Battle of Long Lake (near Spirit Lake), when a Yanktonai Sioux camp was attacked by the U.S. Army.[36] Rain-in-the-Face extended his quirt to the daughter and swung her up onto his own horse. His life-saving action created bonds with Black Prairie Dog and

Fig. 90. Rain-in-the-Face holding a shield, circa 1902. Photograph by Frank B. Fiske (1883–1952). (Photo courtesy of AZUSA Publishing, LLC)

Black Prairie Dog's half-brother Brave Bear, so that when Brave Bear lost his own son, he ceremonially adopted Rain-in-the-Face through a *hunka* ceremony.[37] Brave Bear, whose insignia was bear claws, was a "thunder dreamer," a distinguished man who could see visions. After the adoption, Rain-in-the-Face gained the right to wear bear claws. The shield depicted here is similar to one he holds in a formal photographic portrait by Frank Fiske (fig. 90).

SCENE 4: Center, third from right (fig. 91). This enigmatic vignette may show a Sioux being taken prisoner by two Crow warriors, identified through their hairstyle and the bead necklace on the front warrior. They pull an unidentifiable man on a rope—presumably a Sioux whom they have captured. Since Captain Tom Custer (the brother of General George Custer) is the only person known to have captured Rain-in-the-Face,[38] the precise event represented in the scene cannot be determined.

Directly below this prisoner scene, a man rides a black horse while one roan-colored horse runs ahead with a tether dangling from its neck. It is difficult to tell if the horse and rider belong with this vignette or are separate from it. The horse has a military saddle, blanket, and bridle. The Native rider, identified as such by his long

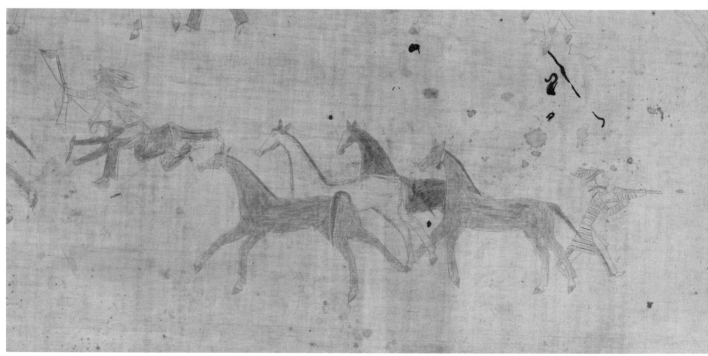

braids, wears a military coat with chevrons and white striped pants indicating trade-cloth leggings. This style of garb was worn by a federally appointed Native policeman or a Native scout for the U.S. Army. Rain-in-the-Face was never a scout, and at the time the liner was painted, he had not yet become a Native policeman.

(opposite, above)
Fig. 91. Detail of Rain-
in-the-Face's tipi liner
depicting two Crow
warriors capturing an
unidentifiable prisoner

(opposite, below)
Fig. 92. Detail of Rain-
in-the-Face's tipi liner
depicting a Lakota warrior,
possibly Rain-in-the-Face,
counting coup on a Crow
warrior

SCENE 5: Bottom, right (fig. 92). The coup-taking scene describes two fighters and a horse. One man has dismounted and staked his roan-colored horse. The side of his face toward the viewer is painted red, indicating that he may represent Rain-in-the-Face, who painted half his face red and the other black in preparation for battle. He is counting coup, using his rifle butt to touch the other protagonist, who is falling to the ground in front of him. The coup taker, stripped to his breechcloth, or loincloth, with a knife at his waist, holds a lance wrapped in otter fur. His braided hair may also be wrapped with fur. The prostrate man is bleeding from his head. He, too, is stripped for war, wearing only his black-striped breechcloth and his cross-laced moccasins, both of the type worn by Crow.[39]

THE RAIN-IN-THE-FACE TIPI LINER AND THE RESERVATION PERIOD

Janet Berlo has written of the subversive character of some ledger art in the face of governmental control: "To make a picture can be a revolutionary act, an autobiographical act, an act of covert resistance. It can be a way of mourning the past, and fixing it in historical time as well. . . . It is an act of resistance to chronicle the old ways and keep them alive."[40] It is likely that Rain-in-the-Face's tipi liner also functioned as a form of subtle resistance to the federal government's acculturation policies by preserving and honoring the warrior-artist's memories of a lifestyle irrevocably gone. Since the liner was not commissioned, it is reasonable to suppose that the subject matter was entirely of Rain-in-the-Face's own choosing, although perhaps slanted to impress Deming. Thus, the liner stands apart from smaller muslin paintings commissioned from other Native artists in the late nineteenth century that mirrored the style of the larger tipi liners and featured subject matter that appealed to a non-Native client. A dominant theme for such battle tipi liners was the Battle of Little Bighorn of 1876, depicted in a liner-style painting (fig. 93) by One Bull (Húnkpapa Lakota).[41] Another popular commission theme was the arrest of Chief Sitting Bull at Standing Rock on December 15, 1890, just a year after Rain-in-the-Face painted his liner—a disastrous event resulting in the death of the chief, his son, several other followers, and several Native policemen.[42] Sitting Bull had long been considered an obstruction to the federal government's control of Sioux lands, and when he became an advocate of the Ghost Dance, a practice the army considered warlike, his arrest was ordered. James McLaughlin, the Standing Rock agent, convinced the army to use the Native police force rather than federal troops to make the arrest. This event was closely followed, on December 29, by the Massacre of Wounded Knee, when three hundred men, women, and children were slaughtered as they were surrendering at Pine Ridge. The combination of these events signaled the end of the warrior era for the Lakota.

Very few personal tipi liners like Rain-in-the-Face's have survived from earlier Reservation times.[43] In fact, to judge from the vivacity and sure line demonstrated in this work, Rain-in-the-Face may have produced other liners with similar depictions that are now lost. Many tipis and their contents were destroyed during the numerous conflicts throughout the Plains region in the nineteenth century.[44] Other liners were ravaged by time and the environment. The practice of painting liners almost ceased as the Plains people were forced onto reservations. When their homes began to change from tipis to log cabins, the liners were moved inside onto the cabin walls and were still admired as artworks and historical documents. Liners were also taken down and brought into wooden dance halls for celebrations.[45] When homes changed to contemporary styles, generally built with federal funding, however, their walls were painted or wallpapered rather than hung with tipi liners.

At the same time that log cabins were replacing tipis, younger Lakota males born on the reservation had no opportunity to perform war deeds to enhance their status, and thus had no need to depict them.[46] Older male warrior-artists, in turn, assumed radically different cultural roles as agriculturalists, ranchers, or business-people. Paintings on muslin, ledger arts, and winter counts became artworks that were often commissioned by army personnel or collectors. Such paintings certainly had historical and mnemonic value to the Native artist and reinforced cultural pride, but the practical and social role of the painted tipi liner was altered drastically. Today, when tipis are set up for fairs and ceremonial events, their liners are often commercial fabrics and hangings that are displayed in the traditional manner inside the tipi, but their designs rarely include pictographs. Instead, pictographic art lives on in the form of contemporary paintings, drawings, and collages produced by artists such as Sherman Chaddlesone (Kiowa; see figs. 156, 157, and Palmer and Palmer interview in this volume) and Arthur Amiotte (Oglala Lakota). A new tipi liner by Harvey Pratt (Southern Cheyenne/Arapaho) depicting his experiences in the Vietnam War continues warrior traditions, portraying values of honor, bravery, and pride revered by Native people serving in the armed forces today (see Pratt essay in this volume).

Continuing research and consultations with the Standing Rock Húnkpapa Lakota and the descendants of Rain-in-the-Face will explore whether additional oral histories can offer further insights concerning the Brooklyn Museum's tipi liner. Pictographic drawings and paintings remain primary agents for intercultural understanding today, and perhaps such communication was the intention of Rain-in-the-Face as he related his exploits to Deming in 1889. Rain-in-the-Face's act of giving the liner to Deming cemented cross-cultural relationships, and now the Brooklyn Museum's preservation of the liner and sharing it back with the Native artist's descendants acknowledge the reciprocal obligation of his gift.

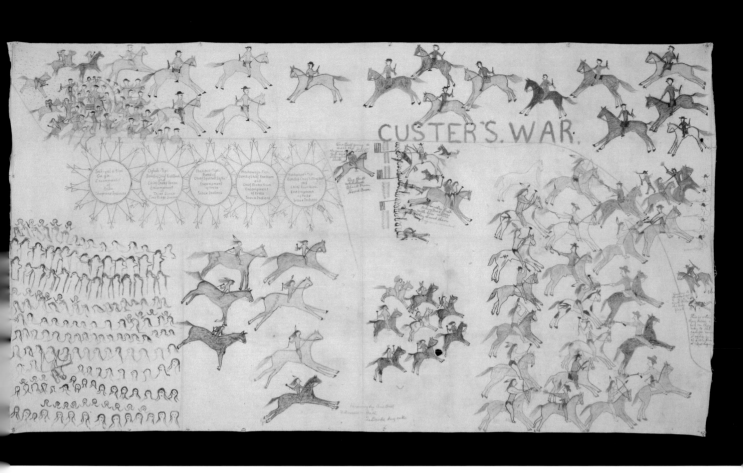

Fig. 93. One Bull (Húnkpapa
Lakota, dates unknown).
*Custer's War (Battle of
Little Bighorn)*, circa 1890.
Muslin, pigment, 39½ ×
69¼ in. (100.3 × 175.9 cm).
Minneapolis Institute of Arts,
The Christina N. and Swan J.
Turnblad Memorial Fund

A MODERN CHEYENNE-ARAPAHO TIPI LINER

HARVEY PRATT

THE NATIVE AMERICAN TIPI LINER IS BOTH A DECORATIVE WORK OF ART and a pictorial history that traditionally depicts family and tribal events as well as warriors' military exploits. As an artist, a Cheyenne and Arapaho tribal member, and a Vietnam veteran, I painted a tipi liner (figs. 94–96) to present a history of my war experiences from 1963 to 1965. In the tradition of Native warriors who displayed their painted liners and narrated the deeds shown, I will relate here the stories behind some of the scenes I depicted on my liner, in which I combined modern images with traditional ledger-style ones that parallel the scenes from the Vietnam War. The six vertical panels of the liner are numbered left to right in the descriptions below.

PANELS 1, 2: I joined the U.S. Marines in 1962. The liner illustrates events beginning in 1963, when I served in the military police of the Third Marine Division (whose emblem appears at the top of Panel 2), training in arrest and security techniques. The ledger-style Native figure with his back turned in Panel 1 is standing guard, reflecting my duties in the military police. I volunteered to become part of a special security-and-rescue unit, but we were not told that we were going to Vietnam. Before we were stationed there, we were sent for cold-weather training in Korea (Panel 1, top). There was a storm at sea, and our ships were tossed all over the ocean before we landed on the west coast of Korea near the 38th parallel. We did an exercise with the Korean Marines during a time when the snow was deep and the weather was extremely cold.

We slept in two-man pup tents, and I took only one hot bath in a month. Later, in Vietnam, I did another exercise with the Korean Marines. One night on leave, when I missed the last bus from Da Nang to the base, a team of armed Korean marines escorted me back, and I gave them my collar brass for helping me. They also secured the door of the club in a downtown bar and wouldn't allow anyone in but marines. The Korean marines liked to prove their fearlessness by biting off pieces of their glass after they'd finished a drink, and they invited us to do the same.

After Korea, we went to Okinawa for several months of guerrilla-warfare training, which included rappelling from helicopters (Panel 1, top). I represented the helicopter by an eagle, a bird that—like a chopper—flies and attacks. In Okinawa we were also trained in weapons, escape and evasion, rescue of military personnel from downed aircraft in enemy areas, language, and special techniques of reconnaissance and patrolling. We flew to Da Nang, attached to the Third Marine Reconnaissance Unit known as Hughes Hellions, which was the first marine ground-combat unit in Vietnam. Our unit's motto was *Vox Mortis* (Voice of Death). I was the only American Indian in the platoon, so I always considered myself the first Native American in a Marine Corps ground-combat unit in the war. For Native warriors, it is traditionally extremely important to be the first to participate in a military action, just as it was important for our ancestors to count coup.

Before we arrived, the South Vietnamese military secured the large air base at Da Nang. Our first duty was to secure the American portion of the base and the airfield where the helicopter squadron maintained a large array of aircraft and fuel. The base was several square miles interlocking with other Vietnamese military facilities. The perimeter of the base, including the aircraft and tarmac, became the active patrol area for the unit. Our duties were carried out by two-man patrols with fixed bayonets (Panel 1, lower right).

PANEL 3, BOTTOM: On one patrol on the airstrip during a monsoon, we captured a Vietnamese male inside one of the attack helicopters. Once we got him into custody, we marched him back to the security tent. We never saw or heard what happened to him or found out if anything was taken from or planted in the helicopter. My patrol partner was R.D. Pratt, who was a nonsmoker and nondrinker. R.D. was my alert; he could sense the Vietnamese as well as they could sense us. He had actually stopped me at the helicopter and put me on alert. I had learned to trust his ability and knowledge about weapons. We worked well together because he was very left-brained and

Fig. 94. Harvey Pratt painting his tipi liner, 2008 (Photo: Gina Pratt)

I was very right-brained. At the bottom of the panel, I included a red hand, which for the Cheyenne and Arapaho is a sign painted on tipi liners and on horses to indicate that a warrior has met his enemy in battle.

PANEL 4, TOP: My fire team was assigned to assist a South Vietnamese military strike against the Viet Cong somewhere in the region called I Corps. I never knew where we were during these missions, and I always depended on my sergeant to take care of me. We flew in and landed in a valley with fires and gunfire all around us. It was our job to go in when someone was hurt or a helicopter or military craft was shot down, or if someone was in danger and needed to be rescued. We were on the ground along a tree line in the valley when an army chopper came in and circled us and then fired or dropped a series of rockets within a few yards of us. All we could do was watch the rockets fall and pray they did not hit our ammunition, which was stored near us. I stood and watched the rockets fall so close to us that we didn't have time to run for cover. It was an "oh, shit!" experience. The airship never landed, and there was never an acknowledgment that it was friendly fire. It was a lucky day for my fire team.

PANEL 4, BOTTOM: On another occasion after a strike on the Viet Cong, four of us were dropped off at an abandoned Vietnamese Ranger camp and were waiting for a transport truck to return us to the Marine base in Da Nang. I was the only marine with any ammunition left—one magazine (twenty rounds). When I was growing up in Oklahoma, we always hunted wild game for food, and ammunition was expensive and hard to get. We never wasted our shots and were very mindful of our ammunition. That time in Vietnam, I was thankful that I had been conservative with my ammunition, because it gave us a little feeling of hope. We were twenty or more miles from the base along an area that was controlled by the Viet Cong and sympathetic to them. I passed out my remaining ammunition so that we all might have a few rounds if we got in trouble. If that happened, we were going to get killed. Soon afterward, we stopped a troop transport truck traveling down the road. The driver and passenger were Vietnamese military, and when our corporal made them understand we wanted to go to the Da Nang base, they motioned us into the back. As we came to Highway One, they continued east into an area heavily controlled by the Viet Cong. They drove us through several hamlets and back roads, eventually returning to Highway One and continuing to the Vietnamese Ranger camp. We began to realize that there had probably been some type of miscommunication, but we were thankful for the lesson learned. We were inexperienced and had relied on others for our safety. From that point on, I carried extra ammunition, hand grenades, and any other means of protection I could keep with me.

PANEL 5, MIDDLE: One day when we had been on a strike with the South Vietnamese army, we were airlifted back to the Vietnamese base. We were being trucked back to our base, about two miles from Highway One, when we passed an unoccupied American bulldozer. Our sergeant called the base and was told to secure the bulldozer and place a guard on it. I was selected as the guard and took a position on the hillside

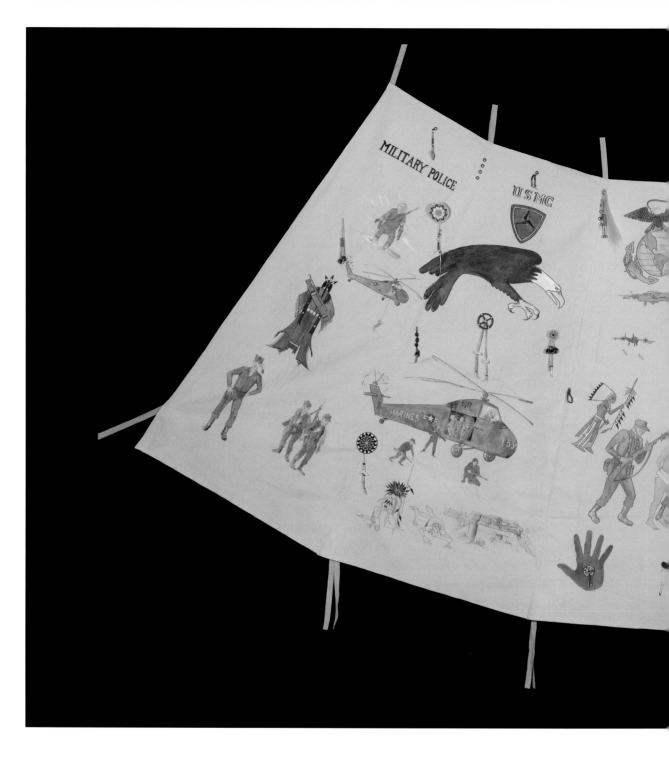

overlooking the area but close enough to use the bulldozer for cover in the event of an attack. (The ledger-style figure at the top of the panel, wearing a buffalo war cap and holding a spear—and also standing guard—refers to my experience.) I stayed on the site for about an hour, watching several vehicles and a truckload of Vietnamese Rangers pass. A truck carrying combat Vietnamese Rangers pulled up and deployed around the machine, pointing their weapons in my direction. They were about to fire on me when they realized I was an American marine. They all started laughing and waving at me, but I stayed in my little fighting hole until I saw a U.S. Marines jeep approach and saw my fire team waving me to the jeep. I was never so glad to see

Fig. 95. Harvey Pratt (Southern Cheyenne/ Arapaho, b. 1941). *Vietnam War Experiences Tipi Liner,* 2008. Cotton canvas, textile and acrylic paint, beads, metal, dyed horsehair, 75 × 168 in. (190.5 × 426.7 cm). Collection of the artist (Photo: Sarah Kraemer, Brooklyn Museum)

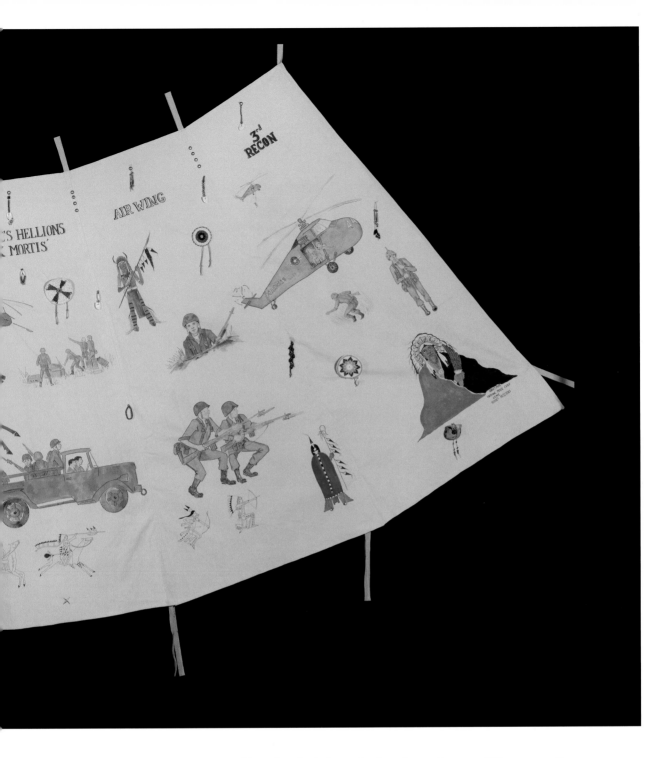

marines and later laughed about the fact that a platoon of Vietnamese Rangers was sent to relieve one marine. To this day, I have never understood why my command chose to leave one man instead of a four-man fire team to secure the equipment on the road.

PANEL 5, BOTTOM: On one patrol after dark, two of us walked a four-hour shift around the compound of sleeping marines. Some of the other recon marines were patrolling an area of the airfield about a mile away from the compound. The North Vietnamese also had patrols in areas to the west and north. We were walking along

HARVEY PRATT
CHEYENNE PEACE CHIEF
USMC
HUGHES HELLIONS

the west fence line when we noticed, just in front of us, a South Vietnamese ARVN (Army of the Republic of Vietnam) guard with a war dog. When the dog turned and charged us, we both dropped to our knees and met the eighty-pound German shepherd with our fixed bayonets. The handler called the dog back, but the sight of that charging animal terrified me. In Korea I had heard stories of war dogs killing people in just a few seconds.

PANEL 6, MIDDLE RIGHT: While stationed at Da Nang, I stood an honor guard for the Commandant of the Marine Corps. We were dressed in combat fatigues with loaded weapons and hand grenades. The commandant was surprised that we were armed during the honor guard but recognized the situation and was proud that we were prepared to defend the base. After I returned from Vietnam, I had the rare honor of being chosen a second time to serve as a member of the honor guard for the commandant, at the Marine Corps air station in Yuma, Arizona.

Fig. 96. Detail of figure 95 showing artist's signature self-portrait as a Cheyenne peace chief (Photo: Sarah Kraemer, Brooklyn Museum)

Fig. 97. Harvey Pratt, 2006
(Photo: Gina Pratt)

PANEL 6, TOP: After a particularly quiet afternoon, we were called into the patrol area and told by the lieutenant that there was a dangerous mission deep in the Viet Cong area where an airplane had been shot down. We were going to send in a rescue team. I could not believe all the hands that went up; many men volunteered for the mission, and I was surprised when the sergeant said the volunteers would be Pratt, Pratt, Corporal Carter, and Sergeant Edwards. We were assigned to two helicopters because we were going to pick up several injured crewmen. We flew for about an hour, and I could tell we were deep into enemy territory by the rounds that hit our choppers. My patrol partner, R.D. Pratt, and I sat on our helmets to protect against fire from below, and I became aware that we were the only men there, including the crew, without flak jackets. Our patrol was set down outside the area of the downed plane to provide protection. After we heard that the survivors had been loaded on the other helicopter by Carter and Edwards, we were airlifted back to our chopper. As we flew down a stream, I saw that Sergeant Edwards was on the ground in the tall grass, with his helicopter hovering over him. I thought he was wounded and jumped off our chopper to help him. He was not wounded, but we were lucky to find him. He and I boarded the chopper and flew along the creek as the second chopper came into view, with Corporal Carter on the safety line. When we landed at the Da Nang air base, the captain of Sergeant Edwards's helicopter said we were going to be recommended for decorations.

The wartime experiences that I painted on the tipi liner shaped my life, and they have great meaning to me as a Native American. After returning from Vietnam in 1965, I began a career in law enforcement and have spent more than thirty-five years with the Oklahoma State Bureau of Investigation. I have worked as a narcotics agent, undercover agent, forensic artist, instructor, trainer, and assistant director. I am also an artist who works in many media and lectures about Native American art and culture. In 1995 I was greatly honored to be inducted into the Southern Cheyenne Chief's Lodge as one of its traditional peace chiefs (Panel 6, bottom; see fig. 96). Two sentinel figures of chiefs on the liner (Panel 5, bottom) represent those who honored me with this appointment: I imagined them watching to see what kind of a man I was becoming. Decades after my tour of duty in Vietnam, my role as a peace chief is that of a mediator who does not take sides and has given up warlike ways.

OF TIPIS AND STEREOTYPES

BENTLY SPANG

MISCONCEPTIONS ABOUT THE TIPI ARE CUT FROM THE SAME questionable cloth as other stereotypes about Native Americans. Woven by non-Natives, this cloth supposedly represents the objective study of the Native peoples of the North American continent. For hundreds of years countless threads have been spun, spooled, woven, and warehoused by non-Native anthropologists, archaeologists, historians, and federal-government officials in their search for the authentic Native American. This cloth is marketed as genuine but is available only at a non-Native-owned cultural outlet near you.

Some ethnographers have spun their thread with good intentions, armed only with human curiosity, compassion, and enough humility to act as a conduit for the Native voice. Their valuable contributions provided my people, the Northern Cheyenne, and others with mostly unfiltered access to the voices of our ancestors: a precious resource for any living Native person such as myself, but exceptionally rare. One such ethnographer was Thomas B. Marquis, whose book *The Cheyennes of Montana* is a compilation of interviews he conducted in the 1920s to present the voices, lives, and stories of several venerable Northern Cheyenne elders such as Iron Teeth, a woman who lived through many amazing and horrendous moments in my people's history.[1]

These Native voices have not been sufficiently heard, however. Stereotypes about Native Americans and the tipi—ingrained in non-Native language and history— exist in the halls of academia and the realm of popular culture alike. As an enrolled member of the Northern Cheyenne Nation and an artist, curator, educator, and writer, I have direct experience with the effects of these stereotypes on my own psyche and on the Native community as a whole.

To explore the stereotype of the tipi, we can begin with the three English spellings in use to describe this structure. *Tipi, tepee,* and *teepee* are the only words I have ever seen applied to this architectural form in the United States. All three have, at their root, the non-Native transliteration of the oral Santee (Dakota) word for tipi,[2] to the exclusion of all other Native nations and their words for the same structure.

The Northern Cheyenne—or, as we call ourselves, Tsististas and Suhtaio—have an entirely different word for the conical dwelling of our ancestors. I am not a fluent speaker of our language, but my father, Zane Spang, is, and I asked him what the word for *tipi* would be in Cheyenne. As is typical protocol in my community, he consulted a number of other fluent speakers and confirmed that the word for *tipi*, spelled phonetically, is *ve eh*, a term most often used, in a social context, to ask where one lives. The limitations of identifying this word in a phonetic English spelling become evident when one hears a Native speaker pronounce it. As my father told me, there is a rush of air at the end of the word that cannot be spelled in English but is crucial to the proper pronunciation. This rush of air can be represented in transliterated form, but Cheyenne speakers who grew up speaking the language have great difficulty reading such transliterations. Ours is an oral tradition, and the spoken word has always had the most meaning and power to us. There have been numerous attempts over the years to capture the spoken language and convert it to a written phonetic form based on the English alphabet. The earliest of these dictionaries was created by a non-Native Mennonite preacher and linguist named Rodolphe Petter in the early 1900s. The first book he chose to translate into phonetically written Cheyenne was, not surprisingly, the Bible. My family owns one of the few surviving original Cheyenne Bibles, and numerous times while I was growing up, I saw my father and other fluent speakers of Cheyenne ponder the curious phonetic notations on its pages.[3] One might think of Petter's accomplishment as a heroic act, bridging a crucial communication gap between cultures. I see it somewhat differently.

By renaming our language word by word, Petter effectively captured it for his use as a tool for his Christian proselytizing to the Cheyenne people. Forcing Christian names on Native people during the Early Reservation period was another way to undermine Native cultures, as Cornel Pewewardy, a Comanche-Kiowa scholar, has observed: "[N]aming was a strategy to commit 'cultural genocide,' a dispersed strategy to destroy ethnic family solidarity, an isolation emphasis on individual rather than family behavior and a disformative strategy to confuse Indigenous Peoples about their ethnic identity."[4]

What one names one owns and can control. The triumvirate of *tipi/tepee/teepee* joins the countless other words—tomahawk, moccasin, breechcloth, travois, and others—created by outsiders to corral all facets of Native experience into a single, misrepresented culture identified as "Indian," "Native American," "American Indian," or indigenous. Gone, in this renaming, are the unique experiences of each culture; gone, too, are the brutal acts inflicted upon Native people by those who desired to own their lands outright. In the mainstream, a lack of knowledge prevails about the history and diversity of Native culture and experience.[5] The limited and sometimes blatantly inaccurate definitions assigned to the tipi today are one example. The good news is that it is not too late to seek out, consult, and appreciate the knowledgeable members of Native communities. Much of the knowledge of the *ve eh* and its uses still exists among the Cheyenne, and the tipi traditions of other Native communities are alive and available for study as well.

Meanwhile, however, Western popular culture has produced a plethora of misconceptions, gross exaggerations, and dehumanizing depictions often defended as attempts to "honor" our tribes. I imagine that Chief Wahoo, the perpetually grinning, single-feathered, tiny-craniumed mascot of the Cleveland Indians baseball team, lives in the stereotypical tipi with his wife, the Land O'Lakes Butter maiden. Chief Wahoo is the patriarch of a huge, dysfunctional extended family of stereotypes, including his great-grandfather, depicted on the Indian Head nickel; his uncle, the Indian-head logo for the Mutual of Omaha insurance company; and his sister-in-law, Disney's Pocahontas. Cornel Pewewardy has written of the effect of such depictions:

The colonizer's falsified stories have become universal truths to mainstream society and have reduced indigenous culture to a cartoon caricature. This distorted and manufactured reality is one of the most powerful shackles subjugating Indigenous Peoples. It distorts all indigenous experiences, past and present, and confounds the road to self determination.[6]

Today the tipi stereotype appears in various forms and materials that are both absurd and insidious, especially on the Internet.[7] Among them are the wacky, tipi-shaped spaceship that was part of the stage set for a musical performance by the rap group Outkast at the 2004 Grammy Awards;[8] a device called the Pee-pee Teepee, designed to cover an infant boy's penis to prevent him from spraying his parents when they change his diaper;[9] and, most visibly, a retail chain of concrete and steel tipi-shaped motel units called variously the Wigwam Village, the Wigwam Motel, and the Wigwam Village Inn (fig. 98).[10] They are all tipis Chief Wahoo and his ilk would be proud to inhabit.

The motel chain was the brainchild of a man named Frank Redford, who in 1935 constructed the first of what would eventually become seven motels based on his "original" tipi design. His first effort, Wigwam Village, was built in Horse Cave, Kentucky, and consisted of a circle of cone-shaped concrete motel rooms, with a larger tipi-shaped building serving as the motel office. The Wigwam Village was a product of Redford's fascination with the conical form. He had seen an ice-cream business housed in a building shaped like an inverted ice-cream cone, and he was also impressed by tipis he saw on a South Dakota reservation.[11] He received a U.S. patent for his tipi design in 1936, built the second Wigwam Village in 1937 in Cave City, Kentucky, and began licensing his design to others (fig. 99). Redford built one more motel in 1947 in California. Four other motels based on the tipi form, also incorrectly called wigwams, were built by licensees of Redford's patented design. Only three of the seven still exist.[12]

Redford's erroneous description of his cone-shaped structures as wigwams is a byproduct of unreliable non-Native renaming (fig. 100). To confuse the tipi with the wigwam, or wickiup, is to have no understanding of the traditional Plains way of life. The *ve eh,* like other tipi forms, was designed as a portable family home that supported the survival of my people as we followed the buffalo, our food source, through the Great Plains. In the past, the tipi cover was made of buffalo hides, and it was stretched over lodgepole pine poles to create the conical shape. Like every object we possessed, household or otherwise, the tipi was designed to be moved quickly, in support of our nomadic lifestyle. The *ve eh* was, and still is, also a dwelling for one of our most venerated spiritual objects, the Sacred Hat.[13] Although we do not live in *ve eh*s anymore, many Northern Cheyenne families own them and use them during the warmer months of the year.

The wigwam is a very different structure—a more permanent, domed form made of bent saplings covered with earth, grasses, or animal hides that was the dwelling of Great Lakes and northeastern United States tribes. Like the word *tipi,* however, the term *wigwam* has replaced the various Native words for similar dwellings of different tribes, and their cultural significance has also been overlooked. Calvin Grinnell, a member of the Hidatsa Nation in North Dakota, has eloquently expressed the meaning assigned to the permanent earth lodges (called *ati*) of his people:

They were unique. Our people thought that they had a spirit, that there was life to everything and that there should be respect given to people's homes, to people's living quarters, because they were made out of natural things. . . . Everything was natural. Then, [there was] the spirit imbued upon it by the people living in there. There was a respect for a person's way of life, a person's individuality and entire families who lived in these earth lodges, earth households.[14]

Fig. 98. Wigwam Motel #6, Route 66, Holbrook, Arizona (Photo: Paul Cloutier)

Fig. 99. Wigwam Village #2,
Cave City, Kentucky (Photo:
Jennifer Bremer)

Fig. 100. *Have You Slept in a Wigwam Lately?*, Wigwam Motel #6, Route 66, Holbrook, Arizona (Photo: Brian Butko)

Curiosities like the Wigwam Villages have reduced the tipi from a cultural position of respect to novelty architecture (fig. 101). Debra Jane Seltzer, an enthusiast of what she calls roadside architecture, devotes a category to tipi-shaped buildings on her Web site, which documents motels, souvenir stands, restaurants, and gas stations across the United States.[15] On the Wikipedia page for "novelty architecture," an image of a tipi-shaped motel unit from the Wigwam Motel in Holbrook, Arizona, is juxtaposed with a building shaped like a milk bottle; giant dinosaur sculptures next to Wall Drug in South Dakota; and the world's largest muskie in Hayward, Wisconsin, a 143-foot-long fish whose lunging body houses the National Freshwater Fishing Hall of Fame (fig. 102).[16] I have been inside the giant muskie and found the experience both fascinating and exhilarating. Is the design based on a venerated architectural form that is symbolic of cultural identity? No. This big-fish building is an affront to no one. On the other hand, I have never stayed in any of the Wigwam Motels or Villages, and I would have a difficult time doing so. The *ve eh* is the cradle of civilization as I know it. It was the core of my community and my extended family. Within its confines were taught the values of love and respect that sustain and guide the community I know today.

The stereotypes extend beyond roadside attractions, of course. Filmmakers, advertisers, writers, government officials, and Native American hobbyists have all created characters for non-Native consumption that reduce hundreds of distinct, living, brilliant cultures to reductive stereotypes. These caricatures—of simpleminded, savage, mystical, bloodthirsty, and drunken people—were regarded as tragic, ultimately flawed representatives of a culture doomed to disappear.

These fictional characters, outfitted with rubber tomahawks and machine-beaded headbands with a single, upright feather, were taught the Hollywood "woo-woo-woo" dance and became part of a script that was delivered to movie theaters,[17]

Fig. 101. South Dakota rest-
stop tipi, May 27, 2002
(Photo: Kelly Martin)

sports complexes,[18] schools, libraries, television stations, and retail shelves the world over. These scripted characters appear in grade-school classrooms and Thanksgiving plays, not to mention the cigar-store Indians outside trading posts that hawk more stereotypes inside.

The social cost of these stereotypes is lost dignity and opportunity for hundreds of Native nations whose peoples number in the millions, and even lost lives, with Native youth suicide rates reaching epidemic proportions. Further, there is the loss of a deep and meaningful relationship between Natives and non-Natives, as we each grapple with the unresolved grief and guilt that permeate each side of our social divide.[19]

Native scholars, artists, writers, and educators across the continent are engaged in reclaiming their heritage and freeing it from stereotypes, whether in the form of oversimplifications, gross generalizations, or offensive caricatures. The next step is to seek out and support the voices of Native peoples in framing our own existence. This essay is certainly part of that reclamation process. The general public must make a sustained effort to reject existing stereotypes and seek out the Native voice as the final word in defining Native existence. Native and non-Native people in this country have achieved progress toward this goal, as exemplified by the recent repeal of the "Indian Family" as the emblem of the state of Arkansas.[20] But there is more work to be done. The result will be a new age of enlightenment and awareness of the complexity of human life on this continent.

Elsie Wick, a Northern Cheyenne elder, recently related a story to me that her grandmother told her about the *ve eh*. She said the old Cheyennes used to heat pieces of mica, the crystalline white mineral, and pulverize and mix them with pine gum. They would then rub the mixture on the tipi cover to waterproof it, but it also created a beautiful visual effect. Elsie said that when the first light of the day struck the *ve eh*s in camp, they glowed like stars in the sky—hence our other name, "the Morning Star people." Like that glowing *ve eh*, the words of Native people and the willingness of non-Natives to listen can mark the dawn of a new era of understanding between our peoples.

Fig. 102. The Hayward Muskie (The World's Largest Muskie), Hayward, Wisconsin (Photo: Bobak Ha'Eri)

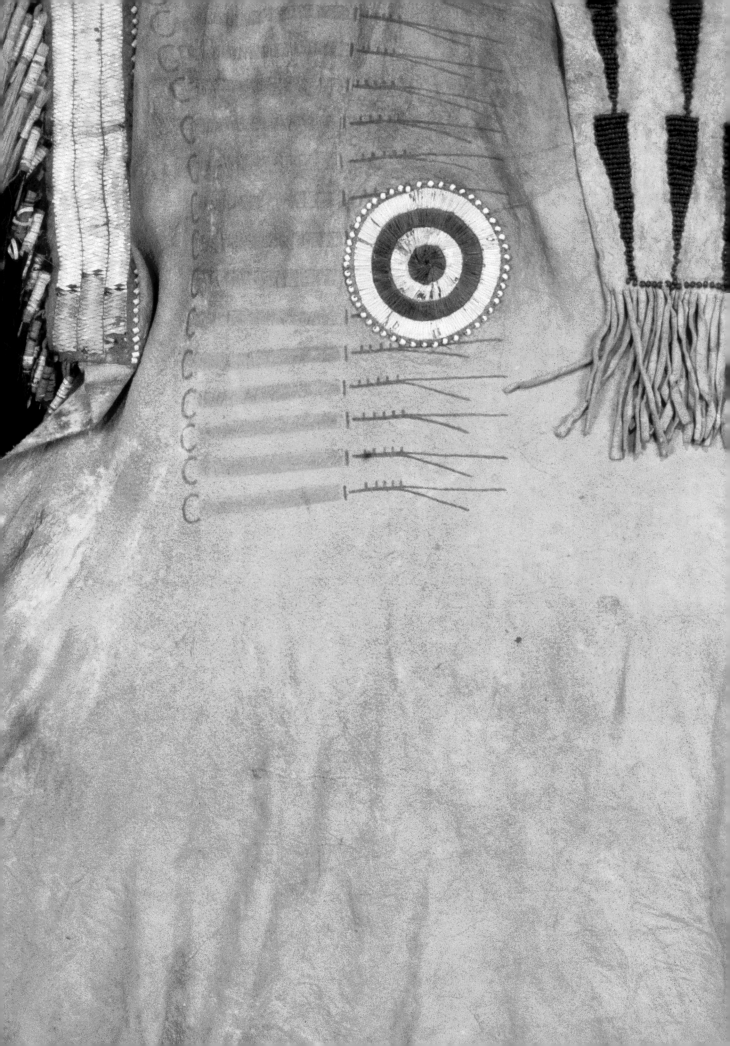

PART 2 / THE CENTER OF FAMILY LIFE

"TO HONOR HER KINDRED"

WOMEN'S ARTS CENTERED IN THE TIPI

BARBARA A. HAIL

IN THE HISTORIC TIMES OF PLAINS NOMADISM, THE TIPI WAS THE center of family life. Tipis were set up in circular camps—the circle representing a way of life in which people related harmoniously to one another and to the spirit world. At the center was the woman, the life-giver; around her, the family. In Lakota words: "Women are the grandmothers and mothers, the matriarchs of the *tiwahe* (family), *tiyospaye* (extended family), and *oyate tipi* (the nation)."[1] Because of the interrelation of home, family, and community, Plains women's arts have constituted a continually vital force both domestically and publicly.

These interconnections were perfectly reflected in the achievements of Fire Wood, a late nineteenth-century Northern Arapaho quillworker whose parents encouraged her to begin to quill cradles, tipis, robes, and various other articles when she was fifteen years old in order "to keep her home surroundings and honor her kindred."[2] She eventually made sixty cradles, fourteen buffalo robes, five decorated tipis and many more standard ones, ten robes, and one buffalo backrest. These domestic works of art were made as gifts to relatives, sometimes to publicly honor war deeds, sometimes in fulfillment of vows for a loved one's recovery from illness, and sometimes as prayers for long life. All solidified the extended kinship relationships upon which Native community life was based.[3]

Women made and owned the family tipi and its furnishings. The historic tipi was composed of hides of the cow (female) bison, sewn together by women who usually worked in extended family groups under the direction of a specialist in tipi construction. When a newly married young woman created her first home, her husband or other men in the family usually supplied the hides, which the woman would scrape and tan. She would then call upon female relatives and close friends to help shape and fit together the tipi cover. Eleven to fifteen hides were needed for a medium-size tipi. The women would sew these together with sinew and make a separate skin door for the opening and a tipi liner for the inside. Sometimes they applied quill or bead decorations to the outside of the tipi and created furnishings of backrests, bedding, and storage containers.

Some objects were made cooperatively by men and women. Men might paint the covers with vision-inspired symbolic designs or the covers and liners with images of their war exploits, but the division of labor by sexes was not always rigidly defined. For example, a man might outline the symbolic designs on a tipi cover, and his wife and children put on the color. Or a woman might prepare the rawhide shape for a container to hold sacred objects, and a man apply the painted designs.[4]

SOCIETIES

Among certain Plains groups, women's societies, or guilds, controlled the making of a tipi and its symbolic decoration in quills—or, later, beads. Quillwork, using both split bird-feather quills and porcupine quills, was developed as a high art in the historic Northern Plains, and quillworking societies existed until very recently among the Hidatsa-Mandan, Arikara, and Dakota women (fig. 103).[5] Early twentieth-century anthropologists made intensive studies of the Arapaho, Gros Ventre (Atsina), Cheyenne, and Oglala Lakota societies and compiled much information.[6] They found that older women served as instructors to younger ones, passing down secrets of both tipi making and porcupine-quill working. Society membership was restricted to women of high moral character and carried prestige. Women of the society worked together to learn to make tipis, liners, and furnishings such as parfleches (flat, envelope-like containers), backrests, and pillows. The arrangement of designs and colors was prescribed, and such designs were considered vows or prayers when applied to a tipi, cradleboard, or robe. A woman kept records of the number of buffalo hides she had tanned and decorated, sometimes inscribed as lines or notches in her fleshing tools (fig. 104) and sometimes as painted marks on her face and body or on a tipi liner.[7] The Northern Cheyenne quillworkers were ranked by the degree of difficulty of the objects they had decorated—exemplified, from lowest to highest, by moccasins, cradles, tipi discs or "stars," buffalo robes, tipi liners, backrests, and storage bags (fig. 105).[8] When first assembling for a meeting, the members would formally recite the work they had done, paralleling the men's ritual of publicly reciting their coups[9]—courageous acts such as touching an enemy with a stick or other object and escaping unharmed.

Women's societies protected information about quillwork used in decorating tipis, robes, bedding, moccasins (fig. 106), and cradles because of its sacred origins. Among the Oglala Lakota, the art of quill embroidery was considered *wakan*, or "sacred," a gift from the culture heroine Double Woman.[10] In the Northern Cheyenne

Fig. 103. Eagle Woman (Mandan, 1858–1928) sewing quill designs with young girl sitting beside her, early 20th century, North Dakota. Photograph by Frances Densmore (1867–1957). National Anthropological Archives, Smithsonian Institution, Washington, D.C., 56.831

(Suhtaio) origin story, a man who had a Buffalo Wife brought knowledge of quill embroidery on both tipis and robes to women and introduced the rituals and pre-scribed techniques and designs of the quilling society.[11] It was necessary to make the designs correctly for them to be efficacious; and the designs, like all art tied to ritual, were slow to change stylistically.[12]

By the mid-nineteenth century glass seed beads had become an important trade item on the Plains. As beads began replacing quills as an embroidery medium, some sewing societies adapted the patterns and traditions of the earlier quilling societies when decorating tipis and their furnishings with beads. The bead-decorated canvas tipi shown in figure 107, for example (which carries the name "Imogene Whitebull" and the date "2–11–04" penciled on its cover), has been decorated in a style typical of the Cheyenne women's sewing society.[13] Southern Cheyenne beading societies con-tinued into the twentieth century.[14] For example, Kathryn Bull Coming, a Southern

Fig. 104. Plains artist. Hide Scraper, 19th century. Northern, Central, or Southern Plains. Buffalo bone, pigment, hide, l. 8¹¹⁄₁₆ in. (22 cm). Brooklyn Museum, Brooklyn Museum Collection, 13.17

Fig. 105. Northern Cheyenne woman using a smoother on a finished piece of quillwork, Lame Deer, Northern Cheyenne Reservation, Montana, circa 1902–4. Photograph by Elizabeth C. Grinnell (1876–?). National Museum of the American Indian, Smithsonian Institution, Washington, D.C., N13627

Fig. 106. Sioux, Hidatsa, or Arikara artist. Man's Moccasins, circa 1882. Northern Plains. Hide, dyed porcupine quills, 10⁷⁄₁₆ × 3¹⁵⁄₁₆ in. (26.5 × 10 cm). Brooklyn Museum, Anonymous gift in memory of Dr. Harlow Brooks, 43.201.66a, b

Cheyenne bead artist, recalled that when her brother returned from World War II, her mother created a set of tipi furnishings to honor him:

Women had to say "welcome home" when men came home from wars or a long journey. . . . [T]hey put up a ceremonial feast for women only. Then the instructor always instructs the woman that is going to make a tipi.

My mother thought "my son's going to come home. I'm going to make a tipi, and on the back, bead it all the way down, and put decorations on there; I'm going to make a spread, make pillows, and moccasins, and his blanket, and willow back sticks, to welcome him when he comes home from World War II." She did it. She had to go through a ceremony. She completed everything. . . . She has to give a feast and invite some society men. Before they go in that tipi, some veteran has got to tell his war story. They eat in there.[15]

For the star ornaments on the outside of the tipi, Kathryn Bull Coming said, "they use cornhusk, and goat fur, and sinew, buckskin. I know how they go, but ceremonial women have to give me [permission] to do those things."[16] It is clear that, at the time of this interview in 1983, at least among some Southern Cheyenne, the rules for creating and ornamenting tipis were still controlled by the tipi makers' society, and a woman needed to earn the right to learn them.

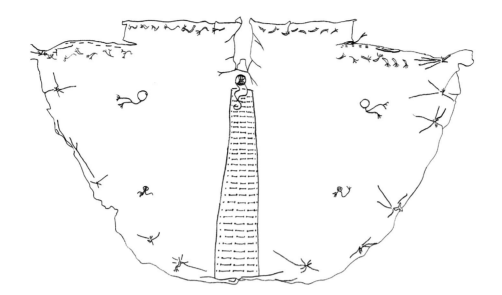

Fig. 107. Drawing of Southern Cheyenne Beaded Tipi Cover (circa 1904, Milwaukee Public Museum, E66373), 1997. Milwaukee Public Museum, Curatorial Files. Matching backrest, tipi door, and pillows are illustrated in figures 108 and 109a, b.

Among Plains societies in general, however, the women's sewing societies became less important over time as a result of several historical and cultural developments. Traditional methods of teaching and learning, previously carried out within extended family groups, were disrupted when an entire generation of young girls was sent away to boarding schools for years at a time, thus losing the opportunity to learn quilling, beading, hide-sewing, and painting skills from older women in their families. When the girls' educations were completed, moreover, economic conditions on reservations forced many of them to look for employment outside their own communities. Older members of the sewing societies were often loathe to pass on valued knowledge because they did not feel the younger women had the skills or the interest to carry on the traditions.[17]

Other outside forces weakened the internal cultural control over design. Government, church, and private agencies became involved in helping Native women find materials and markets for their arts—but at a cost. One example was the Mohonk Lodge on the Cheyenne/Arapaho Reservation in Colony, Oklahoma, which was founded in 1898 by Rev. and Mrs. Walter K. Roe, missionaries of the Dutch Reformed Church.[18] The goal was to help Cheyenne and Arapaho women, as well as those from nearby Kiowa, Comanche, and Fort Sill Apache tribal groups, to earn money by making and selling their traditional beadwork through mail-order catalogues distributed in the East. Soon, however, the women found that, in return for free materials, their designs were to become the property of the center and were to be called "Mohonk Lodge Designs." Such economic colonialism appropriated Native ownership rights and imposed external, commercial standards for creating and judging designs.[19]

Today the knowledge imparted in the sewing societies continues among only a few women. A 2008 exhibition of Cheyenne cultural objects, curated by a Southern

Fig. 108. Southern
Cheyenne artist. Backrest,
circa 1904. Oklahoma.
Wood, sinew, pigment,
hide, beads, tin cones,
horsehair, 53⅛ × 38½
in. (134.9 × 97.8 cm).
Milwaukee Public
Museum, E66378a
(Photo: Joanne Peterson)

Cheyenne, includes a woman's tipi-making medicine bag, of the kind owned by society instructors and often passed from generation to generation. The curator hopes its presence will encourage Cheyenne elders to recall and share society information that is in danger of being lost.[20]

TIPI FURNISHINGS

Women made the furnishings for their tipi homes. Willow-rod backrests, sometimes called lean-backs or lazy-backs, formed relaxing seats or, when two were used together, comfortable beds (fig. 108). They were made of peeled willow rods strung together with cords of heavy sinew to form a mat wider at the bottom than at the top. The mat was hung from a tripod of thin poles four to five feet high. Part of the lower end was laid on the ground, or on skins, and served as the seat of the chair.[21] Backrests might be decorated with paint, quills, beads, or cloth. Cheyenne and Sioux examples

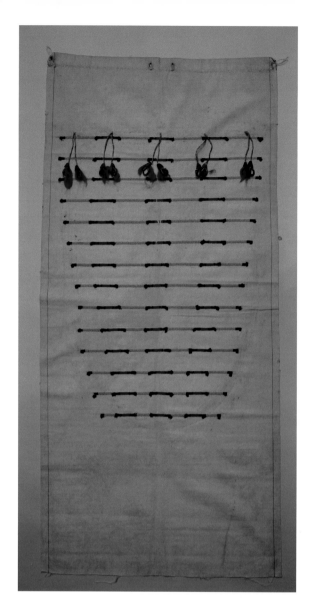

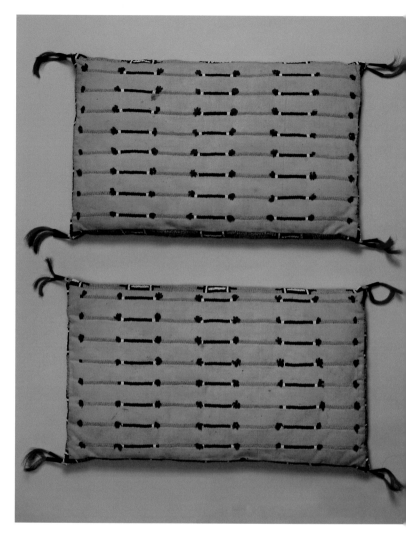

were shorter and wider than those of the Crow and Blackfeet. Backrests were light and could be rolled up when not in use, so they were easily portable.

Pillows of soft antelope hide stuffed with bison hair were part of nineteenth-century tipi furnishings. The Cheyenne and Arapaho decorated them with lines of quills and, later, beads, following the prescribed designs of the women's societies. In the twentieth century pillows were more often made of canvas duck, stuffed with horsehair or chicken feathers and beaded in lines of the sacred colors (white or light blue, red, yellow, and black) formerly used in quillwork produced by the women's societies.[22] The tipi door was often decorated in the same design as the pillows (figs. 109a, b).

Tipi liners added both decoration and warmth. Liners were originally composed of tanned hides pieced together but were later made of canvas duck or other fabric, and were attached with thongs to the poles of the tipi about four feet above the ground. Sometimes a liner was painted by a man with scenes of his war exploits (see essay by Kennedy Zeller in this volume), and sometimes it was decorated in geometric designs by a woman.

Figs. 109a, b. Southern Cheyenne artists. Tipi Door and Pillows, circa 1904. Oklahoma. Canvas, glass beads, wool yarn, hide, deer hooves, tin cones, horsehair, cotton thread, unidentified pillow stuffing, door 61³⁄₈ × 28½ in. (156 × 72.4 cm), pillow 12½ × 17¹¹⁄₁₆ in. (31.8 × 45 cm). Milwaukee Public Museum, E66375, E66377a, b (Photos: Joanne Peterson)

Tipi ornaments, called "stars" by the Cheyenne, were medallions of quills or beads, sometimes with dangles made of horse or buffalo hide or hair. These ornaments were sewn to the outside of society-decorated Cheyenne and Arapaho tipis and represented the four earthly directions. The Cheyenne placed a larger medallion, representing the sun, at the top back of the tipi.[23]

Painted rawhide containers in many sizes and shapes were used to store clothing, food, and sacred medicines. The rectangular containers that folded like an envelope (figs. 110, 111) were called parfleches, a term originally applied by French traders to Plains rawhide shields or the body armor worn by some northwestern tribes because it was strong enough to *parer flèche*, or "parry an arrow."[24] Later the term became synonymous with this particular kind of rawhide container, also sometimes known as an "Indian suitcase." Parfleches were usually made as matched pairs, because a buffalo hide was large enough to yield two containers. Often two women—one seated at each end of a hide—worked together to apply the paint. This was both companionable and efficient, since the painting had to be done while the hide was wet and pliable (fig. 111). Parfleches had holes for thongs, which allowed them to be tied onto the pack saddles women used for easy carrying when moving camp. The bags held dried meat, pemmican, dried berries and roots, or clothing.

Rawhide containers of other sizes and shapes were created for specific objects: a fringed, cylindrical tube for a man's war bonnet might hang from a backrest tripod

Fig. 110. Southern Arapaho artist. Pair of Parfleches, late 19th century. Oklahoma. Rawhide, pigments, cloth; 50/370a: 15⁹⁄₁₆ × 9⁷⁄₁₆ × 1⁹⁄₁₆ in. (39.5 × 24 × 4 cm), 50/370b: 15¹⁄₁₆ × 9¹³⁄₁₆ × 1⁹⁄₁₆ in. (38.3 × 25 × 4 cm). Division of Anthropology, American Museum of Natural History, New York, 50/370a, b

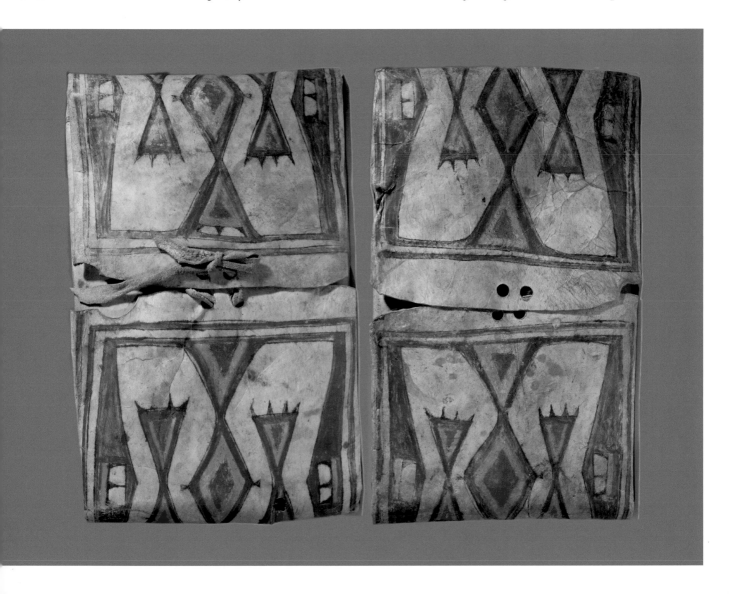

Fig. 111. Crow woman painting parfleche designs on a staked hide, 1890, Montana. National Museum of the American Indian, Smithsonian Institution, Washington, D.C., P09341

(see fig. 137); side-fringed square or rectangular cases often held herbal and sacred medicines (fig. 112); large rawhide boxes were used to store clothing and utensils (see fig. 51). A small, square flat bag might hold women's sewing equipment such as porcupine quills, washed, sorted for size, and dyed, and then placed, along with an awl, in a small pouch made of very tough bison pericardium or animal bladder, which could not be pierced by the quills' sharp points (fig. 113).[25] Soft bags of tanned elk, deer, or bison hide were used to store clothing and other small household possessions (fig. 114). These were sometimes called "possible bags," since they held every possible thing. When a tribe moved camp, these containers became saddlebags. They were made in matching pairs and were tied with thongs to the sides of a pack saddle and behind it. The bags might be decorated with quills or beads in geometric designs of lines, triangles, diamond shapes, concentric boxes, bars, and forks; the side designs were usually transverse bars or elongated checker patterns (figs. 115a, b). They were made largely by Arapaho, Gros Ventre (Atsina), Cheyenne, and Sioux women. Crow and Blackfeet women also made them with differences in design and color palette.

Fig. 112. Comanche artist. Case, circa 1900. Southern Plains. Rawhide, pigments, 9¹³⁄₁₆ × 10⅝ in. (25 × 27 cm). Brooklyn Museum, Brooklyn Museum Collection, X1120

Fig. 113. Plains artist. Sewing Pouches for Storing Porcupine Quills, late 19th century. Northern or Southern Plains. X1126.13 (above): animal bladder, porcupine quills, sinew, pigment, 4 × 11½ in. (10.2 × 29.2 cm), X1126.12 (below): animal bladder, beads, porcupine quills, linen thread, 3½ × 13 in. (8.9 × 33 cm). Brooklyn Museum, Brooklyn Museum Collection, X1126.12, X1126.13

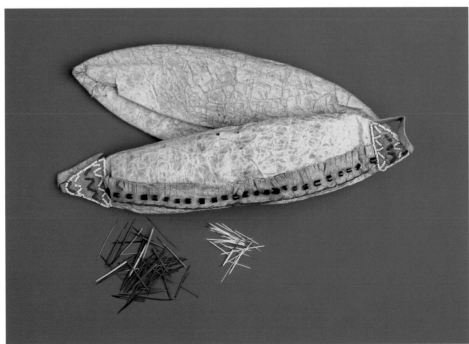

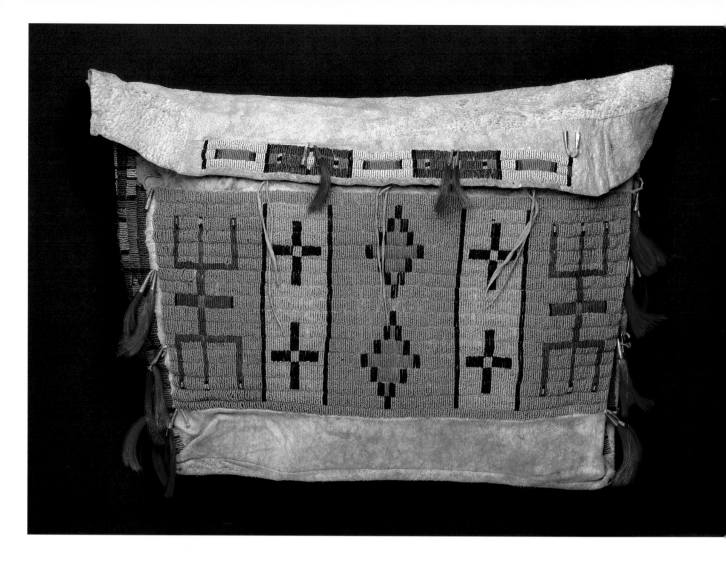

Decorated buffalo robes were among the most prized items made by women in the sewing societies. They were worn over the back and shoulders and were also used as bedding. A hide from a large buffalo might have to be split in order to work with it more easily. The split was then sewn up and covered with a strip of quillwork. The hide was worn with head and tail meeting at the wearer's front, with the quilled strip

(opposite, above)
Fig. 114. Sioux artist. Storage Bag, late 19th century. Central Plains. Hide, beads, tin cones, horsehair, 15½ × 20½ in. (39.4 × 52.1 cm). Brooklyn Museum, Brooklyn Museum Collection, X1111.1

(opposite, below)
Figs. 115a, b. Lakota artist. Pair of Storage Bags, 1885. Northern Plains. Hide, beads, tin cones, horsehair, each 14⅞ × 23 in. (37.8 × 58.4 cm). Buffalo Bill Historical Center, Cody, Wyoming, Gift of Richard W. Leche, NA.106.295a, b

(above)
Fig. 116. Northern Cheyenne artist. Blanket Strip, late 1880s. Northern Plains. Hide, glass beads, metal, brass, twine, sinew, 6 × 62 in. (15.2 × 157.5 cm). Brooklyn Museum, Brooklyn Museum Collection, X1181.1

wrapping horizontally at the waist. Later, beaded strips were sewn to wool and elk-hide wearing blankets in a similar way (fig. 116).

Traditionally women made the clothing for the family.[26] Each woman carried her personal hide-working and sewing tools with her, often as part of a belt set (fig. 117). Even little girls had their own tools, in imitation of their mothers. The tools usually included a bone or metal awl, a small sharp knife, and a strike-a-light (flint and steel for fire-making), each tucked securely into small hide cases that hung from thongs tied to the belt (fig. 118). Small bags might also hold paint, used by both men and women for ceremonial decoration and personal adornment (figs. 119, 120). Garments included shirts, dresses, leggings, and moccasins, originally of animal hide decorated with quills and beads (figs. 121–27). Plains dresses might be made of hide or trade cloth. One of the earliest Northern Plains styles was the side-fold dress, constructed of tanned hide wrapped around the wearer, sewn closed on one side. Six pieces of hide were cut and joined together to make the early nineteenth-century Yankton example shown in figure 121. The two bottom tabs at the proper left side of the dress may be decorative reminders of the forelegs of the animal. The quilled decoration on this dress is of parallel horizontal stripes intersected with tufts of red yarn; the tinned iron and copper cones sewn to the bottom of the dress were valued trade goods, and therefore prestige ornamentation for a woman on the Plains at that time. Another early dress probably related in style and origin to the side-fold dress is the strap dress (fig. 122), which has similar horizontal strips of dyed quillwork across the body of the garment and iron and copper cones at the hem that tinkled as the wearer moved.[27] Early nineteenth-century Plains men's shirts were made of two skins of deer, elk, antelope, bighorn sheep, or small buffalo in poncho style, with open sides and little tailoring. Northern shirts were more likely to have the sleeves sewn closed for warmth. An early nineteenth-century Yanktonai warrior's shirt (fig. 123), with blue pony beads on the bib and porcupine quills and maidenhair fern stems on the shoulder and chest strips, is painted with pictographs said to represent horse whips and blankets. The images probably represent the coups of the wearer and would have been painted by him.

In late nineteenth-century Reservation times, Sioux women covered entire articles of clothing with glass-bead embroidery. They took special pride in creating clothing for their children or making clothes as gifts to honor other children in their

Fig. 117 . Kiowa artist. Woman's Belt Set (partial), 1880–1900. Southern Plains. Harness leather, hide, beads, silver, tin cones, metal buckle, cowrie shell, mirror, 17¾ × 24 in. (45.1 × 61 cm). Haffenreffer Museum of Anthropology, Brown University, Providence, Rhode Island, 58-189

Fig. 118. Sioux or Cheyenne artist. Small Bag, late 19th or early 20th century. Northern Plains. Beads, metal, and hide, 4¾ × 3½ in. (12.1 × 8.9 cm). Brooklyn Museum, Brooklyn Museum Collection, X1126.9

Fig. 119. Kiowa artist. Paint Bag, 1880–90. Southern Plains. Commercial leather, metal, beads, pigment, 4¾ × 3¾ in. (12.1 × 9.5 cm). Brooklyn Museum, Gift of Margaret S. Bedell, 30.1459.9

Fig. 120. Northern Arapaho artist. Paint Bag, circa 1900. Wyoming. Hide, beads, pigment, metal, sinew, 11 × 7 × 2³⁄₁₆ in. (27.9 × 17.8 × 5.6 cm). Division of Anthropology, American Museum of Natural History, New York, 50/928

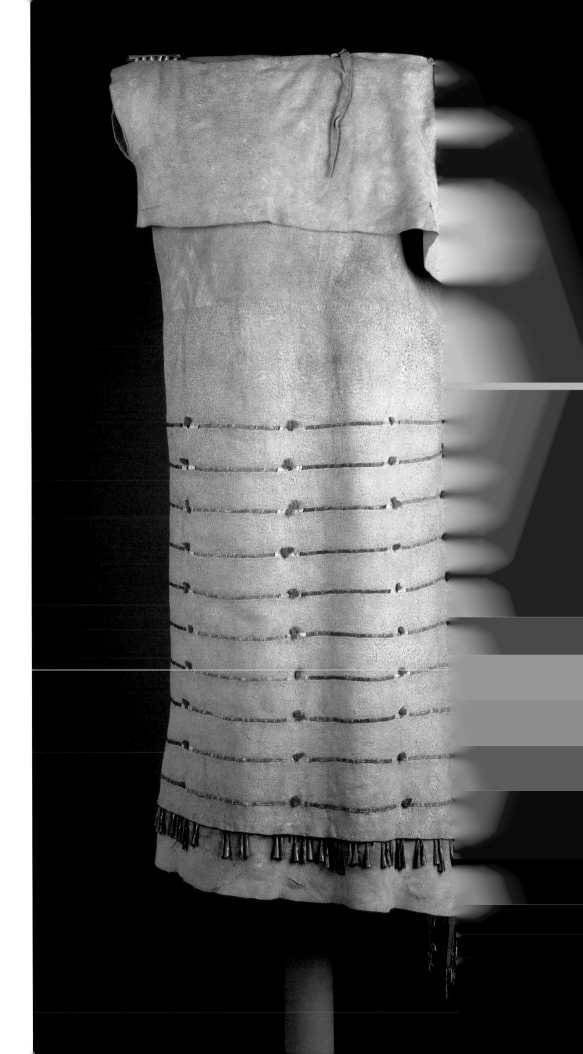

Fig. 121. Yankton artist. Side-Fold Dress, early 19th century. Collected by Dr. Nathan Sturges Jarvis, Sr., Fort Snelling, Minnesota. Hide, dyed bird and porcupine quills, tinned iron and copper cones, glass pony beads, yarn, pigment, sinew, 50 × 16 in. (127 × 40.6 cm). Brooklyn Museum, Henry L. Batterman Fund and the Frank Sherman Benson Fund, 50.67.6

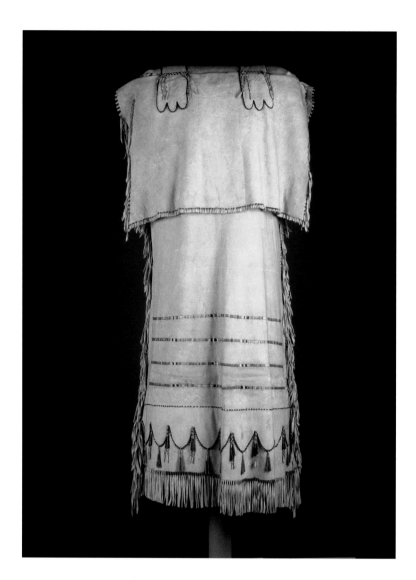

Fig. 122. Yanktonai artist. Strap Dress, early 19th century. Collected by Dr. Nathan Sturges Jarvis, Sr., Fort Snelling, Minnesota. Hide, dyed porcupine quills, glass beads, tin and copper tinklers, thread, sinew, and pigment, 46 × 21 in. (116.8 × 53.3 cm). Brooklyn Museum, Henry L. Batterman Fund and the Frank Sherman Benson Fund, 50.67.2

extended families (see Burke essay in this volume). By the 1870s Sioux women had moved from creating simple geometric designs of bars, circles, triangles, squares, and crosses to making more complex designs, with extensions of lines and forks (fig. 124). By 1890 they had begun beading representational forms, which had formerly been the prerogative of male artists in paint and in pipestone sculpture. In Late Reservation times, owing to the scarcity of game, trade cloth of cotton and wool replaced hide. Early cloth dresses were simply lengths of material folded at the shoulder and sewn down the sides, with a slit cut for the neck opening and sleeves added at right angles to the torso, creating a T-shape. Triangular gussets were added to the sides as needed. Among the Crow, woolen dresses were decorated with accretions of elks' teeth, or their imitations in bone and antler, in curved lateral rows. Among the Kiowa, cowrie shells were applied to best dresses; and among the Sioux, dentalium shells were popular as prestige ornamentation (fig. 128). A long tradition of embroidering dress clothing in a variety of materials—shells, beaks, claws, quills, teeth, and feathers—preceded the use of glass seed beads in the late nineteenth century, a high point of embroidery art.[28]

Fig. 123. Yanktonai artist. Warrior Shirt, early 19th century. Collected by Dr. Nathan Sturges Jarvis, Sr., Fort Snelling, Minnesota. Buckskin, dyes, pigment, glass beads, porcupine quills, maidenhair fern stems, sinew, 30 × 20 in. (76.2 × 50.8 cm). Brooklyn Museum, Henry L. Batterman Fund and the Frank Sherman Benson Fund, 50.67.11

Fig. 124. Lakota artist. Woman's Leggings, circa 1870–95. Central Plains. Hide, glass and metal beads, each 15 × 8 in. (38.1 × 20.3 cm). Brooklyn Museum, Charles Stewart Smith Memorial Fund, 46.96.10a, b

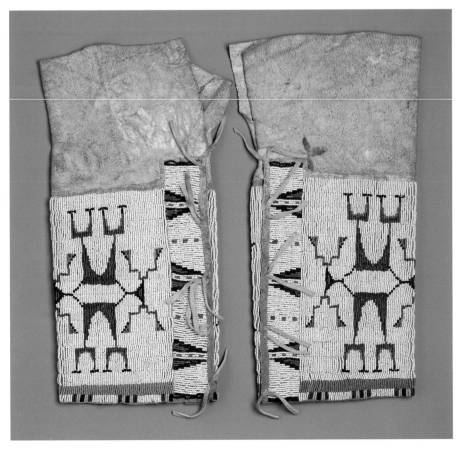

Fig. 125. Eastern Sioux artist. Puckered Moccasins, early 19th century. Collected by Dr. Nathan Sturges Jarvis, Sr., Fort Snelling, Minnesota. Smoked and unsmoked deer skin, deer hair, dyed porcupine quills, copper, 11 × 4 in. (27.9 × 10.2 cm). Brooklyn Museum, Henry L. Batterman Fund and the Frank Sherman Benson Fund, 50.67.20a, b

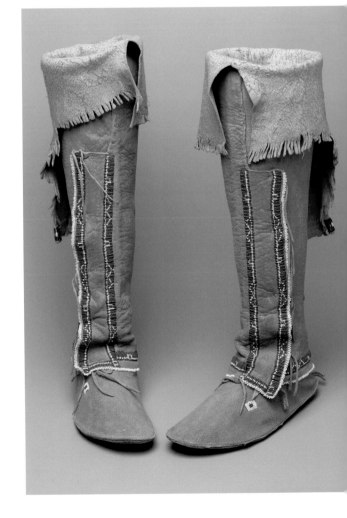

Fig. 126. Kiowa artist. Man's Moccasins, mid-20th century. Southern Plains. Hide, beads, pigments, 10¼ × 3¹³⁄₁₆ in. (26 × 9.7 cm). Brooklyn Museum, Gift of the estate of Ida Jacobus Grant, 44.116.11a, b

Fig. 127. Comanche artist. Woman's Tall Moccasins, early 20th century. Pawhuska, Oklahoma. Hide, pigment, glass beads, sinew, 24½ × 3¾ × 9½ in. (62.2 × 8.3 × 24.1 cm). Brooklyn Museum, Museum Expedition 1911, Museum Collection Fund, 11.694.9055a, b

Fig. 128. Sioux artist. Woman's Dress, 1875–1900. Central or Northern Plains. Wool cloth, dentalium shells, ribbon, glass beads, brass bells, cotton, 43⁵⁄₁₆ × 33⁷⁄₁₆ in. (110 × 85 cm). Brooklyn Museum, Charles Stewart Smith Memorial Fund, 46.96.12

QUILTING

Among Plains women the tradition of working together to produce artistic creations has continued into the present with a new art form—quilting. In Early Reservation times, teachers in day and boarding schools, missionaries' wives, and extension workers began teaching Native girls to quilt, using commercial cotton cloth and sewing thread. The art form became popular, especially in the Northern Plains among Sioux women, who often worked in groups of extended family and/or friends to create quilts with star designs.

The star quilt design has dual origins, reflecting both the Anglo-American "Star of Bethlehem" and "Lone Star" quilting patterns, which were taught to Native girls by their non-Native teachers, and the Sioux "Feather Bonnet" and "Morning Star" designs of early painted bison robes. The morning star symbolizes immortality and a continuing link between the living and the dead. Because of this meaning, star quilts have replaced the red buffalo hide of former days for ceremonial use in Sioux Yuwipi ceremonies, in which the spirits of the dead are summoned to assist in curing and prophecy.[29]

Star quilts are also very popular "giveaway" items that honor special events such as a high school or college graduation, a birth, a marriage, a naming ceremony, a return from war, or an award received from outside the community. As with tipi makers and quill and bead artists, quilters are specialists and are called on by others in their communities to provide quilts for special occasions. Edna Little Elk (Sićanǧu Lakota) of Rosebud Sioux Reservation had made more than a thousand star quilts on her treadle sewing machine by the time she passed away in 2007 at the age of ninety-one. She used to say that she did not have a single quilt in her own house; she had given them all away.[30] In 2007 the Lakota mother of a recent Brown University graduate from Standing Rock, South Dakota, commissioned sixteen star quilts as gifts for her daughter's wedding party and her new in-laws. The quilts bestowed recognition and respect on the couple's marriage. In both examples above, making and giving away artworks reflect the tribes' shared values of industry, generosity, humility, and hospitality.[31]

Since the 1980s quilts have also become a part of traditional Native arts competitions such as the Northern Plains Tribal Arts, an economic development program held annually in South Dakota. In 1994 the winning quilt, "Waterbirds" (fig. 129), was designed by Claire Anne Packard (Yankton Dakota and Sićanǧu Lakota). In her words, "my quilt was inspired by and created to honor the spring season. After the snow melts, the lowlands on the prairie fill with water and the great flocks passing through rest for a while in these areas."[32] Packard followed an old tradition of intergenerational learning by working closely with an aunt, Mabel Greeley (Yankton Dakota), who in turn had learned from her mother in the early 1900s. Packard and Greeley each create their own quilt-top designs, which include variations on the star pattern and other forms taken from nature; they then work together to finish the quilts, all of which are sewn by hand.

Through time, Plains women have created functional and beautiful domestic objects as well as arts that are dream-inspired and sacred. These works were suited to a mobile lifestyle when that life existed. When faced with the confinement and limited opportunities of reservation life, the women found cultural strength in an expanded artistic output, especially in the decoration and reciprocal gift giving of both domestic and sacred objects. With the home as their center, they have maintained close ties to family, to community, and to spiritual needs. They have stood as proud equals to men in reciting their coups of tipis decorated, robes quilled, and quilts sewn, ensuring themselves and their creations honor and prestige in their community. Their art continues to combine the cultural ideals of beauty, sacredness, and harmony.

KIOWA BEADWORK IN THE TWENTY-FIRST CENTURY

TERI GREEVES

MY LOVE OF BEADWORK BEGAN WITH MY KIOWA GRANDMOTHER AND mother. My grandmother, Sarah Ataumbi Big Eagle, was a beadworker her entire life. My mother, Jeri Ah-be-hill, had a trading post in Fort Washakie, Wyoming, on the Wind River Indian Reservation for twenty-five years. I grew up in her store surrounded by the beautiful beadwork she sold and collected.

When I was eight years old, I really wanted to learn how to bead. Zedora Enos, my mother's adopted Shoshone sister, was working for my mom and agreed to teach me. The first stitch I learned was the hump stitch, the typical lane (or lazy) stitch that is done on Plains beadwork; five, seven, or eleven beads are strung together to form a row, which is stitched down at either end. (Eventually I learned other stitches, and the main types I use now are a two-needle appliqué commonly called tackdown, a one-bead-at-a-time method called peyote stitch, various forms of edgework beading, and a leather-sewing technique called welt stitch.)

Years later, my mother moved to Santa Fe and had another store. By that time I was attending the University of California, Santa Cruz, and my mother was buying and selling my beadwork to help me pay school expenses. I was mostly beading small things—hatbands, belt buckles, medallion necklaces. She suggested that I bead a pair of tennis shoes similar to the ones a Lakota woman had brought into her shop in Wyoming years before. I agreed, and the first pair I made was beaded in hump stitch with traditional designs. My second pair was a commission with a pictorial design,

Fig. 130. Teri Greeves (Kiowa, b. 1970). *Saynday's Family Coming Along into the New Millennium: Tennis Shoes Series*, 1998. Beads, tennis shoes, 24 × 39 × 13 in. (61 × 99.1 × 33 cm) including base. Hampton University Museum, Hampton, Virginia

and it was then that I realized I wasn't limited to geometrical, lane-stitch designs. On my third pair I decided to tell a pictorial story that could be read around each shoe, and like the generations of Kiowa before me who have almost always decorated their footwear, I've continued telling stories on my shoes to this day.

After graduating from college, I decided to try some of the Native art markets. I got into a local show and exhibited mostly traditional objects, but also one pair of fully beaded tennis shoes, for which I won a first-place ribbon. The next year, I got into the SWAIA (Southwestern Association for Indian Arts) Indian Market in Santa Fe and won a first-place ribbon for a series of three pairs of tennis shoes titled *Saynday's Family Coming Along into the New Millennium* (fig. 130). Saynday is a trickster who figures in many Kiowa stories; he pulled the Kiowa into this world from the underworld through a hole in a cottonwood tree and also brought the sun and the buffalo to the Kiowa people. The shoes I decorated were displayed together "dancing" on a pedestal because I wanted the piece to be more of a sculpture than a utilitarian object. With its imagery and form, this piece is a representation of Native survival into the next century. Though I competed in a "traditional" category, I won a first-place ribbon with this nontraditional piece.

In my second year at Indian Market, I made a full-size beaded hide umbrella with a running pictorial scene illustrating an Indian parade (fig. 131). My mother had suggested I try beading an umbrella because many years earlier she had seen an old one, beaded in a geometric pattern, in a museum and thought it would be an interesting object to work with. This piece, which I also viewed as more of a sculptural object than a utilitarian one, won Indian Market's most coveted award, Best of Show.

Soon I decided to stop making traditional objects altogether. The shoes started me on a path where I felt the freedom to express myself with beadwork on nontraditional forms while still respecting material and methodology. Storytelling has become integral to what I choose to illustrate. How I come upon the stories stems from whatever I am most curious about at the moment. Some pieces are very personal, illustrating family history (fig. 132). Some pieces are historical—sometimes I am curious to learn more about a certain Kiowa figure or a moment in time past. Some pieces are about cultural practices: I'll go to a dance and see something I'm intrigued to know more about. Some pieces are mythic; these usually grow out of my sons' requests for

Fig. 131. Teri Greeves (Kiowa, b. 1970). *Indian Parade: Umbrella*, 1999. Brain-tanned deer hide, cut beads (size 12 and 13), glass beads, abalone shell, Bisbee turquoise, cloth, brass studs, nickel studs, Indian Head nickels, antique umbrella frame, diam. 42 in. (106.7 cm). Collection of Gil and Nancy Waldman (Photo: Dan Barsotti)

Fig. 132. Teri Greeves (Kiowa, b. 1970). *Great Lakes Girls*, 2008. Glass beads, bugle beads, Swarovski crystals, sterling silver stamped conchos, spiny-oyster shell cabochons, canvas high-heeled sneakers, 11½ × 9 × 3 in. (29.2 × 22.9 × 7.6 cm). Brooklyn Museum, Gift of Stanley J. Love, by exchange, 2009.1a, b

stories about our trickster or the origins of the Kiowa. Some pieces are political, coming from questions I might be asking about how Native people live and navigate the push and pull of tribal sovereignty in the United States.

In the end, I don't think what I do is any different from what other artists have done through the ages. I have found a way to use the materials and techniques of the old masters and mix them up with new materials and techniques for my generation, all in an attempt to interpret this twenty-first-century world I live in.

TIPIS AND THE WARRIOR TRADITION

DANIEL C. SWAN AND MICHAEL P. JORDAN

ALTHOUGH THE ETHNOGRAPHIC LITERATURE FOR THE PLAINS REGION
frequently identifies the tipi and the domestic space within it as the domain of
women, the tipi also occupied an essential place in the lives of Plains men and in
their warrior tradition. At the most basic level, the tipi was the home that the warrior
defended. Because the destruction of a man's tipi and the provisions that it contained
could lead to disaster, especially in the wintertime, the U.S. military routinely burned
the tipis of captured camps.[1] Warriors' awareness of this tactic intensified their moti-
vation for defending their villages during the late nineteenth century. In addition,
the tipi and the area around it were where war clothing and accessories, as well as a
warrior's medicine objects—his possessions imbued with supernatural power—were
stored or displayed. Warrior societies met in their members' tipis to socialize and to
dance. Furthermore, some men owned the rights to painted tipi designs, which were
passed on to male heirs or, on occasion, to men outside the family. Some of these
designs depicted martial exploits, while others were more enigmatic images received
in personal visions. Painted tipi liners also served as canvases on which men recorded
their war exploits, calling attention to their bravery. Focusing primarily on the Kiowa
of the Southern Plains, this essay will explore the relationship between the tipi and the
warrior tradition from the late nineteenth century to the present.

MEN'S CLOTHING AND ACCESSORIES

Plains men created a visual account of their military heroism on their clothes and accoutrements; these were displayed and stored inside the tipi, in the men's area opposite the doorway. Shirts from the tribes of the Upper Missouri region bore depictions of battle scenes and symbols that represented slain enemies as well as captured horses and weapons.[2] An example in the Brooklyn Museum (fig. 133) is decorated with flintlock muskets, quirts, and semicircles (representing horse tracks), referring to combat and horse raids by the shirt's owner. Locks of hair, such as those fringing this shirt, symbolized war honors, captured horses, and scalps; the hair might be human (taken from an enemy or provided by the warrior's relatives), or horsehair might be substituted. A Northern Plains shirt, also in the Brooklyn Museum's collection, is decorated with locks of hair, beaded panels with bear paws, and an eagle feather (fig. 134). Although the practice of depicting war honors on clothing seems to have been more widespread on the Northern Plains, it was not unknown in the south. Thomas Kavanaugh reports that Comanche men painted stripes on their leggings to represent their martial exploits.[3] Hugh L. Scott, a military officer stationed at Fort Sill beginning in 1889, documented the same practice among the Kiowa; the warrior Big Bow told him that each of the marks painted on his leggings represented an enemy he had vanquished.[4] The stripes on a pair of leggings in Brooklyn's collection probably had similar significance (fig. 135). Painted bison robes also drew attention to acts of valor, as seen in one garment's depiction of a lone Kiowa warrior surrounded by non-Native adversaries (fig. 136).[5] Eagle-feather bonnets, worn in battle and on special occasions by distinguished warriors known as *kataiki*, were stored in cylindrical

Fig. 133. Yanktonai artist. Shirt for Chief's War Dress, early 19th century. Collected by Dr. Nathan Sturges Jarvis, Sr., Fort Snelling, Minnesota. Buckskin, pony beads, porcupine quills, maidenhair fern stems, human hair, horsehair, dye, feather, 44 × 68 in. (111.8 × 172.7 cm). Brooklyn Museum, Henry L. Batterman Fund and the Frank Sherman Benson Fund, 50.67.1a

rawhide containers and hung in the tipi (fig. 137).[6] After embarking on his first raid at fifteen or sixteen, a young man might be recognized as a *kataiki* and earn the right to wear such a bonnet by age twenty if he demonstrated exceptional daring (figs. 138, 139).[7] Kiowa women often donned their husbands' bonnets when they participated in victory dances celebrating the return of successful warriors; the practice is illustrated in an 1875–78 drawing in which several women wear such headdresses (fig. 140).[8]

Fig. 134. Sioux artist. Warrior Shirt, 19th century, Northern Plains. Buckskin, pigment, beads, hair, feather, fiber, 46 × 67 in. (116.8 × 170.2 cm). Brooklyn Museum, Dick S. Ramsay Fund, 38.629

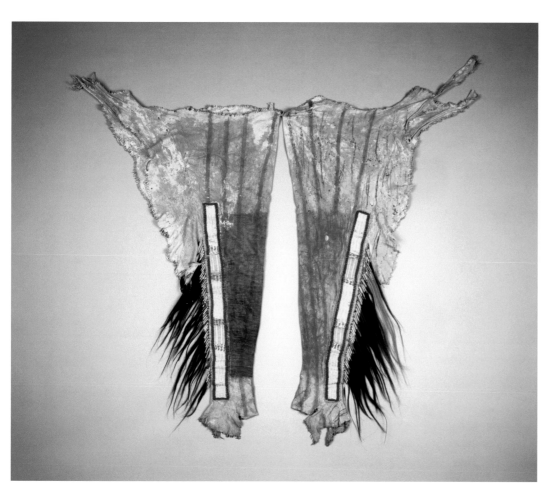

Fig. 135. Yanktonai artist. Warrior Leggings (worn with fig. 133), early 19th century. Collected by Dr. Nathan Sturges Jarvis, Sr., Fort Snelling, Minnesota. Buckskin, pony beads, porcupine quills, maidenhair fern stems, hair, horsehair, dye; (50.67.1b) 42¾ × 29 in. (108.6 × 73.7 cm), (50.67.1c) 45 × 27½ in. (114.3 × 69.2 cm). Brooklyn Museum, Henry L. Batterman Fund and the Frank Sherman Benson Fund, 50.67.1b, c

Fig. 136. Kiowa artist. Buffalo-Hide Robe, 19th century. Southern Plains. Buffalo hide, pigment, 49⅝ × 44⅞ × 1³⁄₁₆ in. (126 × 114 × 3 cm). Department of Anthropology, National Museum of Natural History, Smithsonian Institution, Washington, D.C., E6974

Fig. 137. Blackfeet artist. War Bonnet Case, late 19th century. Northern Plains. Rawhide, pigment, 17½ × 7½ in. (44.5 × 19.1 cm). Brooklyn Museum, Henry L. Batterman Fund and the Frank Sherman Benson Fund, 50.67.30

Fig. 138. Osage or Ponca artist. War Bonnet, early 20th century. Central Plains. Wool, felt, and cotton, golden eagle feathers, horsehair, glass beads, hide, weasel fur, silk, sinew, h. 34½ in. (87.6 cm). Brooklyn Museum, Brooklyn Museum Collection, X1053

Fig. 139. Sioux or Cheyenne artist. War Bonnet, late 19th–early 20th century. Pawhuska, Oklahoma. Feathers, beads, pigment, hide, dyed horsehair, 68½ x 8⁷⁄₁₆ in. (174 × 21.5 cm). Brooklyn Museum, Brooklyn Museum Collection, 05.553

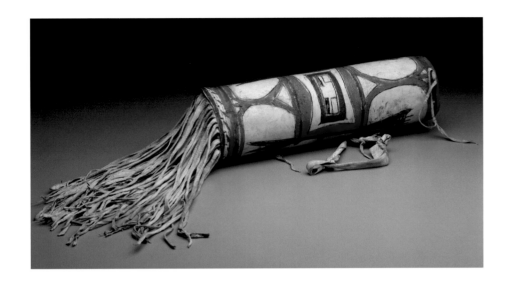

Fig. 140. Kiowa artist. *Kiowa Women Victory Dancing*, from Exercise Book 1875–78. Fort Marion, Florida. Graphite and colored pencil on paper, 6¾ × 7⅞ in. (17 × 20 cm). National Anthropological Archives, Smithsonian Institution, Washington, D.C., 98-54-10

PAINTED TIPIS AND TIPI LINERS

The tipi itself, or its liner, provided a broad canvas on which the warrior could display his war honors, creating a visual backdrop to impress his guests. (For an in-depth discussion of a Lakota tipi liner in the Brooklyn Museum's collection, see Kennedy Zeller essay in this volume.) Among the Kiowa, painted tipis were rare: in the nineteenth century less than 20 percent of the tribe's tipis were painted.[9] Within this relatively small number, a unique design called the Tipi with Battle Pictures celebrated the accomplishments of the Kiowa warriors. The only Kiowa tipi design to feature depictions of combat scenes, the Tipi with Battle Pictures originated among the Cheyenne.[10] The Kiowa chief Dohausan, or Little Bluff, was given the rights to the design in 1845 because of his marriage to a Cheyenne. The design is known through a model created for James Mooney, an anthropologist with the Smithsonian Institution's Bureau of American Ethnology, between 1901 and 1904 by Charley Ohettoint, the son of Dohausan's nephew (fig. 141).[11] Although the deeds depicted by Ohettoint may be fictional, the model does provide an indication of the tipi's general appearance. The south side featured a series of horizontal yellow stripes representing successful war expeditions led by the tipi's Cheyenne owner. Dohausan's design added black stripes to signify the expeditions he himself had led, as well as a series of tomahawks painted down the back of the tipi to represent coup (the act of striking an enemy with a special coup stick, lance, or other weapon) counted by the Kiowa warrior Heart Eater. Pictographs of lances above the door commemorated the exploits of Sitting on

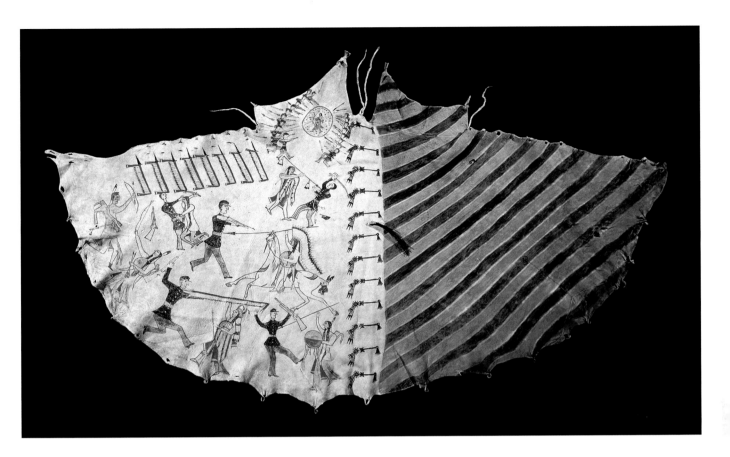

Fig. 141. Charley Ohettoint (Kiowa, dates unknown). Model of the Tipi with Battle Pictures (19th century), circa 1901–4. Southern Plains. Canvas, pigment, h. when erected 26 in. (66 cm), circumference when erected 59 in. (149.9 cm). National Museum of Natural History, Smithsonian Institution, Washington, D.C., 245001

a Tree, another Kiowa warrior. The north side of the tipi featured dozens of combat scenes chronicling the exploits of various Kiowa warriors. A Kiowa man's war record was among his most treasured possessions, and Dohausan had to secure the permission of all the men whose deeds he depicted. When a tipi cover wore out, a new one was made, and a group of men was assembled to paint it. Each time the design was renewed, new deeds were chosen for representation.

WARRIOR SOCIETIES

At the communal level—in the Kiowa warrior societies—the tipi also played a central role. Almost every male was a member of one of the tribe's six societies, which were collectively referred to as *yapahe*.[12] The Polanyi (Rabbit Society) counted all the boys in the tribe as members. Considered a training ground for future warriors, it was led by a distinguished elder who directed the boys' instruction.[13] Upon reaching the age of fourteen or fifteen, most boys joined the Adltoyui (Wild Mountain Sheep Society).[14] For the majority of Kiowa men, the Adltoyui served as a bridge between the Polanyi and the other Kiowa societies.[15] The Tsetanma (Horse Tassels), Tonkongya (Black Leggings), and Diambega (Unafraid of Death, or Skunkberry) societies vied with one another for members, each seeking to attract the wealthiest and most accomplished warriors.[16] The most prestigious society was the Kotsenko (Sentinel Horses), whose members included the ten men considered the bravest warriors in the tribe.[17] As marks of their bravery, these men wore eagle-bone whistles and sashes made from elk hide or trade cloth (figs. 142–44). During battle they staked themselves to the ground by shooting an arrow through the end of the sash or piercing it with a lance, an act that signaled their willingness to die fighting. They could not retreat from this commitment unless released from it by another member of the society.[18]

The warrior societies were inactive during most of the year, when the members were dispersed among different camps. Their only period of activity was during the summer, when all the bands assembled for the Skado, or Medicine Lodge Ceremony.[19] The warrior societies assisted with the preparation of the circular brush arbor in which the ceremony took place and oversaw the layout of the camp circle. In addition, they policed the camp, intervening in disputes that threatened to disturb the peace. During the summer each warrior society also held its meetings, which featured dancing and feasting.[20]

Most of these meetings were held inside tipis, although the societies also paraded on horseback through the camp and occasionally danced outdoors.[21] In the nineteenth century the Kiowa warrior societies, in contrast to those of other tribes, did not have tipis reserved for the use of their members. Instead, members volunteered to host the nightly meetings in their own tipis.[22] On occasion the mother or sister of a society member pledged to provide a daytime feast for the society to express her gratitude for her relative's continued well-being. The leader of a society, a member, or a member's father might also sponsor such a feast. The hosts removed their family's personal belongings from the tipi and moved it to a more prominent and visible position within the camp circle.[23]

A society might also meet in the tipi of one of its officers. This practice is illustrated in two leaves from a Kiowa book of drawings created in 1875 (figs. 145, 146). Visual clues allow us to identify the owners of the tipis and the societies depicted. Each drawing is inscribed "Lodges of Chiefs," and here the term "chief" seems to refer to a *patoki*, or leader of one of the warrior societies, rather than a *topatoki*, or leader of a residence band.[24] The tipi shown in figure 145 is that of Zepkoyet (Big Bow), an accomplished warrior and one of the *patoki* of the Adltoyui.[25] James Mooney collected a model of his tipi design, known as the Tail Picture Tipi (fig. 147).[26] Adding credence to the identification of these drawings as depictions of warrior-society meetings is the presence in figure 145 of the name glyph of a mountain sheep, a clear reference to the Adltoyui, or Wild Mountain Sheep Society.[27] Kiowa and other Plains artists frequently used name glyphs—iconic images that depicted a name in a graphic form—to identify individuals in their drawings. In this case the name glyph is connected not to an individual but to the tipi and serves to identify the group of men gathered there as members of the Adltoyui society.

The scene may show a meeting at which the Adltoyui inducted a new member. Once the members of a society agreed to invite a man to join their ranks, the *adltoki* (two junior officers who carried out the leaders' decisions) located the prospective member and escorted him to the society's meeting.[28] The two men shown arriving at the tipi on horseback in figure 145 probably represent an *adltoki* of the society and a new recruit. The renowned Kiowa flute player Belo Cozad was initiated into the Adltoyui at age sixteen in 1880 and later recalled how the *adltoki* had visited his

(opposite, left)
Fig. 142. Kiowa artist. Kotsenko Society Sash, 19th century. Southern Plains. Hide, pigment, feathers, 81⅞ × 7½ × 2⅜ in. (208 × 19 × 6 cm). National Museum of Natural History, Smithsonian Institution, Washington, D.C., E152897

(opposite, above right)
Fig. 143. Kiowa artist. Kotsenko Society Eagle Bone Whistle, 19th century. Southern Plains. American bald-eagle wing bone, hide, feathers, cord, beads, circumference 18⅛ in. (46 cm). National Museum of Natural History, Smithsonian Institution, Washington, D.C., E152862

(opposite, below right)
Fig. 144. Kiowa artist. *A Member of the Kotsenko Society*, left side of double-page spread from Ledger Book 1875. Fort Marion, Florida. Graphite, colored pencil, and crayon on paper, 7⅛ × 8⅝ in. (18 × 22 cm). National Anthropological Archives, Smithsonian Institution, Washington, D.C., 08528220

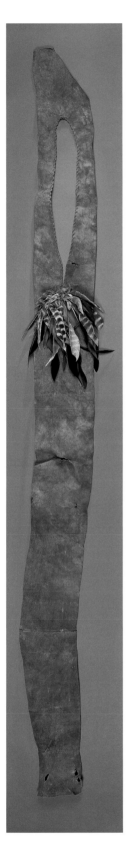

Lodges of Chiefs.

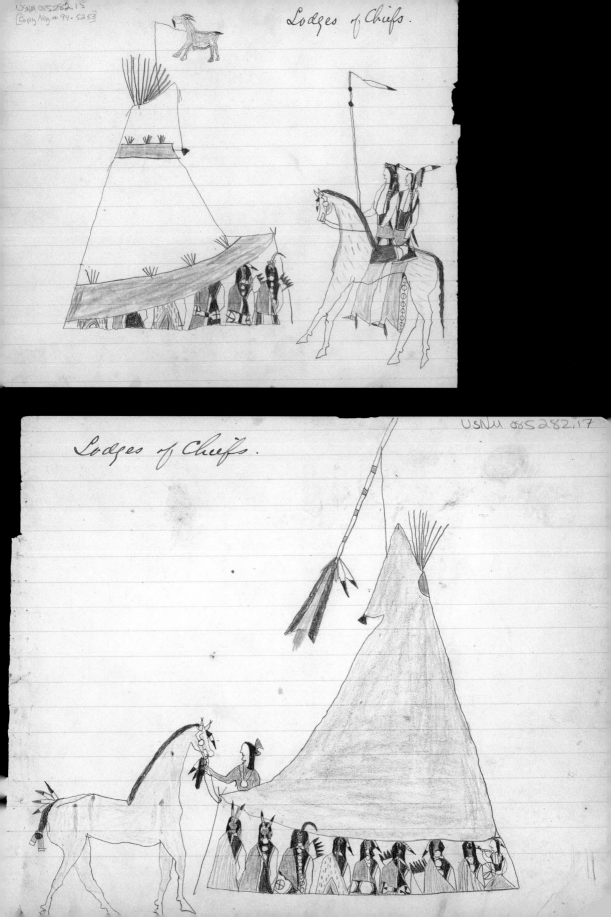

Lodges of Chiefs.

family. After Cozad agreed to join the society, he was directed to sit behind one of the *adltoki* on horseback, and the two rode to the society's meeting.[29] This form of escort on horseback was an allusion to the way a mounted warrior sometimes rescued a dismounted comrade in battle—a deed that was held in high esteem.[30] A Kiowa warrior who had performed such a rescue was allowed to reenact the event by selecting another man to ride behind him when he paraded on horseback through the camp with his society.[31]

The other drawing (fig. 146) depicts a meeting of the Diambega in the tipi of Satanta (White Bear), a *patoki* of the society.[32] Satanta inherited the rights to this design, known as the Red Tipi, from his father.[33] As the name of the design implies, and as a model collected by Mooney illustrates, the entire tipi was painted red, except for a green sun disc placed at the top of the north side (fig. 148).[34] The use of specific

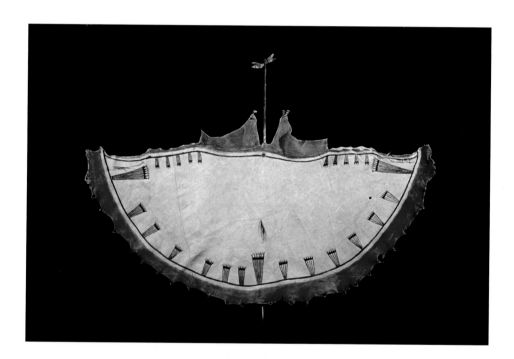

(left and opposite)
Figs. 149a, b. Kiowa artist.
Adltoyui Society, double-
page spread from Exercise
Book 1875–78. Fort Marion,
Florida. Graphite and
colored pencil on paper,
each page 7⅞ × 6¾ in.
(20 × 17 cm). National
Anthropological Archives,
Smithsonian Institution,
Washington, D.C., 98-54-
06, 98-54-07

tipi designs was often part of a larger set of practices associated with a man's med-icine—his power, derived from a supernatural source.[35] When a man received his medicine, he was taught the songs, rituals, and taboos associated with it. These instructions might dictate not only the design painted on his tipi but also those he ritually painted on his shield, his horse, and his body when he prepared for battle.[36] The man depicted standing outside the lodge in figure 146 most likely represents White Bear, who was known for his distinctive red body paint. Further confirmation of his identity is provided by the presence of a *zebat*, or arrow lance, since White Bear owned one of only two such lances that existed among the Kiowa.[37]

During the meeting of a warrior society, the cover of the tipi was rolled up, as seen in another drawing, which shows the members of the Adltoyui on their way to a gathering (figs. 149a, b). Some societies were so large that the assembly overflowed the tipi; rolling up the sides provided additional seating for members and allowed spectators to witness the society's dances.[38] It was also common to open the sides in this way during the summer in order to take advantage of any cool breezes. Figures 149a, b make reference to the feasting and dancing that were central to warrior-society

meetings: the food for the meal is shown inside the tipi, and the mounted figure holds several hand drums, to be used in the dancing that will follow the feast.

THE BLACK LEGGINGS WARRIOR SOCIETY: FROM THE RESERVATION ERA TO TODAY

The Red River War, the U.S. Army's campaign of 1874–75 to force all Southern Plains tribes onto reservations, ended armed resistance to the federal government's encroachment, with immediate and later consequences for the warrior societies. Confinement to a reservation and military surveillance deprived young men of the opportunity to distinguish themselves in combat and to earn social advancement by accumulating war honors.[39] Despite these changes, the warrior societies were maintained primarily through the prominent role they played in the Skado, or Medicine Lodge Ceremony. Over time the destruction of the bison as well as government opposition to indigenous religious practices made it increasingly difficult to hold the Skado. In preparation for the ceremony, a hunter was required to kill a bison bull and

Fig. 150. Gus Palmer, Sr., at the Black Leggings Warrior Society ceremonies, Anadarko, Oklahoma, 1983 (Photo: Daniel C. Swan)

remove a strip of its hide, but by 1880 securing even the single bison needed to satisfy this ritual obligation was problematic. Consequently, the observance of the ceremony became more sporadic, with the last documented Skado taking place in 1887. An attempt was made to hold the ceremony in 1890, but as news traveled that troops were on their way from Fort Sill to stop the event, the assembled crowd dispersed before the preparations were complete.[40] By this time the warrior societies, which had been active only during the annual summer encampment and the Skado, had ceased to function as organized bodies. They remained inactive until the Tonkongya and Diambega societies were revived in 1912, continuing to meet until 1927 and 1928, respectively.[41]

In 1958 the Tonkongya, or Kiowa Black Leggings Warrior Society, was revived a second time, by Kiowa veterans of World War II and the Korean War. The movement to revive the society was led by Gus Palmer, a World War II veteran who sought to honor the memory of Kiowa servicemen who had fallen in battle (fig. 150; see Palmer and Palmer interview in this volume). Among those to be honored was his brother Lyndreth Palmer, who had been killed in World War II. Gus Palmer sought and received the approval and assistance of elders who had participated in the society's ceremonies between 1912 and 1927. These elders taught the members of the newly revived society the songs, dances, and traditions of the Tonkongya. Since its revival in 1958, membership in the organization has been restricted to Kiowa men who have served or are currently serving in the U.S. military. Kiowa women continue to honor their warriors. Some support the organization by participating in the associated Kiowa Veterans' Auxiliary (see fig. 151).[42]

A comparison of a drawing from the late 1800s (fig. 152) with a photograph of contemporary Kiowa Black Leggings Warrior Society members (fig. 153) demonstrates how modern-day members have incorporated elements of nineteenth-century dress and material culture into their practice. Little Henry, a former member of the Tonkongya, recalled in the 1930s that society members painted their lower legs and forearms black and their chests, backs, and upper arms yellow[43]—a recollection substantiated by the historical drawing. Today members of the society paint their lower legs black or wear black stockings to simulate body paint.[44] A few members even employ the more extensive body painting described by Little Henry. The men in the drawing are also depicted wearing hair-pipe (tubular bead) breastplates (fig. 154), ornaments that are still worn by Kiowa Black Leggings Warrior Society members during ceremonies.

The figure in the nineteenth-century drawing wearing a red cape (see fig. 152) may represent Goo-laid-te, a prominent member of the Tonkongya who was killed in a clash with the U.S. military in the 1870s.[45] On an earlier raid Goo-laid-te had captured a red cape from a Mexican officer[46] whom he had defeated in combat. The war trophy became a family heirloom and was passed down from generation to generation.[47] When the society was revived, Gus Palmer and his brothers, descendants of Goo-laid-te, gave the members of the society the right to wear red capes when they

Fig. 151. Kiowa Veterans' Auxiliary participating in Black Leggings Warrior Society ceremonies, Anadarko, Oklahoma, 1983 (Photo: Daniel C. Swan)

Kiowa Chiefs on a road to the Agents.

Fig. 152. Kiowa artist. *Tonkongya Society*, from a ledger book, late 19th century. Southern Plains. Graphite, colored pencil, and ink on paper, 7½ × 12 in. (19.1 × 30.5 cm). The Charles and Valerie Diker Collection, Ledger Drawing #59

Fig. 153. Kiowa Black Leggings Warrior Society dancers, Anadarko, Oklahoma, 2008 (Photo: Daniel C. Swan)

Fig. 154. Plains artist.
Breastplate, late 19th
century. Bone, hide, beads,
metal, 24½ × 10 in. (62.2
× 25.4 cm). Brooklyn
Museum, Brooklyn Museum
Collection, X1104.4

Fig. 155. Black Leggings
Warrior Society tipi,
Anadarko, Oklahoma, 1983
(Photo: Daniel C. Swan)

danced.[48] In this manner they honored not only their fellow veterans but also the memory of their ancestor.

In 1974 Tonkongya members decided that the society needed a tipi of its own. As a record of Kiowa martial history, Dohausan's Tipi with Battle Pictures provided inspiration for the design. The new tipi was painted by Dixon Palmer, a World War II veteran who had joined his brother Gus in leading the 1958 revival of the society (fig. 155). Dixon Palmer preserved the bilateral asymmetry of the original design, which featured black and yellow stripes on the south side of the tipi and depictions of combat scenes on the north side, but he focused on the experiences of Kiowa warriors who served during World War II, with scenes including paratroopers, tanks, and bombers. He also included depictions of the patches of military units in which Kiowa men had served since World War II. Eventually the society outgrew this tipi, and a larger one was constructed in 1993. Dixon Palmer also painted this larger version of the tipi, omitting the combat scenes but retaining the service patches.[49]

In 2008 the Kiowa Black Leggings Warrior Society marked the fiftieth anniversary of the organization's revival. To celebrate this event the society painted a new tipi (fig. 156), whose design features combat scenes that represent each of the wars and conflicts in which Kiowa have fought. Thus, the scenes honor Kiowa men and women who have served the United States in conflicts of the twentieth and twenty-first centuries as well as Kiowa warriors who participated in nineteenth-century intertribal warfare. Kiowa artists Sherman Chaddlesone and Jeff Yellowhair painted the new tipi

Fig. 156. The new Black Leggings Warrior Society tipi, Anadarko, Oklahoma, 2009 (Photo: Susan Kennedy Zeller)

Fig. 157. Sherman Chaddlesone (right) and Jeff Yellowhair (left) painting the new Kiowa Black Leggings Warrior Society tipi, Anadarko, Oklahoma, 2008 (Photo: Daniel C. Swan)

(fig. 157). They were assisted by Russell Bohay, Sr., and Russell Bohay, Jr., who painted the yellow and black stripes on the south side of the tipi. Chaddlesone, a member of the Tonkongya society and a Vietnam veteran, painted several combat scenes[50] in his unique artistic style inspired by nineteenth-century Kiowa ledger drawings. The new tipi provides a visual record of Kiowa military history in a style that recalls tribal records produced more than a hundred years earlier.

THE TIPI TODAY

Although painted tipis are not as prevalent among the Kiowa as they once were, the descendants of several prominent nineteenth-century warriors continue to use their ancestors' designs. For example, the Chief Satanta (White Bear) Descendants, an organization formed by lineal descendants of White Bear—one of the nineteenth-century leaders of the Diambega society—employ the Red Tipi design. The organization displays the latest incarnation of the Red Tipi at events in which its members participate.[51] Dohausan, who owned the rights to the Tipi with Battle Pictures, also owned the rights to a second tipi. This tipi—which was painted yellow except for the upper portion and the smoke flaps, which were painted red—was referred to as Little Bluff's Yellow Tipi to distinguish it from a similar tipi owned by Lone Wolf. The descendants of Dohausan returned his Yellow Tipi design to use in the 1970s.[52] Nelson Big Bow revived the use of the Eagle Tipi, one of the two designs that belonged to his great-grandfather Zepkoyet, a nineteenth-century leader of the Adltoyui warrior society. The design for the Eagle Tipi originated in a vision Zepkoyet received while on a war journey.[53] Big Bow erects the tipi during the annual celebration of the Tia-Piah Society of Oklahoma, a gourd-dance organization of which he is a prominent member. These painted tipis not only evoke the memories of nineteenth-century warriors but also function as tangible reminders of the kinship ties that connect descendants to historic figures.

Today, as in the past, the tipi is intimately associated with the Kiowa warrior tradition. The Black Leggings Warrior Society tipi functions as a record of the tribe's martial history and a tangible symbol of the society itself. For the descendants of prominent Kiowa warriors, the use of tipis bearing hereditary designs is a way of paying homage to ancestors who defended the tribe during the turbulent late nineteenth century. Through these traditions, tipis continue to occupy an honored place in the historical consciousness of the Kiowa community, linking the people to a time when Kiowa warriors gathered in the summer to dance and celebrate their valorous deeds.

THE TIPI OF THE KIOWA TONKONGYA
(BLACK LEGGINGS WARRIOR SOCIETY)

DIXON PALMER, CHARTER MEMBER, KIOWA TONKONGYA,
AND LYNDRETH PALMER, COMMANDER, KIOWA TONKONGYA

From an interview conducted by Michael P. Jordan and Daniel C. Swan, February 12, 2008, Anadarko, Oklahoma

DP: In our organization we didn't have a tipi at the beginning, when we first revived the Tonkongya, my older brother Gus and me. The Black Legs is one of the six war societies of the Kiowa. If you look back, our great-grandfather was the one who captured that cape.[1] He killed a Mexican officer, and he brought it back to his camp.

We have meetings once in a while, and things come up and we would talk about the tipi. We said the society should have a tipi. According to the traditions of the Black Legs Society, you go in the tipi, and everything takes place in there. We pray for the welfare of the members—all veterans—and their families. That's the main reason we get together. That was one of the reasons we decided we should have a tipi. It was based on the Tipi with Battle Pictures that belonged to Dohausan. He was the chief of the Kiowa tribe for thirty-three years, and he had that tipi. And it was handed down.

Dr. Everett Rhodes, one of our members, was the one who sponsored our first tipi, in 1974. We talked about this tipi. They said, "Dixon would paint it." I explained to the organization how I was going to paint this tipi. "We're not going to paint it like the original. I'll paint it to honor our veterans who have gone on. We will put their names on the front of the tipi, and the shoulder patches of all the military units where Kiowa have served will be at the top and down the back." I still used the black and

Fig. 158. Lyndreth Palmer (right), Commander of the Black Leggings Warrior Society, and his uncle, Dixon Palmer, Charter Member of the society, Anadarko, Oklahoma, December 2009 (Photo: Courtesy of Lyndreth Palmer)

yellow stripes from the Tipi with Battle Pictures. I believe it means that the veterans traveled all day and night, as warriors.[2] It's a veterans' tipi. At the top it's red on one side to represent the blood that was given, the boys who were killed. And I drew some military pictures. I had the paratroopers, tanks, B-17s, all from World War II.

LP: Well, that tipi is used in our dance. All the members, we put up the tipi the week before [the dance][3] and clean everything up nice. Nothing is done haphazardly whenever we put up the tipi. That's the beginning of the ceremony. And you look forward to that. Everything functions exactly the way the old people told us. They were the ones who explained to us about the tipi. It was the old people who told us all about the songs. And when we come out of that tipi, there are two songs that we sing, two special songs. We come into the grounds, and then the women do the Scalp Dance. The Scalp Dance is something else that was sacred in those times when those guys come back from battle. When they were victorious, the women danced the Scalp Dance for four days and four nights.

We are about to celebrate the fiftieth anniversary of our organization, and we're making a new tipi. In about a month, when it gets warm, we'll paint it. Uncle Dixon said the way we should do it, this newer tipi, we got to add some names to the front. We'll be adding several new names. He's going to be there to direct us. We commissioned Sherman Chaddlesone to do the painting. He's a member and a Vietnam veteran. The way we are going to do this new tipi, the way that we are thinking, we'll have all those patches, the same way as before. And we will have battle scenes. We're going to have warrior skirmishes in one area. There will be scenes for World War I, World War II, the Korean War, Vietnam, and Desert Storm. And we are going to leave one [place open], because we will have another war to add.

DP: People forget. We don't want people to forget—we want this organization to go forward as long as it can, to remember our members who were killed in combat. You don't forget. You have pictures of them. And when we dance, we call their names. We understand and we talk Kiowa. My younger brother was the first Kiowa killed in World War II. Lyndreth. He was a tank driver with General Patton. Patton was driving through the Bastogne—that's when he got killed. And we honor the members who were killed. The younger generation that is coming up, we explain to them, "You should be proud, very proud of your Tonkongya."

GROWING UP ON THE PLAINS

CHRISTINA E. BURKE

INTO THE EARLY TWENTIETH CENTURY, THE LIVES OF PLAINS CHILDREN revolved around the tipi. From the time a child was born, the tipi was his or her home and refuge—shared by an extended family that might include grandparents, aunts, uncles, and cousins—and a place where daily life and important ceremonies took place. It served to structure a person's behavior from birth to adulthood, when grown children moved out to their own tipis to start their own families.

The tipi was a microcosm of the camp community, and the protocols and values observed there served as a model for an individual's place in the world. Children learned their roles and responsibilities within the family and community from lessons taught inside the tipi. By observing adults, whether related to the child by kinship or not, and by being instructed directly, children learned where to sit, how to behave with the family, and how to welcome and interact with relatives and other visitors. They also absorbed cultural norms and virtues of family pride, respect for elders, and gender-specific roles that were part of everyday life and ritual activities.

Children were catered to and indulged, with misbehavior addressed through gentle reprimand. Corporal punishment was virtually unknown among Plains peoples. Instead, behavioral standards were reinforced through social control; when children misbehaved, adults admonished them, shaming them into acting properly.[1] Behavioral norms were also a common topic of discussion at formal events such as religious ceremonies and social dances, when leaders addressed the community and reiterated such tribal values as bravery, fortitude, generosity, and wisdom to both the young and old.

For Plains children of the nineteenth and early twentieth centuries, youth was a time of great freedom, when they engaged in play with siblings, cousins, and other youngsters in the community. Children's activities honed specific skills and prepared them for responsibilities in later life.[2] These roles were gender-based and served to perpetuate the family, the community, and the tribe. Men hunted for food and protected the community from enemies, for example; women gathered plants, prepared food, managed the household, and made clothing, tipis, and various household goods.[3] Consequently, boys tested their dexterity by practicing hunting with child-size bows and arrows and honed their hand-eye coordination with games of skill that included throwing and shooting at targets. Girls practiced running a household by playing with dolls and toy tipis and helping their mothers with chores and the care of younger children.

Parents were their children's primary instructors on life and behavior, although grandparents, aunts, and uncles were often caregivers and mentors as well. In some communities, one's mother's sisters were considered mothers, and one's father's brothers were regarded as fathers. Among the Lakota, for instance, such role models were addressed with the same kinship term as one's biological mother and father. A Lakota child called his or her father and all uncles *até* and referred to his or her mother and all aunts as *iná*. This kinship system also extended to one's own generation, so that any child of an *até* and *iná* was considered a sibling rather than a cousin.[4] The importance of the extended family, especially in child rearing, continues today, and many children are raised partly or entirely by grandparents or aunts and uncles.

TIPI ARTS FOR CHILDREN: CRADLES AND CLOTHING

Plains families, like those everywhere, showered their children with love, affection, and beautifully made things, from cradles and clothing to toys and dolls. Cradles in particular symbolized the continuity of the family, community, and tribe, and of human life. Babies were swaddled in various types of cradles, from undecorated utilitarian versions to elaborately adorned ones that were passed down through generations. Indeed, some Kiowa people referred to the cradle as "a house for the beginning of life."[5] Whether plain or decorated, cradles made infants feel secure and safeguarded children both physically and spiritually (fig. 159). The infants were wrapped in rawhide, wood, buckskin, and cloth and protected by significant designs, charms, and prayers that were part of the cradle's creation.

Like modern car seats, cradles provided protection when a family was moving as well as in daily camp life, inside and outside the tipi. Cradleboards with wooden frames could easily be leaned against a tree or used inside the tipi as a baby's bed. They could also be slung from a mother's back or suspended from the pommel of a horse's saddle when a family was on the move. Before a child was born, the mother-to-be and/or her female relatives began work on a cradle, in which the infant would be kept swaddled during the first several months of life. Sometimes the father's female

Fig. 159. Lois Smoky
(Kiowa, 1907–1981) in a
cradle, 1907, Oklahoma.
University of Pennsylvania
Museum of Archaeology
and Anthropology,
Philadelphia, 54-141794

relatives made the cradle to show their esteem for him.[6] Among many tribes, including the Comanche, Kiowa, and Lakota, decorated cradles were recognized as masterpieces of women's craftsmanship, and they retain this status today.[7] These objects of prestige were so highly prized that they were used by various family members and handed down from generation to generation. Today many cradles are in public and private collections, having passed out of Native hands during the early part of the twentieth century.[8]

Many tribes made both soft cradles (sometimes referred to as cradle hoods) of tanned hide—and, later, trade cloth—and lattice-style cradles or cradleboards

Fig. 160. Arapaho artist. Cradle, 1870s. Northern or Southern Plains. Muslin, willow, porcupine quills, pigment, deer hide, 32 × 13 in. (81.3 × 33 cm). Brooklyn Museum, Brooklyn Museum Collection, X1126.36

mounted on wooden frames. The style and decoration varied from tribe to tribe, and cradle makers were careful not to duplicate designs; each cradle was unique. Decorative embellishments were done in quill- and/or beadwork, and sometimes the wooden frame was adorned. Design elements might include images of powerful animals, whether real or mythical, or other symbols intended to provide the child with spiritual protection and promote a long, healthy life. An Arapaho example is decorated with a large quilled disc sewn onto the hood (fig. 160). This traditional design represents the child's brain, while the cross-straps signify ribs, and the quilled bands hanging down from the hood stand for hair braids.[9]

Cradleboards with wooden frames covered with tanned hide and/or cloth were usually quilled or beaded or created using a combination of these techniques. The shape of the frame varied according to the tribe. Crow cradleboards traditionally have an elongated and rounded headboard that was wrapped in hide and decorated with beadwork (fig. 161). Kiowa and Lakota examples have wooden slats extending above a baby's head that may be decorated with brass tacks, carving, paint, or, in rare cases, beadwork (fig. 162). A fully beaded cradleboard might require more than a hundred thousand beads in all.[10] Such elaborately beaded cradleboards are still being made, although there are fewer skilled beadworkers than in the past. Consequently, recognized artists are in demand, and their creations are highly prized in Native communities and among collectors and museums alike.

Sometimes trinkets were suspended from the hood to amuse the baby (fig. 163). Many Plains cradles featured a small decorated hide amulet, which held the child's umbilical cord. When a baby's umbilical cord fell off, it was placed inside an amulet as protective medicine. The amulet was often attached to the cradle hood, where it served both practical and spiritual functions: to amuse and stimulate the child and to protect and bless him or her and ensure long life.[11] Such amulets were often in the form of an animal—usually a turtle or lizard, both associated with strength and longevity—and embellished with quill- and/or beadwork (fig. 164). Later the amulet might be sewn into a child's clothing and even kept throughout life as part of a personal bundle.[12]

Infants did not wear clothing. Instead, they were wrapped in soft, tanned hides or cloth lined with dried grass, cattail down, or another absorbent material.[13] Following sustained interaction with non-Natives, Plains people adopted new types of baby clothing and accessories such as bonnets adorned with dyed quills that were embroidered into geometric shapes or zoomorphic designs (fig. 165). These articles illustrate the interaction of cultures and the creative adaptation of nontraditional forms by Native people, who made them their own by decorating them with tribally specific designs. Contemporary examples include a fully beaded bonnet, complete with lacy ruffle, and a matching beaded bib by Todd Yellow Cloud Augusta (Oglala Lakota), a male artist who creates children's garments, which are traditionally made by the mother (fig. 166). Both of these pieces feature depictions of tipis and people in traditional clothing.

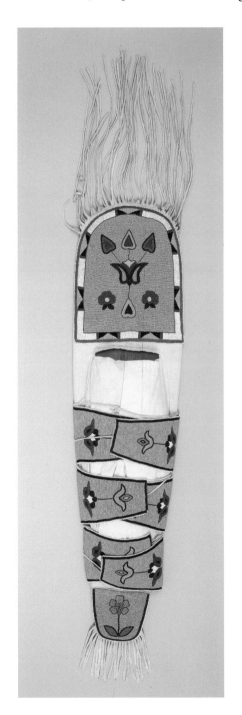

Fig. 161. Crow artist. Cradle, circa 1915. Northern Plains. Wood, hide, glass beads, cotton, 41¾ × 5½ in. (106 × 14 cm). Buffalo Bill Historical Center, Cody, Wyoming, Irving H. "Larry" Larom Collection, NA.111.5

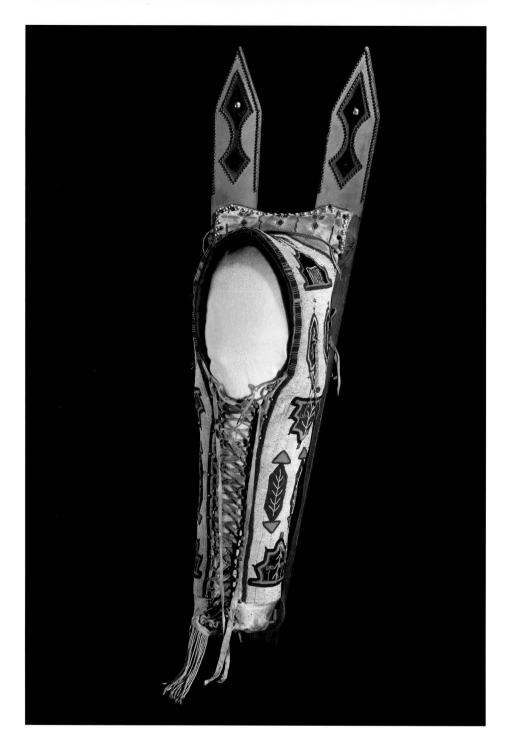

Fig. 162. Doyetone (Kiowa, dates unknown). Cradle, circa 1904. Oklahoma. Hide, glass beads, wood, cloth, pigment, metal, 45⅝ × 12¼ × 9 in. (115.8 × 31.1 × 22.9 cm). Milwaukee Public Museum, E57416

    As children learned to walk, they wore more clothing, some of it richly decorated in quill- and beadwork. In the past, mothers took animal hides brought home by their husbands and male relatives, and prepared them for use either by tanning or smoking, processes that made the hides pliable for sewing. Everyday clothing—shirts and long leggings for boys, and dresses and short leggings for girls—was plain with little embellishment. Both boys and girls wore moccasins (such as the quilled and beaded baby and child's moccasins shown in figures 167 and 168), which were constructed and decorated according to tribal aesthetics. Boys and men usually wore short moccasins that did not go above the ankle (fig. 169). Among some tribes,

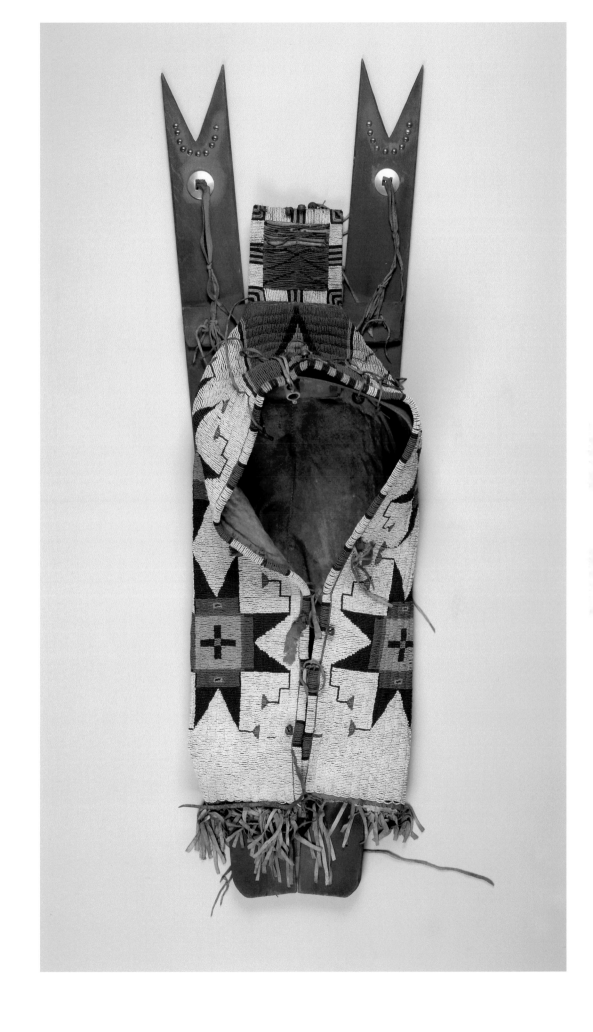

Fig. 163. Sioux artist. Cradle, 1870–1900. Northern Plains. Buffalo hide, wood, beads, metal, ceramic, porcupine quills, brass nails, pigment, 32 5/16 × 12 3/16 × 7 in. (82.1 × 31 × 17.8 cm). Brooklyn Museum, Dick S. Ramsay Fund, 38.630

Fig. 164. Standing Rock Sioux artist. Turtle-Shaped Amulet, early 20th century. Northern Plains. Hide, beads, porcupine quills, metal, horsehair, 4¹³⁄₁₆ × 3³⁄₁₆ in. (12.2 × 8.1 cm); Teton Sioux artist. Lizard-Shaped Amulet, 1890–1904. Rosebud Indian Reservation, South Dakota. Hide, beads, 6⅛ × 3⁵⁄₁₆ in. (15.5 × 8.4 cm); Teton Sioux artist. Lizard-Shaped Amulet, circa 1900. Rosebud Indian Reservation, South Dakota. Hide, quills, beads, 5⅞ × 3½ in. (15 × 8.9 cm). Milwaukee Public Museum; top to bottom, E40711, E59772, E263 (Photo: Joanne Peterson)

Fig. 165. Sioux artist, probably Lakota. Baby Bonnet, circa 1900. North or South Dakota. Hide, dyed porcupine quills, sinew, 7½ × 5⅞ × 6¹¹⁄₁₆ in. (19 × 15 × 17 cm). National Museum of the American Indian, Smithsonian Institution, Washington, D.C., 1/3337

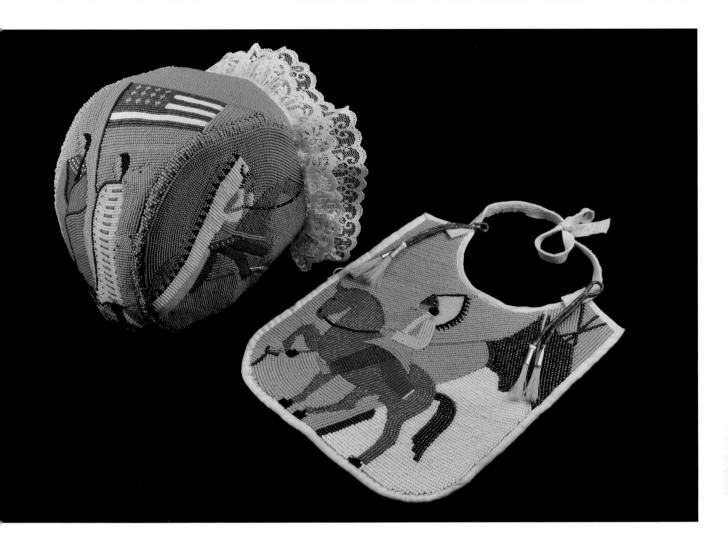

Fig. 166. Todd Yellow Cloud Augusta (Oglala Lakota, dates unknown). Baby Bonnet, 1993; Bib, 1994. Pine Ridge Reservation, South Dakota. Bonnet: canvas, glass seed beads, lace, 7¹⁄₁₆ × 6⅛ in. (18 × 15.5 cm); Bib: glass seed beads, cotton, porcupine quills, metal, horsehair, 9¹⁄₁₆ × 7⅞ in. (23 × 20 cm). Haffenreffer Museum of Anthropology, Brown University, Providence, Rhode Island, 93-216, 94-290

Fig. 167. Santee artist. Baby Moccasins, circa 1890–1920. Niobrara Reservation (now Santee Sioux Reservation), Nebraska. Hide, porcupine quills, glass beads, sinew, 4⁵⁄₁₆ × 2⁹⁄₁₆ in. (11 × 6.5 cm). National Museum of the American Indian, Smithsonian Institution, Washington, D.C., 18/2122

Fig. 168. Crow artist. Child's Moccasins, 1885–95. Montana. Smoked hide, glass beads, cut steel beads, 7½ × 3⅛ in. (19 × 8 cm). Brooklyn Museum, Anonymous gift in memory of Dr. Harlow Brooks, 43.201.72a, b

Fig. 169. Cheyenne artist. Man's Moccasins, early 20th century. Pawhuska, Oklahoma. Hide, glass beads, $10^{13}/_{16}$ × $4^{5}/_{16}$ in. (27.5 × 11 cm). Brooklyn Museum, Museum Expedition 1911, Museum Collection Fund, 11.694.9035a, b

Fig. 170. Cheyenne artist. Girl's Moccasins, late 19th or early 20th century. Central Plains. Hide, glass beads, 18 × 2³⁄₁₆ × 5⅞ in. (45.7 × 5.6 × 14.9 cm). Brooklyn Museum, Brooklyn Museum Collection, 13.15a, b

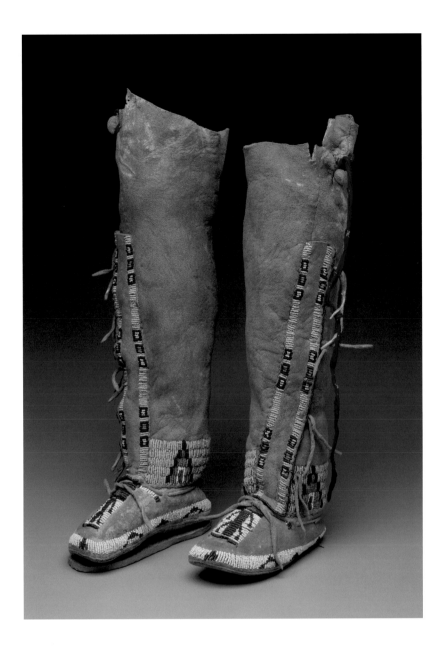

including the Lakota, girls and women also wore low-top moccasins, but with leggings that came up to the knee. Among other groups such as the Kiowa and the Cheyenne, girls and women wore knee-high moccasins, often decorated with quilled or beaded designs on the upper and lower sections (fig. 170).

Special outfits for ceremonies or for honored individuals were elaborately adorned in a variety of ways. Preparing the materials and creating such clothing took days and weeks, if not months. The birth of a baby was cause to celebrate life and the future of the family and the tribe, and women expressed their joy by lavishing a great deal of time and care on clothes for the child, despite the fact that the garments would quickly be outgrown. Fully beaded clothing for boys (fig. 171) and girls (fig. 172) was worn only for special occasions, since the sumptuous beading made the pieces heavy and uncomfortable. Today's versions of such garments are the elaborately decorated powwow outfits with matching moccasins, headdresses, shawls, and accoutrements

Fig. 171. Sioux artist. Boy's Vest, late 19th century. Northern Plains. Hide, glass beads, 13½ × 12¼ in. (34.3 × 31.1 cm). Brooklyn Museum, Brooklyn Museum Collection, X98

Fig. 172. Sioux artist. Girl's Dress, circa 1900. Rosebud Reservation, South Dakota. Hide, glass beads, 22⅜ × 24⅜ in. (56.9 × 62 cm). Milwaukee Public Museum, E28

Fig. 173. Crow Fair, Crow Agency, Montana, 2008 (Photo: Susan Kennedy Zeller)

that many families make for their children. These outfits continue the tradition of heaping affection on children in ways that are visible to the community at large. Reflecting Native life in contemporary American society, powwow clothing for young children may include such imagery from popular culture as Mickey Mouse, Spiderman, and Dora the Explorer (fig. 173).

CHILDREN'S TOYS AND FAMILY GAMES

Childhood was a time for freedom and play, but toys and games also helped prepare children for their adult roles. Such recreational activities taught skills and accuracy and improved endurance and fortitude, traits expected of both sexes.[14] In construction and decoration, toys were miniature replicas of the objects used by adults in everyday life—tipis, clothing, tools, and weapons. Around the age of four or five, children were given their own clothing, utensils, and even their own beds. It became their responsibility to store and care for their belongings.[15]

In general, girls' games were played close to the family tipi. Girls played house and practiced cooking, gathering food, sewing clothing, caring for dolls, and moving camp. They set up toy tipis for their dolls and occasionally had play tipis that were large enough to crawl inside (fig. 174). Toy tipis were often adorned just like the family tipi, with beaded rosettes, quilled tabs, and even pictographs documenting the military exploits of male relatives (fig. 175). Girls also had toy travois, the sledges that were used to transport household goods when communities moved camp.

Dolls were soft-bodied, made of tanned hide stuffed with dry grass or other material. Hair, either human or from a horse, was attached to the head. Facial features might be minimal or nonexistent, leaving it to the child to imagine the face on her doll, but many examples had painted or beaded eyes, nose, and mouth (figs. 176, 177). Dolls did have very detailed, removable clothing and accoutrements. They sometimes had their own cradles, which were exact replicas of those in which the girls themselves had been swaddled and were made with the same care and artistry as the full-size versions (fig. 178). Doll clothing and accessories were tribally specific, created using the construction techniques, colors, and design elements of a particular community. Female dolls sometimes wore belts that held the sewing tools that were ubiquitous among Plains women (see fig. 117). There are even examples of male dolls with their own horses and horse trappings (fig. 179). Today very few Native people make dolls for the children in their lives, partly because of the labor- and time-intensive process of creating such pieces. In addition, many Native children prefer to play with commercial dolls. Like cradleboards and other traditional arts, dolls are now often created for the art market; they have been transformed from children's toys to

Fig. 174. Cheyenne girls and their playhouses, Northern Cheyenne Reservation, Montana, 1907. Photograph by Julia E. Tuell (1886–1960). Library of Congress Prints and Photographs Division, Washington, D.C., LC-USZ62-120768

Fig. 175. Lakota artist. Toy Tipi, circa 1880–1900. North or South Dakota. Hide, wood, pigments, porcupine quills, metal cones, feathers, horsehair, sinew, silk floss, string, h. 33¹⁄₁₆ in. (84 cm). National Museum of the American Indian, Smithsonian Institution, Washington, D.C., 2/9535

sculptures that replicate the traditional regalia worn by Plains peoples (figs. 180a, b). Such carefully made soft sculptures are sought by collectors, garner high prices at galleries, and win top awards at such juried competitions as the Southwestern Association for Indian Arts (SWAIA) market in Santa Fe.

In contrast to girls, boys were encouraged to roam and play away from the tipi. They learned to ride horses and use bows and arrows made by their fathers and uncles (fig. 181). With these weapons they hunted small game like rabbits, birds, and turtles—foods that supplemented the family's diet and made the child feel that he was making a contribution.[16] Like their male relatives, boys kept their weapons in the tipi (perhaps with the men's weapons at the back) in tanned hide quivers that were quilled

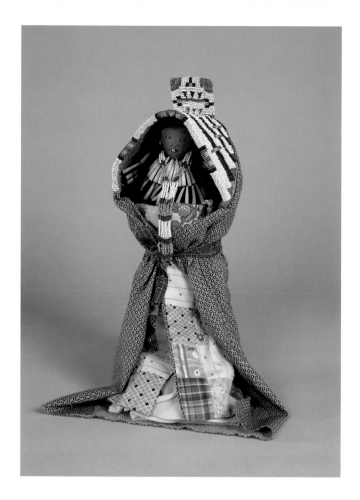

and/or beaded (fig. 182). Boys and men also competed in games of skill, throwing spears into moving targets made of wood hoops strung with sinew in a weblike pattern and sent rolling down a hillside (figs. 183, 184).[17] The entire family could play another game that involved tossing a type of dart referred to as an "ice glider" across a frozen river or lake (fig. 185). The object was to see whose glider could go farthest with the greatest accuracy (fig. 186). The gliders were made of wood or bone, usually buffalo or deer ribs, to which two feathers, or "flights," were attached.[18] Boys and girls also practiced dexterity and eye-hand coordination by playing the pin-and-bone game, in which one tried to catch a bone on the end of a metal pin (fig. 187).[19]

Both boys and girls also engaged in team sports, including shinny, a game similar to field hockey. Points were scored by passing a buckskin ball through a goal using long shinny sticks that were curved and flattened at one end. Players could also kick the ball, but the use of hands was strictly forbidden. Sometimes tipis were used as "goalposts," and there were no boundaries, so the entire camp might become the playing field.[20] Girls also played a complicated game in which runners tossed a double ball (two hide balls tied together by a thong) back and forth with a stick five or six feet long in order to score a goal (fig. 188). The game was played in teams—two defensive and one offensive—and the goalposts were about a quarter mile apart.[21]

Today these games of skill have evolved into official sports within school curricula and community youth-center activities. Boys and girls often play the same sports, with baseball, softball, volleyball, and particularly basketball as the favorite choices. Organizations such as the NABI (Native American Basketball Invitational) Foundation sponsor "Rez Ball" as a highly competitive sport. Track events and cross-country running are also highly regarded by Native people because they highlight individual skills respected in their traditions and cultures.

Games of chance were also played by girls and boys, as well as adults. One of the most prevalent—the "hand game"—was popular among tribes across North America. Although it is unknown how old the game is, during the Lewis and Clark Expedition in April 1806, William Clark and Sergeant John Ordway both recorded in their journals that they had observed the Skillutes and the Skid-datts (tribes that lived where the Cowlitz River joins the Columbia River) playing hand games.[22] This guessing game involves both dexterity (hiding a game piece in the hand) and luck (guessing the hand in which the opponent has hidden the piece). Hand-game pieces—cylinders of bone or wood—were made in pairs, and one piece from each pair was marked with notches, incised designs, or paint, or sometimes tied with string. The object of the game was for the guessing team to identify which hand the player of the hiding team was using to conceal the unmarked piece (or the marked piece, depending on the rules adopted).[23]

The hand game and its variations are still played by men, women, and children, usually in teams. In the past, the genders were separated, with women competing against women and men playing against other men.[24] Among some groups such as the Kiowa, the hand game was played in a tipi, where teams sat in a circle around the fire.[25] The hider put both hands behind his or her back and moved the piece back and forth before bringing forward both closed fists. The hider's teammates

Fig. 181. Blackfeet boy carrying a bow case and quiver on his back, circa 1900–1920, Montana. Photograph by Roland Reed (1864–1934). Denver Museum of Nature and Science, Neg 2-036

Fig. 182. Sioux artist. Boy's Bow Case and Quiver, circa 1890. Northern Plains. Hide, porcupine quills, beads, sinew?, 13¾ × 29 in. (34.9 × 73.7 cm). The Field Museum, Chicago, A114801d (Photo: John Weinstein)

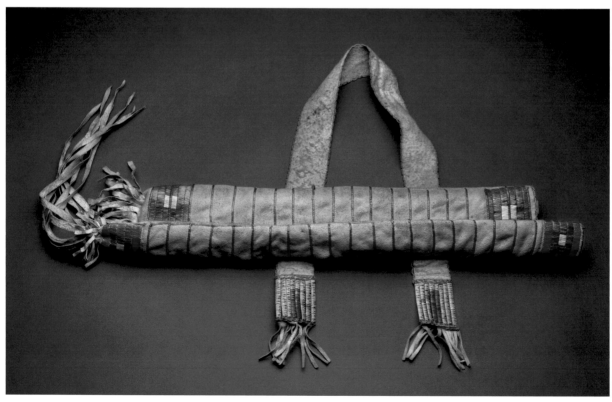

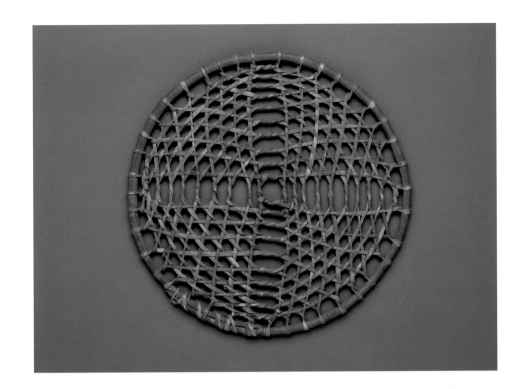

Fig. 183. Plains artist. Game Hoop, 19th or 20th century. Northern, Central, or Southern Plains. Wood, rawhide, diam. 13¾ in. (34.9 cm). Brooklyn Museum, Brooklyn Museum Collection, X1126.31a

Fig. 184. Southern Cheyenne boys playing the hoop and stick game, 1902, Spotted Horse's Camp, Oklahoma. Photograph by Elizabeth C. Grinnell (1876–?). McCracken Library Collection, Buffalo Bill Historical Center, Cody, Wyoming, MS 37, box 1, p.37.1.14 73

meanwhile distracted their opponents and entertained spectators by singing, drumming, and swaying.²⁶

A guesser from the opposing team pointed to the hand thought to hold the game piece. If the guess was correct, the opposing team scored a point and the chance to take a turn at hiding the piece. If the guesser was wrong, the first team scored a point and was allowed another turn. Score was kept with a set of tally, or counting, sticks. Historically, wagers were made, and prizes included tobacco, a quiver, a yard of

Fig. 185. Arikara artist. Ice Glider Set, circa 1920. Fort Berthold Reservation, North Dakota. Bones, wood, feathers, pigment, l. of each 5⅞ in. (15 cm). National Museum of the American Indian, Smithsonian Institution, Washington, D.C., 13/2857

Fig. 186. Amos Bad Heart Bull (Oglala Lakota, 1869–1931). *Feathered Bone Glider Game*, circa 1890. Ink, pencil, and watercolor on paper, 7 × 12 in. (17.8 × 30.5 cm). Drawing no longer extant (Photo from Helen Blish, *A Pictographic History of the Oglala Sioux* [Lincoln: University of Nebraska Press, 1967])

Fig. 187. Cheyenne artist. Bone and Pin Game, circa 1900. Cheyenne Indian Reservation, Lame Deer, Montana. Bone, beads, metal, pigment, sinew, 2¾ × 13¾ in. (7 × 34.9 cm). The Field Museum, Chicago, A114803d (Photo: John Weinstein)

Fig. 188. Arikara artist. Double Ball, circa 1923. North Dakota. Hide, dyed porcupine quills, sinew, unknown stuffing, 2¹¹⁄₁₆ × 2³⁄₁₆ × 13 in. (6.8 × 5.5 × 33 cm). National Museum of the American Indian, Smithsonian Institution, Washington, D.C., 12/6170

cloth or a blanket, leggings, or even—in high-stakes games—a horse.[27] Hand-game sets came to be elaborate works of art with carved game pieces, beaded and tasseled counting sticks, and rattles (fig. 189).

The hand game has evolved into a major winter pastime, with teams competing in intertribal tournaments held in community centers. Players of all ages become known for their craftiness, while audience members participate by becoming cheerleaders, performing special songs and dances composed to distract the opponents while their team is in possession of the hiding pieces. Side bets go on for each play as well as for the final outcome.[28]

YOUTH TO ADULTHOOD

In Plains communities, children were considered adults when they began behaving like adults and taking on adult responsibilities. Certain events marked a child's entry into manhood or womanhood, however. For a boy this was usually his first participation in a hunting party or a war party, a brave deed that entailed the new responsibilities of providing for one's family and protecting one's people. Before he reached his teens, a boy would probably go on his first hunting party, and around the age of thirteen to fifteen, he would accompany a war party to take care of the horses and/or fetch water or firewood when needed.[29] During such trips, a boy effectively served as an apprentice to his father and male relatives, observing them, obeying their requests, and training for a time when he and his cohorts would hunt or go into battle.

For a girl, womanhood began when she experienced her first menstrual period. On that occasion she was secluded in a small tipi made specifically for this ritual and was instructed in the creation and decoration of moccasins and other clothing by her mother and female relatives. This instruction indicates how the women's responsibility for clothing their families was vitally important to the well-being of the community. Following her seclusion, a girl's family would host a coming-out party, announcing to the community that she was eligible for marriage. Such ceremonies were significant life events for young women and constituted community celebrations of the female virtues of industry, modesty, and generosity.[30]

Today the role that tipis play in Plains children's lives differs significantly from that of a hundred years ago. Most families buy canvas tipis to house guests, provide shelter during powwows, and serve as cultural symbols on formal and ritual occasions. Tipis are ubiquitous at graduation ceremonies at tribal colleges and at ceremonial events such as adoptions, dances, and rituals (figs. 190a, b). They are also crucial to the growing cultural revitalization movement taking place in Native communities across the Plains. During summer cultural exploration camps, tipis are where the children sleep, hear traditional stories in their tribal language, and learn such arts as hide tanning and beadwork. For contemporary Plains children, these traditional structures continue to be a part of their lives, reinforcing cultural identity and values.

Figs. 190a, b. Sinte Gleska University graduation held in Christian Life Fellowship building, Rosebud Indian Reservation, South Dakota, August 25, 2007 (Photos: Susan Kennedy Zeller)

NOTES

NOTES TO "TIPI: HERITAGE OF THE GREAT PLAINS"

1. Iris Pretty Paint, personal communication to the author, Dec. 11, 2007. Pretty Paint, née Heavy Runner, is codirector of research opportunities in science for Native Americans at the University of Montana, Missoula. She was also one of the consultants on the planning team for the exhibition *Tipi: Heritage of the Great Plains.*

2. The Sioux Nation consists of three major divisions: Dakota, Nakota, and Lakota. The Dakota are subdivided into the Santee and the Eastern Dakota. The Nakota include Yankton and Yanktonai. The Lakota, who are also called Teton or Western Dakota, are further subdivided into seven bands: Blackfeet (Sihásapa); Two Kettle (Óʹóhenunpa); Sans Arc (Itázpčo); Brule (Sićanǧu Oyate); Oglala; Minicónjou; and Húnkpapa.

3. There are various spellings of the word *tipi.* The one used here is based on the work of Stephen R. Riggs (1812–1883), who wrote the first Dakota–English dictionary in 1852 and transliterated the oral Santee (Dakota) word for "tent" or "dwelling" as *tʰípi.* See Stephen Return Riggs, *Grammar and Dictionary of the Dakota Language. Collected by the Members of the Dakota Mission and Edited by the Rev. Stephen R. Riggs,* Smithsonian Contributions to Knowledge 4 (Washington, D.C.: Smithsonian Institution, 1852). See also the enlarged edition: James Owen Dorsey, ed., *A Dakota–English Dictionary by Stephen Return Riggs,* Contributions to North American Ethnology 7 (Washington, D.C.: Government Printing Office, 1890).

4. Smallpox epidemics occurred in 1780 and 1837–38. The latter outbreak was particularly devastating, almost wiping out the Mandan, killing two-thirds of the Blackfeet, half the Assiniboine and Arikara, a third of the Crow, and a quarter of the Pawnee.

5. The Medicine Lodge Treaty of 1867 was negotiated with the Comanche, Kiowa, Cheyenne, Arapaho, and Plains Apache at Medicine Lodge Creek in southern Kansas; the Fort Laramie Treaty of 1868 was negotiated with the Oglala and Lakota Sioux at Fort Laramie in Wyoming. Colin F. Taylor, *The Plains Indians: A Cultural and Historical View of the North American Plains Tribes of the Pre-Reservation Period* (London: Salamander Books, 1994), 228, 234–35.

6. For a comprehensive discussion of the tipi, see Reginald Laubin and Gladys Laubin, *The Indian Tipi: Its History, Construction, and Use,* 2nd ed. (Norman: University of Oklahoma Press, 1977).

7. *Painted Tipis by Contemporary Plains Indian Artists*, with an introduction by Myles Libhart and Rosemary Ellison, Blackfeet tipi legends by Cecile Black Boy (Anadarko, Okla.: Oklahoma Indian Arts and Crafts Cooperative, 1973), 9, 11.

8. Domestic tipis had a small altar directly behind the fireplace for daily prayers and offerings of sweetgrass, sage, and cedar smoke. Laubin and Laubin, *The Indian Tipi*, 108–9.

9. Peyotism most likely began in the 1640s when the indigenous Carrezo people of the Texas region brought their Peyote Religion to the Lipan Apache. Peyotism, whose purpose is to assist physical and spiritual well-being, was introduced to the Plains region in the early nineteenth century, and tribes eventually developed a distinctive Peyote Religion called the Native American Church. Originally a family's tipi was used for the ceremony after being temporarily cleared of its daily contents. Today the Peyote tipi is erected on the occasion of a meeting and is disassembled soon thereafter. See Daniel C. Swan, *Peyote Religious Art: Symbols of Faith and Belief* (Jackson: Mississippi University Press, 1999); and Omer C. Stewart, *Peyote Religion: A History* (Norman: University of Oklahoma Press, 1987).

10. These double tipis were probably observed by Prince Maximilian of Wied and the artist George Catlin during their expeditions to the North American interior in the 1830s, because they reported seeing hide tipis as large as fifty feet wide. Laubin and Laubin, *The Indian Tipi*, 215, 240–41.

11. Brian M. Fagan, *Ancient North America: The Archaeology of a Continent* (London: Thames and Hudson, 1991), 126.

12. Thomas F. Kehoe, "Tipi Rings: The 'Direct Ethnological' Approach Applied to an Archeological Problem," *American Anthropologist*, n.s., 60, no. 5 (Oct. 1958): 861–73. See also Carling Malouf, "The Tipi Rings of the High Plains," *American Antiquity* 26, no. 3 (Jan. 1961): 381–89.

13. Julie E. Francis and Lawrence L. Loendorf, *Ancient Visions: Petroglyphs and Pictographs from the Wind River and Bighorn Country, Wyoming and Montana* (Salt Lake City: University of Utah Press, 2002), 175–77.

14. Laubin and Laubin, *The Indian Tipi*, 4.

15. Juan de Oñate, "1549–1624 Account of the Discovery of the Buffalo," in Herbert Eugene Bolton, ed., *Spanish Exploration in the Southwest, 1542–1706* (New York: Charles Scribner's Sons, 1916), 226.

16. John C. Ewers, *Artists of the Old West*, enl. ed. (Garden City, N.Y.: Doubleday, 1973), 26, 30. The current location of this watercolor by Peale (*Sioux Lodges,* 1819) is unknown, but it is reproduced in Ewers on page 30.

17. Ibid., 77–97.

18. Catlin displayed artifacts and paintings in exhibitions of his Indian Gallery in New York, Boston, Baltimore, Philadelphia, and Washington, D.C., in 1837

and 1838. He also included a twenty-five-foot Crow buffalo-hide tipi when the exhibition opened in London in 1840. Brian W. Dippie, "Green Fields and Red Men," in George Gurney and Therese Thau Heyman, eds., *George Catlin and His Indian Gallery* (Washington, D.C.: Smithsonian American Art Museum; New York: W. W. Norton, 2002), 58–61; Christopher Mulvey, "George Catlin in Europe," in ibid., 64–66.

19. The army surgeon Nathan Sturges Jarvis was stationed at Fort Snelling, Minnesota, from 1833 to 1836. His collection of 157 objects, primarily from Plains Cree, Yankton, Yanktonai, and Métis tribes, features men's and women's clothing, pipes, clubs, personal accessories, and cradleboards. The Brooklyn Museum purchased this rare and early collection from the New-York Historical Society in 1950.

20. A buffalo can weigh up to eighteen hundred pounds. Janet Catherine Berlo, *Spirit Beings and Sun Dancers: Black Hawk's Vision of the Lakota World* (New York: George Braziller in association with New York State Historical Association, 2000), 111.

21. By 1850 bison herds were virtually extinct east of the ninety-fifth meridian, the eastern border of Indian Territory that extended south from the Minnesota-Canada border, slicing through the states of Minnesota and Iowa, and then along the western borders of Missouri, Arkansas, and Louisiana, to Galveston Bay, Texas. Taylor, *The Plains Indians*, 9.

22. Ken Zontek, *Buffalo Nation: American Indian Efforts to Restore the Bison* (Lincoln: University of Nebraska Press, 2007), 17.

23. Ibid., 9.

24. Ibid., 9–10.

25. Ibid., 3.

26. Ibid. For additional creation stories, see Larry Barsness, *Heads, Hides & Horns: The Complete Buffalo Book* (Fort Worth: Texas Christian University Press, 1985), 75–84.

27. Taylor, *The Plains Indians*, 84.

28. Marsha C. Bol, "Gender in Art: A Comparison of Lakota Women's and Men's Art, 1820–1920" (Ph.D. dissertation, University of New Mexico, 1989), 181. See also Beatrice Medicine, "Women's Roles," in Emma I. Hansen, *Memory and Vision: Arts, Cultures, and Lives of Plains Indian People* (Cody, Wyo.: Buffalo Bill Historical Center in association with University of Washington Press, Seattle, 2007), 95–96.

29. Barsness, *Heads, Hides & Horns*, 82.

30. Taylor, *The Plains Indians*, 84.

31. Zontek, *Buffalo Nation*, xv.

32. Hansen, *Memory and Vision*, 115–16; Herman J. Viola, "Introduction: Freedom, Bravery, and Generosity: Native Americans and the Horse," in George P. Horse Capture and Emil Her Many Horses, eds., *A Song for the Horse Nation: Horses in Native American Cultures* (Washington, D.C.: National Museum of the American

Indian, Smithsonian Institution, 2006), 7; John C. Ewers, *Plains Indian History and Culture: Essays on Continuity and Change* (Norman: University of Oklahoma Press, 1997), 206.

33. John C. Ewers, *The Horse in Blackfoot Indian Culture*, Smithsonian Institution, Bureau of American Ethnology, Bulletin 159 (Washington, D.C.: Government Printing Office, 1955), 314–16; Hansen, *Memory and Vision*, 124.

34. Ewers, *The Horse in Blackfoot Indian Culture*, 314.

35. Viola, "Introduction: Freedom, Bravery, and Generosity," 9–10.

36. Herman J. Viola, "The Art of Capturing Horses: Joe Medicine Crow Counts Coup During World War II," in Horse Capture and Her Many Horses, *A Song for the Horse Nation,* 61.

37. Viola, "Introduction: Freedom, Bravery, and Generosity," 10.

38. Frances Densmore, *Teton Sioux Music*, Smithsonian Institution, Bureau of American Ethnology, Bulletin 61 (Washington, D.C.: Government Printing Office, 1918), 298, 388.

39. Hansen, *Memory and Vision*, 121.

40. Ewers, *Plains Indian History and Culture,* 207.

41. Hansen, *Memory and Vision*, 124.

42. For example, during the Paleo-Indian period, alibates flint, a mottled or banded red, blue, and purple stone, was traded from its Texas quarry starting around 9000 B.C. through the historic period; obsidian, from a quarry in British Columbia that was in use from 8000 B.C. until European contact, has been found in archaeological sites far from its place of origin; and olivella shells from the California coast dating to about 6000 B.C. were excavated from a Nevada site. Lois Sherr Dubin, *North American Indian Jewelry and Adornment: From Prehistory to the Present* (New York: Harry N. Abrams, 1999), 29.

43. The Plateau culture area extends from the Cascade Mountains in Washington to the Rocky Mountains in Idaho and Montana and from southern British Columbia to northern California. The Eastern Woodlands region encompasses the entire eastern part of the United States from the Atlantic Ocean to the Mississippi River and from the Great Lakes to the Gulf Coast of Mexico.

44. Dubin, *North American Indian Jewelry*, 243.

45. Ewers, *Plains Indian History and Culture,* 24.

46. These mercantile centers, which consisted of both strategic locations and villages, included Kettle Falls in Washington State; the Dalles and Celilo Falls on the Columbia River between Oregon and Washington; Mandan-Hidatsa in North Dakota; Arikara and Dakota Rendezvous in South Dakota; Shoshone Rendezvous in Wyoming; Pawnee in Nebraska; Hopi and Zuni in Arizona; and Pecos in New Mexico. Dubin, *North American Indian Jewelry*, 243.

47. Ibid.

48. Castle McLaughlin, *Arts of Diplomacy: Lewis and Clark's Indian Collection* (Cambridge, Mass.: Peabody Museum of Archaeology and Ethnology, Harvard University; Seattle: University of Washington Press, 2003), 39.

49. Peace medals, struck by the Jefferson administration as symbols of state power and mutual allegiance, were given to tribal leaders. On one side the words "Peace and Friendship" are surrounded by two clasped hands, and a peace pipe overlies a tomahawk. On the reverse side Thomas Jefferson's profile introduces recipients to the new "Great Father," or president of the United States. Ibid., 44–45.

50. Lois Sherr Dubin, *The History of Beads from 30,000 B.C. to the Present* (New York: Harry N. Abrams, 1987), 271, 274. Castle McLaughlin (*Arts of Diplomacy*, 38) points out that glass trade beads were so fully integrated into Native life that today they are considered symbolic of Native American identity.

51. Dubin, *The History of Beads*, 274.

52. McLaughlin, *Arts of Diplomacy*, 38.

53. Dubin, *The History of Beads*, 274–75.

54. Hansen, *Memory and Vision*, 253.

NOTES TO "THE ART OF TIPI LIVING"

1. Joseph Medicine Crow, *From the Heart of the Crow Country: The Crow Indians' Own Stories* (New York: Orion Books, 1992), 120.

2. Mary Helen Medicine Horse, *A Dictionary of Everyday Crow* (Crow Agency, Mont.: Bilingual Materials Development Center, 1987), 42, 126.

3. Dale D. Old Horn and Timothy P. McCleary, *Apsáalooke Social and Family Structure* (Crow Agency, Mont.: Little Big Horn College, 1995), 51. In the Big Day interview in this volume the word is transliterated as *ashtáahile*, in accordance with the spelling used by Randolph Graczyk, who worked with Crow people in the vicinity of Pryor, Montana; see Randolph Graczyk, *A Grammar of Crow = Apsáalooke Aliláau* (Lincoln: University of Nebraska Press; Bloomington: in cooperation with the American Indian Studies Research Institute, Indiana University, 2007).

4. Ibid., 54; Timothy P. McCleary, *The Stars We Know: Crow Indian Astronomy and Lifeways* (Prospect Heights, Ill.: Waveland Press, 1997), 64.

5. Carl Sweezy, quoted in Althea Bass, *The Arapaho Way: A Memoir of an Indian Boyhood* (New York: Clarkson N. Potter, 1966), 12.

6. John C. Ewers, *The Blackfeet: Raiders on the Northwestern Plains* (Norman: University of Oklahoma Press, 1958), 116.

7. Gene Weltfish, *The Lost Universe: Pawnee Life and Culture* (Lincoln: University of Nebraska Press, 1977), 144–45, 379–81.

8. Just as the number of poles used in tipis varied, so did the number of hides and, consequently, the overall size of the lodges. Once horses became available to Plains tribes by the eighteenth century, women were able to construct larger lodges to be carried on horse-drawn travois. According to Robert H. Lowie, Crow tipi covers required fourteen to eighteen buffalo hides. Lowie, *The Crow Indians* (Lincoln: University of Nebraska Press, 1983), 87. Royal B. Hassrick asserts that the size of a Lakota tipi depended as much on the man's ability to

provide hides as the woman's ability to prepare them. Hassrick, *The Sioux: Life and Customs of a Warrior Society* (Norman: University of Oklahoma Press, 1964), 15.

9.   Weltfish, *The Lost Universe*, 144.

10. Ewers, *The Blackfeet*, 114–16.

11. Alfred L. Kroeber, *The Arapaho* (Lincoln: University of Nebraska Press, 1983), 60–65; Hassrick, *The Sioux*, 214.

12. Frank B. Linderman, *Red Mother: The Life Story of Pretty-Shield, Medicine Woman of the Crows* (New York: John Day Company, 1932), reprinted as *Pretty-Shield: Medicine Woman of the Crows* (Lincoln: University of Nebraska Press, 1972), 32–34. Citations are to the 1972 edition.

13. Alma Hogan Snell, interview with the author, Jan. 22, 2000.

14. Ibid.

15. Ibid.

16. Weltfish, *The Lost Universe*, 145–46.

17. Ralph T. Coe, *Sacred Circles: Two Thousand Years of North American Indian Art: Nelson Gallery of Art–Atkins Museum of Fine Arts* (Kansas City: Nelson Gallery Foundation, 1977), 161.

18. Sweezy, in Bass, *The Arapaho Way*, 13–14.

19. Alma Hogan Snell, interview with the author, Jan. 22, 2000.

20. Linderman, *Pretty-Shield*, 138–39.

21. Sweezy, in Bass, *The Arapaho Way*, 8–9.

22. Ibid., 11.

23. Ibid., 9.

24. Ibid., 10.

25. Ella C. Deloria, *Speaking of Indians* (Vermillion: University of South Dakota Press, 1992), 56.

26. The General Allotment Act (Dawes Act) of 1887 gave the president of the United States discretionary power to allot parcels of reservation lands of varying sizes to individuals; allotments ranged from 160 acres for heads of families to 40 acres for infants. The allotted land was to be held in trust (it could not be sold or taxed) for twenty-five years. After allotment, the remaining lands of each reservation were to be available for sale to non-Natives in parcels of 160 acres. The purpose of the Dawes Act was to break up communal lands and require Native families to live on individual allotments as farmers or ranchers. The act resulted in a major diminishment of Native lands from 155,632,312 acres in 1881 to 104,314,349 acres in 1890 and 77,865,373 acres in 1900. Richard White, *"It's Your Misfortune and None of My Own": A History of the American West* (Norman: University of Oklahoma Press, 1991), 115.

27. Deloria, *Speaking of Indians*, 56–57.

28. Beatrice Medicine, "Lakota Star Quilts: Commodity, Ceremony, and Economic Development," in Marsha L. MacDowell and C. Kurt Dewhurst, eds., *To Honor and Comfort: Native Quilting Traditions* (Santa Fe: Museum of New Mexico Press in association with Michigan State University Museum, 1999), 111–17;

Laurie N. Anderson, "Learning the Threads: Sioux Quiltmaking in South Dakota," in MacDowell and Dewhurst, *To Honor and Comfort*, 93–96.

29. Arthur Amiotte, interview with the author, Jan. 20, 2000.

NOTES TO "THE RAIN-IN-THE-FACE TIPI LINER"

1. Deming (1860–1942) visited Crow territory for a few weeks before coming to Standing Rock Reservation. His coauthor for the articles and guide was De Cost Smith, another artist and researcher who had been in Standing Rock several times since 1884 and returned later. See Man-Afraid-of-His-Name [Edwin Willard Deming], "Sketching Among the Sioux," *Outing* 23, no. 1 (Oct. 1893): 3–13; and De Cost Smith, *Indian Experiences* (Caldwell, Idaho: Caxton Printers, 1943).

2. A notarized affidavit by Edwin Deming of February 1, 1942, on file in the Brooklyn Museum Archives verifies that Rain-in-the-Face gave him the tipi liner in 1889 when he was in Standing Rock. See also Edwin Willard Deming, typescript transcript of entries from missing original diaries, n.d., Division of Special Collections & University Archives, University of Oregon Libraries, Eugene; [Alden Deming], "The Life of Edwin Willard Deming," typescript, n.d., p. 9, Edwin W. Deming Papers, 1923–25, Archives of American Art, Smithsonian Institution, Washington, D.C.

3. Therese Deming to Herbert Spinden, circa 1942–43, Records of the Department of African, Oceanic, and New World Art. Objects. 33. Sale/Purchases [05] 1/1942–3/1944, Brooklyn Museum Archives.

4. See James McLaughlin, *My Friend the Indian* (Boston and New York: Houghton Mifflin Company, 1910); Charles A. Eastman, "Rain-in-the-Face, the Story of a Sioux Warrior," *Teepee Book* 2, no. 6 (1916), reprinted as *The Teepee Book: Official Publication, The Fiftieth Anniversary of the Custer Battle: 1876–1926* (Sheridan, Wyo.: Mills Co., 1926); and Smith, *Indian Experiences*.

5. A. Deming, "The Life of Edwin Willard Deming."

6. McLaughlin, *My Friend the Indian*; Eastman, "Rain-in-the-Face, the Story of a Sioux Warrior"; Smith, *Indian Experiences*.

7. The Sioux Nation includes three divisions: the Dakota, the Nakota, and the Lakota. The Lakota (Lakhóta) are sometimes called Western Dakota or Teton. They are made up of seven bands known as Blackfeet (Sihásapa), Two Kettle (Óʼóhenunpa), Sans Arc (Itázpčo), Brule (Sićangu Oyate), Oglala, Minicónjou, and Húnkpapa. The Húnkpapa are primarily located in Standing Rock. The Sićangu are located in Rosebud, South Dakota, and the Oglala in Pine Ridge, South Dakota.

8. E. Deming, typescript transcript of entries from diaries, 6.

9. Marsha C. Bol, "Gender in Art: A Comparison of Lakota Women's and Men's Art, 1820–1920" (Ph.D. dissertation, University of New Mexico, 1989), 84. Bol reports there were even more tipis at the Fort Peck reservation area, where six to seven thousand tipis were set up.

10. E. Deming, typescript transcript of entries from diaries, 12.

11. Bol, "Gender in Art," 346; Ellen Pearlstein, Lynn Brostoff, and Karen Trentelman, "A Technical Study of the Rosebud Winter Count," *Plains Anthropologist* 54, no. 209 (Feb. 2009).

12. A consultation meeting was held at the Brooklyn Museum on September 17, 2007, to examine and review the Rain-in-the-Face tipi liner (see n. 26).

13. John C. Ewers, "Military Art of the Plains Indians" (paper presented at the Cooper-Hewitt Museum, New York, Spring 1984), in Colin F. Taylor and Hugh A. Dempsey, eds., *The People of the Buffalo,* vol. 1, *The Plains Indians of North America—Military Art, Warfare and Change: Essays in Honor of John C. Ewers* (Wyk auf Foehr, Germany: Tatanka Press, 2003).

14. David W. Penney, "The Horse as Symbol: Equine Representations in Plains Pictographic Art," in Evan M. Maurer, ed., *Visions of the People: A Pictorial History of Plains Indian Life* (Minneapolis: Minneapolis Institute of Arts; Seattle: University of Washington Press, 1992), 72.

15. George Catlin, *Illustrations of the Manners, Customs, and the Condition of the American Indians,* 2 vols. (London: Chatto and Windus, 1857).

16. Evan M. Maurer, "Visions of the People," in Maurer, *Visions of the People,* fig. 149; John C. Ewers, "Early White Influence upon Plains Indian Painting: George Catlin and Carl Bodmer Among the Mandan, 1832–34," *Smithsonian Miscellaneous Collections* 134, no. 7 (April 24, 1957).

17. Garrick Mallery, *Picture Writing of the American Indians* (New York: Dover Publications, 1972), originally published as vols. 1 and 2 of *Tenth Annual Report of the Bureau of Ethnology to the Secretary of the Smithsonian Institution, 1888–89* (Washington, D.C.: Government Printing Office, 1893); Henry Rowe Schoolcraft, *The American Indians: Their History, Condition and Prospects from Original Notes and Manuscripts* (Buffalo, N.Y.: G. H. Derby, 1851).

18. James R. Walker, *Lakota Belief and Ritual,* ed. Raymond J. DeMallie and Elaine A. Jahner (Lincoln: University of Nebraska Press, 1980), reprinted (Winnipeg, MB: Bison Books, 1991). Citations are to the 1991 edition. Raymond J. DeMallie and Douglas R. Parks, "Plains Indian Warfare," in Taylor and Dempsey, *The People of the Buffalo,* 1:70.

19. Walker, *Lakota Belief and Ritual*, 109–12; DeMallie and Parks, "Plains Indian Warfare," 70.

20. Bol, "Gender in Art," 127; Frances Densmore, *Teton Sioux Music and Culture* (Lincoln: University of Nebraska Press, 1992), 62, 63, 387, 403. Originally published as *Teton Sioux Music,* Smithsonian Institution, Bureau of American Ethnology, Bulletin 61 (Washington, D.C.: Government Printing Office, 1918).

21. Densmore, *Teton Sioux Music and Culture*, 40.

22. Maurer, "Visions of the People," 39.

23. Bol, "Gender in Art," 127.

24. Ewers, "Military Art of the Plains Indians," 24.

25. Maurer, "Visions of the People," 39.

26. The participants in the consultation meeting at the Brooklyn Museum on September 17, 2007, included Janet Berlo, professor of art history and visual and

cultural studies, University of Rochester; Christina Burke, curator of Native American and non-Western art, Philbrook Museum of Art, Tulsa; Donald Tenoso (Húnkpapa Lakota), research associate, National Museum of Natural History, Smithsonian Institution; Marcella LeBeau, great-granddaughter of Rain-in-the-Face, and her daughter Diane Booth; Tim Mentz (Lakota), Tribal Historic Preservation Office, Standing Rock Sioux Tribe, North Dakota.

27. Joyce M. Szabo, *Howling Wolf and the History of Ledger Art* (Albuquerque: University of New Mexico Press, 1994), 7.

28. Densmore, *Teton Sioux Music and Culture*, 406.

29. Christina Burke, "Waniyetu Wówapí: An Introduction to the Lakota Winter Count Tradition," in Candace S. Greene and Russell Thornton, eds., *The Year the Stars Fell: Lakota Winter Counts at the Smithsonian* (Lincoln: University of Nebraska Press, 2007), 2.

30. See also Janet Catherine Berlo, *Spirit Beings and Sun Dancers: Black Hawk's Vision of the Lakota World* (New York: George Braziller in association with New York State Historical Association, 2000), pls. 3–6.

31. Karen Daniels Petersen, *Plains Indian Art from Fort Marion* (Norman: University of Oklahoma Press, 1971).

32. Berlo, *Spirit Beings and Sun Dancers*, 111.

33. Smith, *Indian Experiences*, 116.

34. The number of vignettes given here is approximate, since it is sometimes difficult to ascertain where one vignette ends and another begins. Moreover, some of the figures are not organized in neat horizontal rows.

35. Whereas Crow warriors painted their foreheads red, Rain-in-the-Face reported to De Cost Smith (*Indian Experiences*, 216) that he often painted one side of his face red and the other black when he prepared for war, so that it is possible that on this liner the viewer can see only the red side. This figure does not wear a Crow hairstyle.

36. Tim Mentz, consultation meeting, Brooklyn Museum, Sept. 17, 2007.

37. A *hunka* ceremony bonded two men as brothers, who would fight together. It is an official ceremony conducted by a medicine man and celebrated with feasts and gift giving. Walker, *Lakota Belief and Ritual*, 198–99.

38. In 1873 Rain-in-the-Face was in a war party against General George Custer along the Yellowstone River when he came across the civilian veterinarian John Honsinger and the civilian sutler Augustus Baliran. Considering his actions part of the war, Rain-in-the-Face killed both of them. In the winter of 1874 the Crow scout Curley Reynolds overheard a tipi camp oration of these killings by Rain-in-the-Face and told General Custer. Custer sent his brother, Captain Tom Custer, to capture Rain-in-the-Face, which he did by grabbing him from behind when he was in the Standing Rock store. Despite a huge uproar from the Húnkpapa camp and several visits by the warrior's brothers to General Custer at Fort Abraham Lincoln, Custer kept Rain-in-the-Face prisoner throughout the winter of 1874–75, intending to charge him with murder. In the spring Rain-in-the-Face managed to escape with either the aid of another prisoner's friends or through a

sympathetic non-Native guard. Supposedly Rain-in-the-Face swore his revenge, so that when both Custers were killed in the Battle of Little Bighorn in 1876, the media vilified Rain-in-the-Face, claiming that he had not only killed General Custer but had eaten the heart of Tom Custer. Henry Wadsworth Longfellow wrote a popular epic poem, "The Revenge of Rain-in-the-Face," with the lines "'Revenge!' cried Rain-in-the-Face / 'Revenge upon all the race / Of the White Chief with yellow hair!'" Throughout the remainder of his life, Rain-in-the-Face verified and denied these allegations on different occasions, giving a final denial to Charles Eastman just before his death.

39. Berlo, *Spirit Beings and Sun Dancers*, 110; consultation meeting, Brooklyn Museum, Sept. 17, 2007.

40. Janet Catherine Berlo, *Plains Indian Drawings, 1865–1935: Pages from a Visual History* (New York: Harry N. Abrams, 1996), 18.

41. For a version, see Maurer, "Visions of the People," 199, fig. 155; for One Bull's version, see ibid., 198, fig. 154; for Red Horse's version on ledger papers, see ibid., 200, figs. 156–61.

42. For Standing Bear's version of Sitting Bull's Ghost Dance and arrest (on muslin), see ibid., 180, fig. 140.

43. Bol, "Gender in Art," 347. Bol mentions liners in public collections at the American Museum of Natural History, New York (50.1-399); Buechel Memorial Lakota Museum, St. Francis Mission, Rosebud Sioux Reservation, S.D. (1980-222); Cincinnati Art Museum (1894-1214); and National Museum of Natural History, Smithsonian Institution, Washington, D.C. (345944). In addition, L. James Dempsey, in *Blackfoot War Art, Pictographs of the Reservation Period, 1880–2000* (Norman: University of Oklahoma Press, 2007), lists Blackfeet examples at the Canadian Museum of Civilization, Gatineau, Quebec (51678); National Museum of the American Indian, Smithsonian Institution, Washington, D.C. (13-2380); and (a rare example combining men's and women's work) Provincial Museum of Alberta, Edmonton (H66.387.1).

44. The nineteenth century is rife with many battles in the Plains region as the Sioux were pushed out from their lands, first by settlers looking for gold in the Dakotas and then by the building of the Northern Pacific Railroad. The U.S. Army built several forts that were intended not only to protect settlers traveling west in the northern Dakotas on what came to be called the Oregon Trail but also to prevent them from straying into Sioux hunting grounds. This army tactic only caused more conflicts. Although a major treaty was signed in 1868, it was broken by the federal government in 1876. Notable Sioux victories were the Fetterman Fight in 1866 and the Battle of Little Bighorn in 1876. The U.S. Army prevailed in the Fort Snelling Indian trials, in which more than three hundred Sioux were convicted of war acts in 1862, the Sand Creek Massacre in 1864, and the Massacre of Wounded Knee in 1890.

45. Luther Standing Bear, *My People the Sioux* (Boston: Houghton Mifflin Company, 1928), 15.

46. Bol, "Gender in Art," 384.

1. Thomas B. Marquis, *The Cheyennes of Montana,* ed. Thomas D. Weist (Algonac, Mich.: Reference Publications, 1978).

2. Stephen Return Riggs, *Grammar and Dictionary of the Dakota Language. Collected by the Members of the Dakota Mission and Edited by the Rev. Stephen R. Riggs*, Smithsonian Contributions to Knowledge 4 (Washington, D.C.: Smithsonian Institution, 1852).

3. Written Cheyenne is always considered somewhat flawed by fluent Cheyenne speakers, who find the notations for pitch marks and glottal stops used by Petter and others very confusing. In our community we tend to use simpler phonetic versions without such marks, and for this reason I have used *ve eh* here. Although the Cheyenne regard the spoken form of the language as the most correct one, dictionaries like Petter's are becoming more acceptable in our community, and the language is being taught at Chief Dull Knife College in Lame Deer, Montana, using a version based on Petter's work.

4. Cornel Pewewardy, "Renaming Ourselves on Our Own Terms: Race, Tribal Nations, and Representation in Education," *Indigenous Nations Studies Journal* 1, no. 1 (Spring 2000), http://www.hanksville.org/storytellers/pewe/writing/Rename.html (accessed May 15, 2008).

5. Bently Spang, "The Process of Self Definition within the Native North American Art Movement," *Journal of Multicultural and Cross-cultural Research in Art Education* 13 (Spring 1996): 49–60.

6. Pewewardy, "Renaming Ourselves."

7. For a discussion of Native American stereotypes found on the Internet, see Bently Spang, "A Cheyenne in Cyber Space," in Emma I. Hansen, *Memory and Vision: Arts, Cultures, and Lives of Plains Indian People* (Cody, Wyo.: Buffalo Bill Historical Center in association with University of Washington Press, Seattle, 2007), 294–97.

8. The stage set was awash with many other offensive Native American stereotypes, including scantily clad female dancers in buckskin miniskirts sporting the Hollywood-inspired headbands over Indian-braid wigs with a single feather, upright, protruding from the back of the head. See Cristina Verán, "Rap, Rage, REDvolution," *Village Voice,* Apr. 13, 2004, http://www.villagevoice.com/news/0416,veran,52833,1.html (accessed June 2, 2008).

9. "Pee-pee Teepee," Beba Bean, http://www.bebabean.com/products/pptp.aspx (accessed May 29, 2008).

10. "Wigwam Motel," Wikipedia, http://en.wikipedia.org/w/index.php?title=Wigwam_Motel&oldid=208436262.html (accessed June 2, 2008).

11. Wigwam Village Inn #2, http://www.wigwamvillage.com (accessed Mar. 31, 2008).

12. "Wigwam Motel," Wikipedia.

13. The sacred hat is one of two sacred objects that govern, guide, and protect both the Northern and Southern Cheyenne peoples. It is housed in a tipi year-round.

14. Calvin Grinnell, quoted in Hansen, *Memory and Vision,* 66.

15. Debra Jane Seltzer, "Roadside Architecture," http://www.agilitynut.com/roadside.html (accessed June 10, 2008).

16. "Novelty Architecture," Wikipedia, http://en.wikipedia.org/w/index.php?title=Novelty_architecture&oldid=214648741 (accessed June 11, 2008). The open mouth of the National Freshwater Fishing Hall of Fame features a viewing deck.

17. In movies the stereotyped Native American is usually cast as the mystical shaman or the doomed Indian.

18. The logo of the new sports complex of the North Dakota Fighting Sioux is an image of the head of a nameless, windblown brave. See M. Underwood, "Fate of University of North Dakota 'Fighting Sioux' Logo Threatens Hockey Arena," *Fox News,* Nov. 6, 2007, http://www.foxnews.com/story/0,2933,308697,00.html (accessed June 9, 2008).

19. See Ashley Murphy, "Stereotyping," a speech delivered to the Washington State Human Rights Commission Forum on Urban Indian Issues, May 25, 2006, Washington State Human Rights Commission, http://www.hum.wa.gov/NativeAmericans/stereotyping.html (accessed June 13, 2008).

20. Shannon Shaw, "Goodbye, Good Riddance, 'Indian Family,'" Reznet, 2008, http://www.reznetnews.org/article/feature-article/goodbye,-good-riddance,-%2526%2523039%3Bindian-family%2526%2523039%3B (accessed June 13, 2008).

NOTES TO "WOMEN'S ARTS CENTERED IN THE TIPI"

1. Exhibition label, Buechel Memorial Lakota Museum, St. Francis Mission, Rosebud Indian Reservation, S.D., 2007.

2. Northern Arapaho quillworker Fire Wood, interview with Cleaver Warden (Southern Arapaho), 1904–5, field notebook of George Dorsey, curator of anthropology, Field Museum of Natural History, quoted in Marsha C. Bol, "The Quilled Art of the Northern Arapaho Woman, Fire Wood" (paper presented at the Plains Indian Art Symposium, University of Tennessee, Nov. 11, 1995), 1–2.

3. Bol, "The Quilled Art," 1–2, 4–7.

4. Mary Jane Schneider, "Women's Work: An Examination of Women's Roles in Plains Indian Arts and Crafts," in Patricia Albers and Beatrice Medicine, *The Hidden Half: Studies of Plains Indian Women* (Washington, D.C.: University Press of America, 1983), 104. Painted tipis have been documented for the Kiowa and the Blackfeet by the anthropologist James Mooney, who commissioned a series of model tipis that are now in the Field Museum of Natural History, Chicago, and in the National Museum of Natural History, Smithsonian Institution, Washington, D.C.

5. Mark J. Halvorson, *Sacred Beauty: Quillwork of Plains Women* (Bismarck: State Historical Society of North Dakota, 1998).

6. Alfred L. Kroeber, "The Arapaho," *Bulletin of the American Museum of Natural History* 18 (1902–7), reprinted as *The Arapaho* (Lincoln: University of Nebraska Press, 1983), 70–77. Citations are to the 1983 edition. George Bird Grinnell,

The Cheyenne Indians: Their History and Ways of Life (New Haven: Yale University Press, 1923); Clark Wissler, *Societies and Ceremonial Associations of the Oglala Division of the Teton-Dakota*, Anthropological Papers of the American Museum of Natural History 11 (1912), pt. 1: 92–93 (New York: Published by order of the Trustees [of the American Museum of Natural History]). See also Alice Marriott, "The Trade Guild of the Southern Cheyenne Women," in Marriott and Carol Rachlin, *Dance Around the Sun: The Life of Mary Little Bear Inkanish: Cheyenne* (New York: Thomas Y. Crowell, 1977).

7. Winfield W. Coleman, "The Cheyenne Women's Sewing Society," in Gene Ball and George P. Horse Capture, eds., *Plains Indian Design Symbology and Decoration* (Cody, Wyo.: Buffalo Bill Historical Center, 1980), 51; Schneider, "Women's Work," 112; Kroeber, *The Arapaho*, 26; Loretta Fowler, "The Arapaho," in *Handbook of North American Indians* (Washington, D.C.: Smithsonian Institution Press, 2001), vol. 13, pt. 2: 848.

8. Grinnell, *The Cheyenne Indians*, 1:161.

9. Ibid.

10. Wissler, *Societies and Ceremonial Associations*, 92–93.

11. Grinnell, *The Cheyenne Indians*, 2:385–91.

12. Kroeber, *The Arapaho*, 33–34; Bol, "The Quilled Art," 9.

13. The large beaded ceremonial tipi and its matching furnishings of backrests, pillows, liner, door, and dew cloths were purchased by the Milwaukee Public Museum in 1997 from Richard N. Corrow of Scottsdale, Arizona. The collection history (acc. no. 66373-8) includes a letter dated June 15, 1995, from Bruce Shackleford to Corrow, providing information about the tipi set. In 1983, when Shackleford was director of the Creek Council House in Okmulgee, Oklahoma, his friend the Creek artist Woody Crumbo told him that he believed it was the same set he had seen for sale by Reese Kincaid, proprietor of the Mohonk Lodge in Clinton, Oklahoma, about 1950. The set had been brought in by Cheyennes. A curatorial note by Ann McMullen, curator of North American ethnology at the Milwaukee Public Museum in 1997, states her belief that this is the work of the Southern Cheyenne Women's Society between 1905 and 1935, with various pieces having been made at different times. McMullen notes that beaded tipis are very rare. Curatorial files, Milwaukee Public Museum.

14. Coleman, "The Cheyenne Women's Sewing Society," 51.

15. Kathryn Bull Coming, transcript of taped interview with Daniel C. Swan, Seiling, Okla., Oct. 12, 1983.

16. Ibid.

17. Tim Ramsey, personal communication to the author, Oct. 21, 2007.

18. They successfully sought funds from the Lake Mohonk Conference of Friends of the Indians (New Paltz, New York) to build an arts center and purchase beads, hide, and other materials.

19. Barbara A. Hail, "Mohonk to Mohawk: What's in a Name?: From Mission Outreach to Commercial Venture" (paper presented at Native American Art Studies Association Conference, Portland, Ore., Oct. 25, 2001).

20. Gordon Yellowman, personal communication to the author (regarding *Cheyenne Visions II*, an exhibition organized by the Denver Art Museum), Apr. 16, 2008.

21. Reginald Laubin and Gladys Laubin, *The Indian Tipi: Its History, Construction, and Use* (Norman: University of Oklahoma Press, 1957), 61.

22. Kathryn Bull Coming, interview with Daniel C. Swan; Coleman, "The Cheyenne Women's Sewing Society," 54.

23. Coleman, "The Cheyenne Women's Sewing Society," 61; Adrianne Santini, "Enacting Creation at Home: Quilled and Beaded Tipi Discs of the Cheyenne and Arapaho" (paper presented at Native American Art Studies Association Conference, Portland, Ore., Oct. 25, 2001), 8.

24. Frederick Webb Hodge, ed., *Handbook of American Indians North of Mexico*, Smithsonian Institution, Bureau of American Ethnology, Bulletin 30 (Washington, D.C.: Government Printing Office, 1907–10), 2:203.

25. Grinnell, *The Cheyenne Indians*, 1:219.

26. A mid-nineteenth-century exception was the hair-fringed honor shirt of the Oglala Shirt-Wearer's Society, made by elder society members and presented to four appointed councilors upon their investiture. Wissler, *Societies and Ceremonial Associations*, 7. Men also made their own undecorated moccasins to replace those worn out during long journeys on foot. Some nineteenth-century men assumed the traditionally female role of beadwork expert, but in the absence of extensive documentation, they have seldom received credit for this work. Benson Lanford, personal communication to the author, 1995.

27. Castle McLaughlin, *Arts of Diplomacy: Lewis and Clark's Indian Collection* (Cambridge, Mass.: Peabody Museum of Archaeology and Ethnology, Harvard University; Seattle: University of Washington Press, 2003), 173.

28. Barbara A. Hail, *Hau, Kola! The Plains Indian Collection of the Haffenreffer Museum of Anthropology* (Providence, R.I.: The Museum, 1980), 90.

29. Albers and Medicine, *The Hidden Half*, 138–39.

30. Margaret MacKichan, Art Institute, Sinte Gleske University, Rosebud Indian Reservation, S.D., personal communication to the author, Apr. 16, 2008.

31. Jennifer Edwards Weston to the author, Jan. 15, 2008; Emma I. Hansen, *Memory and Vision: Arts, Cultures, and Lives of Plains Indian People* (Cody, Wyo.: Buffalo Bill Historical Center in association with University of Washington Press, Seattle, 2007), 67.

32. Claire Packard to the author, Sept. 24, 1994.

NOTES TO "TIPIS AND THE WARRIOR TRADITION"

1. Stan Hoig, *The Sand Creek Massacre* (Norman: University of Oklahoma Press, 1961), 158; Wilbur Sturtevant Nye, *Plains Indian Raiders: The Final Phases of Warfare from the Arkansas to the Red River, with original photos by William S.*

Soule (Norman: University of Oklahoma Press, 1968), 21, 72, 137, 175; Ernest Wallace, *Ranald S. Mackenzie on the Texas Frontier* (College Station: Texas A&M University Press, 1993), 79–81, 140–43, 173; William Y. Chalfant, *Cheyennes at Dark Water Creek: The Last Fight of the Red River War* (Norman: University of Oklahoma Press, 1997), 188.

2. James D. Keyser and Timothy J. Brady, "A War Shirt in the Schoch Collection: Documenting Individual Artistic Expression," *Plains Anthropologist* 41, no. 155 (1993): 29–52; Joseph D. Horse Capture and George P. Horse Capture, "From Museums to Indians: Native American Art in Context," in Joseph D. Horse Capture and George P. Horse Capture, *Beauty, Honor, and Tradition: The Legacy of Plains Indian Shirts* (Washington, D.C.: National Museum of the American Indian, Smithsonian Institution; Minneapolis Institute of Arts; distributed by the University of Minnesota Press, 2001), 19, 43, 53–54, 66; Castle McLaughlin, *Arts of Diplomacy: Lewis and Clark's Indian Collection* (Cambridge, Mass.: Peabody Museum of Archaeology and Ethnology, Harvard University; Seattle: University of Washington Press, 2003), 163–68; Michael G. Johnson, "Wanata's Costume in Edinburgh: An Early Example of Yanktonai Sioux Ceremonial Warrior Costume?" in Colin F. Taylor and Hugh A. Dempsey, eds., *The People of the Buffalo*, vol. 2, *The Plains Indians of North America — The Silent Memorials: Artifacts as Cultural and Historical Documents* (Wyk auf Foehr, Germany: Tatanka Press, 2005), 174–84.

3. Thomas W. Kavanaugh, *The Comanches: A History, 1706–1875* (Lincoln: University of Nebraska Press, 1996), 30.

4. Gillette Griswold, *Big Bow* (Lawton, Okla.: Fort Sill National Historic Landmark and Museum, n.d.), 5.

5. Candace S. Greene, "Southern Plains Graphic Art before the Reservation," *American Indian Art Magazine* 22, no. 3 (1997): 44–45.

6. Gaylord Torrence, *The American Indian Parfleche: A Tradition of Abstract Painting* (Seattle: University of Washington Press, 1994), 69–70; William L. Merrill et al., *A Guide to the Kiowa Collections at the Smithsonian Institution,* Smithsonian Contributions to Anthropology 40 (Washington, D.C.: Smithsonian Institution Press, 1997), 27.

7. Bernard Mishkin, *Rank and Warfare Among the Plains Indians* (New York: J. J. Augustin, 1940), 38.

8. Maurice Boyd, *Kiowa Voices*, vol. 1, *Ceremonial Dance, Ritual, and Song* (Fort Worth: Texas Christian University Press, 1981), 62; James Mooney, *Calendar History of the Kiowa Indians* (Washington, D.C.: Smithsonian Institution Press, 1979), 291. Originally published as *Seventeenth Annual Report of the Bureau of American Ethnology, 1895–96* (Washington, D.C.: Government Printing Office, 1898); Mishkin, *Rank and Warfare,* 30.

9. John C. Ewers, *Murals in the Round: Painted Tipis of the Kiowa and Kiowa-Apache Indians: An Exhibition of Tipi Models Made for James Mooney of the Smithsonian Institution During His Field Studies of Indian History and Art in*

Southwestern Oklahoma, 1891-1904 (Washington, D.C.: Published for the Renwick Gallery of the National Collection of Fine Arts by Smithsonian Institution Press, 1978), 8.

10. The origin of the design among the Cheyenne is unknown. The initial inspiration for the Tipi with Battle Pictures and the rudimentary aspects of its design may have been received by a Cheyenne in a vision, but this cannot be verified. It is clear, however, that Dohausan, the first Kiowa owner of the design, was free to select the combat scenes he wished to depict on the tipi cover, provided he was able to secure permission from the men who had accomplished these deeds. In this sense, the Tipi with Battle Pictures was unique. It differed from other Kiowa tipi designs, which originated in visionary experiences and whose forms were strictly prescribed by the spiritual power encountered by the supplicant. Candace S. Greene and Thomas D. Drescher, "The Tipi with Battle Pictures: The Kiowa Tradition of Intangible Property Rights," *Trademark Reporter* 84, no. 42 (1994): 421–23; Candace S. Greene, *Silver Horn: Master Illustrator of the Kiowas* (Norman: University of Oklahoma Press, 2001), 19–21.

11. Greene and Drescher, "The Tipi with Battle Pictures," 421–26; Ewers, *Murals in the Round*, 14–17; Karen Daniels Petersen, *Plains Indian Art from Fort Marion* (Norman: University of Oklahoma Press, 1971), 23–24.

12. Weston LaBarre et al., typescript of students' notes (combined notes of William Bascom, Donald Collier, Weston LaBarre, Bernard Mishkin, and Jane Richardson of the 1935 Laboratory of Anthropology Field School, led by Alexander Lesser), 524, Papers of Weston LaBarre, National Anthropological Archives, Smithsonian Institution, Washington, D.C.; Robert H. Lowie, *Societies of the Kiowa,* Anthropological Papers of the American Museum of Natural History 11 (1916), pt. 11: 837–51 (New York: Published by order of the Trustees [of the American Museum of Natural History]); William C. Meadows, *Kiowa, Apache, and Comanche Military Societies: Enduring Veterans, 1800 to the Present* (Austin: University of Texas Press, 1999), 38.

13. LaBarre et al., typescript, 1194; Lowie, *Societies of the Kiowa,* 844.

14. LaBarre et al., typescript, 1197, 1243; Meadows, *Kiowa, Apache, and Comanche Military Societies*, 41.

15. LaBarre et al., typescript, 1196; Mishkin, *Rank and Warfare*, 38.

16. LaBarre et al., typescript, 558; Lowie, *Societies of the Kiowa,* 842; Meadows, *Kiowa, Apache, and Comanche Military Societies*, 41.

17. LaBarre et al., typescript, 531; Lowie, *Societies of the Kiowa,* 848; Meadows, *Kiowa, Apache, and Comanche Military Societies*, 40–41.

18. LaBarre et al., typescript, 531–32, 534, 538, 1221; Lowie, *Societies of the Kiowa,* 848–49; Meadows, *Kiowa, Apache, and Comanche Military Societies*, 40.

19. LaBarre et al., typescript, 527, 556, 750, 1208. The Skado, or Medicine Lodge, was the Kiowa version of the Sun Dance, a religious ritual shared by many Plains tribes. It was held to ensure the proliferation of the buffalo and success in war. During the ceremony supplicants fasted and danced for four days. Their suffering demonstrated their sincerity and increased the efficacy of their prayers.

Through their prayers the dancers sought to secure the blessings of health and prosperity for their families and for the tribe as a whole. Hugh L. Scott, "Notes on the Kado, or Sun Dance of the Kiowa," *American Anthropologist* 13, no. 3 (1911): 345, 347, 353, 364–65; Benjamin Kracht, "Kiowa Religion in Historical Perspective," *American Indian Quarterly* 21, no. 1 (1997): 18–19. For an analysis of Kiowa drawings depicting aspects of the ceremony, see Greene, *Silver Horn*, 110–19.

20. Scott, "Notes on the Kado," 353, 357, 360–61; Jane Richardson, *Law and Status Among Kiowa Indians* (New York: J. J. Augustin, 1940), 9–10, 22–27; LaBarre et al., typescript, 527.

21. LaBarre et al., typescript, 1209–11.

22. Ibid., 1208–9.

23. Ibid., 536, 538, 547, 749–50, 1211.

24. Mishkin, *Rank and Warfare*, 41–42; LaBarre et al., typescript, 1205.

25. Richardson, *Law and Status*, 23.

26. Merrill et al., A *Guide to the Kiowa Collections*, 45.

27. Greene, *Silver Horn*, 17.

28. LaBarre et al., typescript, 524, 526, 536–38.

29. Ibid., 539.

30. Mishkin, *Rank and Warfare*, 39–40.

31. LaBarre et al., typescript, 1211.

32. Richardson, *Law and Status*, 23.

33. Warriors owned the rights to the tipi designs, which were in essence a form of intellectual property. Men typically transferred the rights to these designs to their male heirs, and designs came to be associated with particular families. Greene and Drescher, "The Tipi with Battle Pictures," 421–24; Ewers, *Murals in the Round*, 19–20.

34. Ewers, *Murals in the Round*, 19–20; Mooney, *Calendar History*, 337.

35. While all medicine ultimately derived from a supernatural source, this does not imply that individuals invariably received their power through visions or dreams. A man might inherit his medicine from a male relative. Men from wealthy families preferred to obtain medicine from successful older men who had proven their powers by distinguishing themselves in combat. Only wealthy men could afford the gifts necessary to seal such a transaction, however. Mishkin, *Rank and Warfare*, 49–50. In battle a warrior's medicine protected him from harm and empowered him to overcome his opponents. Men who possessed medicine that enabled them to heal wounds or to prophesy were often asked to accompany raiding parties. Kracht, "Kiowa Religion in Historical Perspective," 16–18; Boyd, *Kiowa Voices*, vol. 2, *Myths, Legends, and Folktales* (1983), 95–96; Wilbur Sturtevant Nye, *Bad Medicine and Good: Tales of the Kiowas* (Norman: University of Oklahoma Press, 1962), 151.

36. Kracht, "Kiowa Religion in Historical Perspective," 16–17; Greene, *Silver Horn*, 19–21, 79.

37. Mooney, *Calendar History*, 338.

38. LaBarre et al., typescript, 524, 538, 547.

39. Mooney, *Calendar History*, 53; Meadows, *Kiowa, Apache, and Comanche Military Societies*, 97–98.

40. Mooney, *Calendar History*, 346, 355–56, 358–59; Scott, "Notes on the Kado," 358–60; Meadows, *Kiowa, Apache, and Comanche Military Societies*, 100–102.

41. Meadows, *Kiowa, Apache, and Comanche Military Societies*, 103, 108–12.

42. Although female Kiowa veterans cannot join the Kiowa Black Leggings Warrior Society, they may enter the society's tipi to pray and may participate in the society's processional. These women do not wear the distinctive clothing associated with the society. Some choose to wear their uniforms or dance shawls embroidered with information about their military service, however, allowing them to identify themselves as veterans or active-duty members of the armed forces. Dixon Palmer, personal communication to Michael P. Jordan, Feb. 12, 2008; Lyndreth Palmer, personal communication to Jordan, Aug. 31, 2008; Meadows, *Kiowa, Apache, and Comanche Military Societies*, 128, 139–40.

43. LaBarre et al., typescript, 558.

44. Meadows, *Kiowa, Apache, and Comanche Military Societies*, 140.

45. Boyd, *Kiowa Voices*, 1:74; Jane Pattie and Helen McCorpin, "The Kiowa Black Legs: Warriors of a Proud People," *Persimmon Hill* 24, no. 4 (1996): 80.

46. During the nineteenth century the Kiowa frequently conducted raids into Texas and Mexico. Some expeditions went as far as Durango, Mexico. Parties also traveled west into New Mexico and Colorado to raid the Ute and Navajo. Many of the entries in the Kiowa pictographic calendars refer to these expeditions. Mooney, *Calendar History*, 173–74, 181, 186, 188, 337–39; Nye, *Plains Indian Raiders*, 39, 107, 112, 144.

47. Boyd, *Kiowa Voices*, 1:74; Pattie and McCorpin, "The Kiowa Black Legs," 80–81.

48. Meadows, *Kiowa, Apache, and Comanche Military Societies*, 141.

49. Dixon Palmer, personal communication to Jordan, Feb. 12, 2008; Meadows, *Kiowa, Apache, and Comanche Military Societies*, 142; Greene and Drescher, "The Tipi with Battle Pictures," 426.

50. Lyndreth Palmer, personal communication to Jordan, Feb. 12, 2008; Chaddlesone, personal communication to Jordan, Oct. 11, 2008.

51. Betty Sankadota Washburn, personal communication to Jordan, June 28, 2006.

52. Florene White Horse Taylor, personal communication to Jordan, Jan. 7, 2008.

53. Griswold, *Big Bow*, 8–9.

NOTES TO "THE TIPI OF THE KIOWA TONKONGYA"

1. Dixon Palmer and his brothers gave the Black Leggings Warrior Society the right to wear red capes like their family heirloom.

2. In their raids in the nineteenth century, Plains tribes traveled great distances to capture horses. The Kiowa traveled deep into Mexico on raids, and to Colorado and New Mexico to clash with the Ute and Navajo.

3. The revived Black Leggings Warrior Society has generally danced twice a year, in the spring and fall. Beginning in 2009, the society will dance only once a year—in the fall. In the nineteenth century and earlier, the Kiowa warrior societies held their gatherings and dances during the annual Skado, or Sun Dance, in the summer, when all the bands camped together for a week or two.

NOTES TO "GROWING UP ON THE PLAINS"

1. Royal B. Hassrick, *The Sioux: Life and Customs of a Warrior Society* (Norman: University of Oklahoma Press, 1964), 275–76. See also K. N. Llewellyn and E. Adamson Hoebel, *The Cheyenne Way: Conflict and Case Law in Primitive Jurisprudence* (Norman: University of Oklahoma Press, 1941), 264.

2. Edwin L. Wade, Carol Haralson, and Rennard Strickland, *As in a Vision: Masterworks of American Indian Art: The Elizabeth Cole Butler Collection at Philbrook Art Center* (Norman: University of Oklahoma Press, 1983), 84.

3. Raymond J. DeMallie, "Teton," in *Handbook of North American Indians* (Washington, D.C.: Smithsonian Institution Press, 2001), vol. 13, pt. 2: 794–820.

4. James R. Walker, *Lakota Society*, ed. Raymond J. DeMallie (Lincoln: University of Nebraska Press, 1982), 57–58. See also Fr. Eugene Buechel and Fr. Paul Manhart, *Lakota Dictionary: New Comprehensive Edition* (Lincoln: University of Nebraska Press, 2002).

5. Barbara A. Hail, ed., *Gifts of Pride and Love: Kiowa and Comanche Cradles* (Bristol, R.I.: Brown University, Haffenreffer Museum of Anthropology, 2000), 17.

6. Hassrick, *The Sioux*, 272 .

7. Ibid., 42. See also Hail, *Gifts of Pride and Love*.

8. Hail, *Gifts of Pride and Love*, 19.

9. Emma Hansen, personal communication to the author, Mar. 2007.

10. William C. Orchard, "Indian Porcupine Quill and Beadwork," in *Introduction to American Indian Art* (New York: Exposition of Indian Tribal Arts, 1931), 2:13.

11. See catalogue entries by Evan M. Maurer and Louise Lincoln in Evan M. Maurer, ed., *Visions of the People: A Pictorial History of Plains Indian Life* (Minneapolis: Minneapolis Institute of Arts, 1992), 136–38.

12. Ibid., 138.

13. Hassrick, *The Sioux*, 275.

14. Ibid., 278.

15. Ibid., 277.

16. Ibid., 278.

17. For a comprehensive discussion of Native American games, see Stewart Culin, *Games of the North American Indians*, vol. 1, *Games of Chance*, and vol. 2, *Games of Skill* (Lincoln: University of Nebraska Press, 1992). Originally published as *Twenty-fourth Annual Report of the Bureau of American Ethnology, 1902–1903* (Washington, D.C.: Government Printing Office, 1907). For a specific discussion of the hoop game, see Culin, 2:420–527.

18. Culin refers to this game as Snow-Snake. Ibid., 2:399–420.

19. Culin refers to this game as Ring and Pin. Ibid., 2:527–61.

20. Hassrick, *The Sioux*, 131; Culin, *Games*, 2:616–47.

21. Culin, *Games*, 2:647–65.

22. See dated entries for Friday, Apr. 18, 1806, in Meriwether Lewis, *The Journals of Lewis and Clark*, ed. Bernard DeVoto (New York: Houghton Mifflin Company, 1997).

23. Culin, *Games*, 1:267.

24. Ibid.

25. Ibid., 284.

26. Ibid.; Gloria A. Young and Erik D. Gooding, "Celebrations and Giveaways," in *Handbook of North American Indians* (Washington, D.C.: Smithsonian Institution Press, 2001), vol. 13, pt. 2: 1011–25.

27. Culin, *Games*, 1:276.

28. Informal conversations between Susan Kennedy Zeller and Derek Big Day (Crow) during Crow Fair, Aug. 17–19, 2007.

29. Hassrick, *The Sioux*, 77; Hugh A. Dempsey, "Blackfoot," in *Handbook of North American Indians*, vol. 13, pt. 1: 604–28; Dempsey, "Sarcee," in *Handbook of North American Indians*, vol. 13, pt. 1: 629–37.

30. Hassrick, *The Sioux*, 113; DeMallie, "Teton," 807, 809.

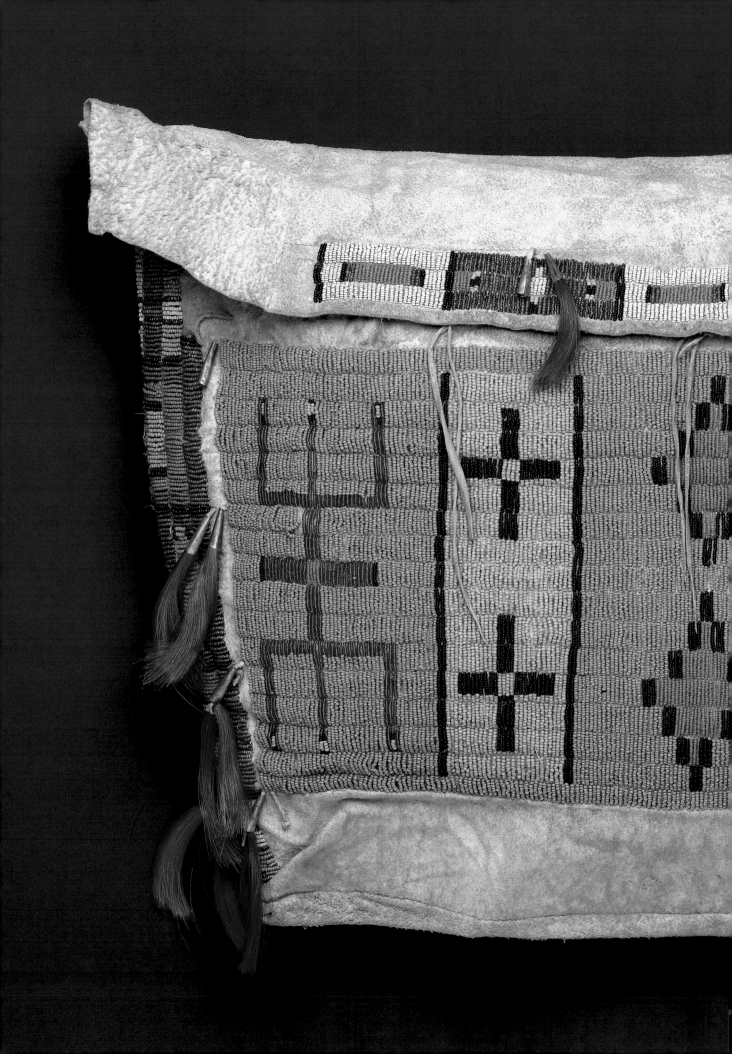

SELECTED BIBLIOGRAPHY

Albers, Patricia, and Beatrice Medicine. *The Hidden Half: Studies of Plains Indian Women.* Washington, D.C.: University Press of America, 1983.

Ball, Gene, and George P. Horse Capture, eds. *Plains Indian Design Symbology and Decoration.* Cody, Wyo.: Buffalo Bill Historical Center, 1980.

Barsness, Larry. *Heads, Hides & Horns: The Complete Buffalo Book.* Fort Worth: Texas Christian University Press, 1985.

Bass, Althea. *The Arapaho Way: A Memoir of an Indian Boyhood.* New York: Clarkson N. Potter, 1966.

Berlo, Janet Catherine. *Spirit Beings and Sun Dancers: Black Hawk's Vision of the Lakota World.* New York: George Braziller in association with New York State Historical Association, 2000.

Bol, Marsha C. "Gender in Art: A Comparison of Lakota Women's and Men's Art, 1820–1920." Ph.D. dissertation, University of New Mexico, 1989.

Bolton, Herbert Eugene, ed. *Spanish Exploration in the Southwest, 1542-1706.* New York: Charles Scribner's Sons, 1916.

Boyd, Maurice. *Kiowa Voices.* Vol. 1, *Ceremonial Dance, Ritual, and Song,* and Vol. 2, *Myths, Legends, and Folktales.* Fort Worth: Texas Christian University Press, 1981, 1983.

Buechel, Fr. Eugene, and Fr. Paul Manhart. *Lakota Dictionary: New Comprehensive Edition.* Lincoln: University of Nebraska Press, 2002.

Catlin, George. *Illustrations of the Manners, Customs, and the Condition of the American Indians.* 2 vols. London: Chatto and Windus, 1857.

Chalfant, William Y. *Cheyennes at Dark Water Creek: The Last Fight of the Red River War.* Norman: University of Oklahoma Press, 1997.

Coe, Ralph T. *Sacred Circles: Two Thousand Years of North American Indian Art: Nelson Gallery of Art–Atkins Museum of Fine Arts.* Kansas City: Nelson Gallery Foundation, 1977.

Culin, Stewart. *Games of the North American Indians.* Vol. 1, *Games of Chance,* and Vol. 2, *Games of Skill.* Lincoln: University of Nebraska Press, 1992. Originally published as *Twenty-fourth Annual Report of the Bureau of American Ethnology, 1902-1903.* Washington, D.C.: Government Printing Office, 1907.

Deloria, Ella C. *Speaking of Indians.* Vermillion: University of South Dakota Press, 1992.

DeMallie, Raymond J. "Teton." In *Handbook of North American Indians.* Vol. 13, pt. 2: 794–820. Washington, D.C.: Smithsonian Institution Press, 2001.

Dempsey, Hugh A. "Blackfoot." In *Handbook of North American Indians.* Vol. 13, pt. 1: 604–28. Washington, D.C.: Smithsonian Institution Press, 2001.

———. "Sarcee." In *Handbook of North American Indians.* Vol. 13, pt. 1: 629–37. Washington, D.C.: Smithsonian Institution Press, 2001.

Dempsey, L. James. *Blackfoot War Art: Pictographs of the Reservation Period, 1880–2000.* Norman: University of Oklahoma Press, 2007.

Densmore, Frances. *Teton Sioux Music and Culture.* Lincoln: University of Nebraska Press, 1992. Originally published as *Teton Sioux Music.* Smithsonian Institution, Bureau of American Ethnology, Bulletin 61. Washington, D.C.: Government Printing Office, 1918.

Dorsey, James Owen, ed. *A Dakota-English Dictionary by Stephen Return Riggs.* Contributions to North American Ethnology 7. Washington, D.C.: Government Printing Office, 1890.

Dubin, Lois Sherr. *The History of Beads from 30,000 B.C. to the Present.* New York: Harry N. Abrams, 1987.

———. *North American Indian Jewelry and Adornment: From Prehistory to the Present.* New York: Harry N. Abrams, 1999.

Eastman, Charles A. "Rain-in-the-Face, the Story of a Sioux Warrior." *Teepee Book* 2, no. 6 (1916). Reprinted as *The Teepee Book: Official Publication, The Fiftieth Anniversary of the Custer Battle: 1876–1926.* Sheridan, Wyo.: Mills Company, 1926.

Ewers, John C. *The Horse in Blackfoot Indian Culture.* Smithsonian Institution, Bureau of American Ethnology, Bulletin 159. Washington, D.C.: Government Printing Office, 1955.

———. "Early White Influence upon Plains Indian Painting: George Catlin and Carl Bodmer Among the Mandan, 1832–34." *Smithsonian Miscellaneous Collections* 134, no. 7 (April 24, 1957).

———. *The Blackfeet: Raiders on the Northwestern Plains.* Norman: University of Oklahoma Press, 1958.

———. *Artists of the Old West.* Enl. ed. Garden City, N.Y.: Doubleday, 1973.

———. *Murals in the Round: Painted Tipis of the Kiowa and Kiowa-Apache Indians: An Exhibition of Tipi Models Made for James Mooney of the Smithsonian Institution During His Field Studies of Indian History and Art in Southwestern Oklahoma, 1891–1904.* Washington, D.C.: Published for the Renwick Gallery of the National Collection of Fine Arts by Smithsonian Institution Press, 1978.

———. *Plains Indian History and Culture: Essays on Continuity and Change.* Norman: University of Oklahoma Press, 1997.

Fagan, Brian M. *Ancient North America: The Archaeology of a Continent.* London: Thames and Hudson, 1991.

Fowler, Loretta. "The Arapaho." In *Handbook of North American Indians.* Vol. 13, pt. 2: 840–62. Washington, D.C.: Smithsonian Institution Press, 2001.

Francis, Julie E., and Lawrence L. Loendorf. *Ancient Visions: Petroglyphs and Pictographs from the Wind River and Bighorn Country, Wyoming and Montana.* Salt Lake City: University of Utah Press, 2002.

Greene, Candace S. "Southern Plains Graphic Art before the Reservation." *American Indian Art Magazine* 22, no. 3 (1997): 44–45.

———. *Silver Horn: Master Illustrator of the Kiowas.* Norman: University of Oklahoma Press, 2001.

Greene, Candace S., and Thomas D. Drescher. "The Tipi with Battle Pictures: The Kiowa Tradition of Intangible Property Rights." *Trademark Reporter* 84, no. 42 (1994): 418–33.

Greene, Candace S., and Russell Thornton, eds. *The Year the Stars Fell: Lakota Winter Counts at the Smithsonian.* Lincoln: University of Nebraska Press, 2007.

Grinnell, George Bird. *The Cheyenne Indians: Their History and Ways of Life.* New Haven: Yale University Press, 1923.

Griswold, Gillette. *Big Bow.* Lawton, Okla.: Fort Sill National Historic Landmark and Museum, n.d.

Gurney, George, and Therese Thau Heyman, eds. *George Catlin and His Indian Gallery.* Washington, D.C.: Smithsonian American Art Museum; New York: W. W. Norton, 2002.

Hail, Barbara A. *Hau, Kola! The Plains Indian Collection of the Haffenreffer Museum of Anthropology, Brown University.* Providence, R.I.: The Museum, 1980.

———, ed. *Gifts of Pride and Love: Kiowa and Comanche Cradles.* Bristol, R.I.: Brown University, Haffenreffer Museum of Anthropology, 2000.

Hansen, Emma I. *Memory and Vision: Arts, Cultures, and Lives of Plains Indian People.* Cody, Wyo.: Buffalo Bill Historical Center in association with University of Washington Press, Seattle, 2007.

Hassrick, Royal B. *The Sioux: Life and Customs of a Warrior Society.* Norman: University of Oklahoma Press, 1964.

Hodge, Frederick Webb, ed. *Handbook of American Indians North of Mexico.* Smithsonian Institution, Bureau of American Ethnology, Bulletin 30. Washington, D.C.: Government Printing Office, 1907–10.

Hoig, Stan. *The Sand Creek Massacre.* Norman: University of Oklahoma Press, 1961.

Horse Capture, George P., and Emil Her Many Horses, eds. *A Song for the Horse Nation: Horses in Native American Cultures.* Washington, D.C.: National Museum of the American Indian, Smithsonian Institution, 2006.

Horse Capture, Joseph D., and George P. Horse Capture. *Beauty, Honor, and Tradition: The Legacy of Plains Indian Shirts.* Washington, D.C.: National Museum of the American Indian, Smithsonian Institution; Minneapolis Institute of Arts; distributed by the University of Minnesota Press, 2001.

Kavanaugh, Thomas W. *The Comanches: A History, 1706–1875.* Lincoln: University of Nebraska Press, 1996.

Kehoe, Thomas F. "Tipi Rings: The 'Direct Ethnological' Approach Applied to an Archeological Problem." *American Anthropologist,* n.s., 60, no. 5 (Oct. 1958): 861–73.

Keyser, James D., and Timothy J. Brady. "A War Shirt in the Schoch Collection: Documenting Individual Artistic Expression." *Plains Anthropologist* 41, no. 155 (1993): 29–52.

Kracht, Benjamin. "Kiowa Religion in Historical Perspective." *American Indian Quarterly* 21, no. 1 (1997): 15–33.

Kroeber, Alfred L. "The Arapaho." *Bulletin of the American Museum of Natural History* 18 (1902–7). Reprinted as *The Arapaho*. Lincoln: University of Nebraska Press, 1983.

Laubin, Reginald, and Gladys Laubin. *The Indian Tipi: Its History, Construction, and Use.* Norman: University of Oklahoma Press, 1957. 2nd ed., 1977.

Lewis, Meriwether. *The Journals of Lewis and Clark.* Edited by Bernard DeVoto. New York: Houghton Mifflin Company, 1997.

Linderman, Frank B. *Red Mother: The Life Story of Pretty-Shield, Medicine Woman of the Crows.* New York: John Day Company, 1932. Reprinted as *Pretty-Shield: Medicine Woman of the Crows.* Lincoln: University of Nebraska Press, 1972.

Llewellyn, K. N., and E. Adamson Hoebel. *The Cheyenne Way: Conflict and Case Law in Primitive Jurisprudence.* Norman: University of Oklahoma Press, 1941.

Lowie, Robert H. *Societies of the Kiowa.* Anthropological Papers of the American Museum of Natural History 11 (1916), pt. 11: 837–51. New York: Published by order of the Trustees [of the American Museum of Natural History].

———. *The Crow Indians.* Lincoln: University of Nebraska Press, 1983.

MacDowell, Marsha L., and C. Kurt Dewhurst, eds. *To Honor and Comfort: Native Quilting Traditions.* Santa Fe: Museum of New Mexico Press in association with Michigan State University Museum, 1999.

Mallery, Garrick. *Picture Writing of the American Indians.* New York: Dover Publications, 1972. Originally published as vols. 1 and 2 of *Tenth Annual Report of the Bureau of Ethnology to the Secretary of the Smithsonian Institution, 1888–89.* Washington, D.C.: Government Printing Office, 1893.

Malouf, Carling. "The Tipi Rings of the High Plains." *American Antiquity* 26, no. 3 (Jan. 1961): 381–89.

Man-Afraid-of-His-Name [Edwin Willard Deming]. "Sketching Among the Sioux." *Outing* 23, no. 1 (Oct. 1893): 3–13.

Marquis, Thomas B. *The Cheyennes of Montana.* Edited by Thomas D. Weist. Algonac, Mich.: Reference Publications, 1978.

Marriott, Alice, and Carol Rachlin. *Dance Around the Sun: The Life of Mary Little Bear Inkanish: Cheyenne.* New York: Thomas Y. Crowell, 1977.

Maurer, Evan M., ed. *Visions of the People: A Pictorial History of Plains Indian Life.* Minneapolis: Minneapolis Institute of Arts; Seattle: University of Washington Press, 1992.

McCleary, Timothy P. *The Stars We Know: Crow Indian Astronomy and Lifeways.* Prospect Heights, Ill.: Waveland Press, 1997.

McLaughlin, Castle. *Arts of Diplomacy: Lewis and Clark's Indian Collection.* Cambridge, Mass.: Peabody Museum of Archaeology and Ethnology, Harvard University; Seattle: University of Washington Press, 2003.

McLaughlin, James. *My Friend the Indian.* Boston and New York: Houghton Mifflin Company, 1910.

Meadows, William C. *Kiowa, Apache, and Comanche Military Societies: Enduring Veterans, 1800 to the Present.* Austin: University of Texas Press, 1999.

Medicine Crow, Joseph. *From the Heart of the Crow Country: The Crow Indians' Own Stories.* New York: Orion Books, 1992.

Medicine Horse, Mary Helen. *A Dictionary of Everyday Crow.* Crow Agency, Mont.: Bilingual Materials Development Center, 1987.

Merrill, William L., et al. *A Guide to the Kiowa Collections at the Smithsonian Institution.* Smithsonian Contributions to Anthropology 40. Washington, D.C.: Smithsonian Institution Press, 1997.

Mishkin, Bernard. *Rank and Warfare Among the Plains Indians.* New York: J. J. Augustin, 1940.

Mooney, James. *Calendar History of the Kiowa Indians.* Washington, D.C.: Smithsonian Institution Press, 1979. Originally published as *Seventeenth Annual Report of the Bureau of American Ethnology, 1895–96.* Washington, D.C.: Government Printing Office, 1898.

Nye, Wilbur Sturtevant. *Bad Medicine and Good: Tales of the Kiowas.* Norman: University of Oklahoma Press, 1962.

———. *Plains Indian Raiders: The Final Phases of Warfare from the Arkansas to the Red River, with original photos by William S. Soule.* Norman: University of Oklahoma Press, 1968.

Old Horn, Dale D., and Timothy P. McCleary. *Apsáalooke Social and Family Structure.* Crow Agency, Mont.: Little Big Horn College, 1995.

Orchard, William C. "Indian Porcupine Quill and Beadwork." In *Introduction to American Indian Art.* Pt 2: 3–13. New York: Exposition of Indian Tribal Arts, Inc., 1931.

Painted Tipis by Contemporary Plains Indian Artists. Introduction by Myles Libhart and Rosemary Ellison. Blackfeet tipi legends by Cecile Black Boy. Anadarko, Okla.: Oklahoma Indian Arts and Crafts Cooperative, 1973.

Pattie, Jane, and Helen McCorpin. "The Kiowa Black Legs: Warriors of a Proud People." *Persimmon Hill* 24, no. 4 (1996).

Pearlstein, Ellen, Lynn Brostoff, and Karen Trentelman. "A Technical Study of the Rosebud Winter Count." *Plains Anthropologist* 54, no. 209 (Feb. 2009).

Petersen, Karen Daniels. *Plains Indian Art from Fort Marion.* Norman: University of Oklahoma Press, 1971.

Richardson, Jane. *Law and Status Among Kiowa Indians.* New York: J. J. Augustin, 1940.

Riggs, Stephen Return. *Grammar and Dictionary of the Dakota Language. Collected by the Members of the Dakota Mission and Edited by the Rev. Stephen R. Riggs.* Smithsonian Contributions to Knowledge 4. Washington, D.C.: Smithsonian Institution, 1852.

Schoolcraft, Henry Rowe. *The American Indians: Their History, Condition and Prospects from Original Notes and Manuscripts.* Buffalo, N.Y.: G. H. Derby, 1851.

Scott, Hugh L. "Notes on the Kado, or Sun Dance of the Kiowa." *American Anthropologist* 13, no. 3 (1911): 345–79.

Smith, De Cost. *Indian Experiences.* Caldwell, Idaho: Caxton Printers, 1943.

Spang, Bently. "The Process of Self Definition within the Native North American Art Movement." *Journal of Multicultural and Cross-cultural Research in Art Education* 13 (Spring 1996): 49–60.

Standing Bear, Luther. *My People the Sioux.* Boston: Houghton Mifflin Company, 1928.

Stewart, Omer C. *Peyote Religion: A History.* Norman: University of Oklahoma Press, 1987.

Swan, Daniel C. *Peyote Religious Art: Symbols of Faith and Belief.* Jackson: Mississippi University Press, 1999.

Szabo, Joyce M. *Howling Wolf and the History of Ledger Art.* Albuquerque: University of New Mexico Press, 1994.

Taylor, Colin F. *The Plains Indians: A Cultural and Historical View of the North American Plains Tribes of the Pre-Reservation Period.* London: Salamander Books, 1994.

Taylor, Colin F., and Hugh A. Dempsey, eds. *The People of the Buffalo.* Vol. 1, *The Plains Indians of North America—Military Art, Warfare and Change: Essays in Honor of John C. Ewers,* and Vol. 2, *The Plains Indians of North America—The Silent Memorials: Artifacts as Cultural and Historical Documents.* Wyk auf Foehr, Germany: Tatanka Press, 2003, 2005.

Torrence, Gaylord. *The American Indian Parfleche: A Tradition of Abstract Painting.* Seattle: University of Washington Press, 1994.

Wade, Edwin L., Carol Haralson, and Rennard Strickland. *As in a Vision: Masterworks of American Indian Art: The Elizabeth Cole Butler Collection at Philbrook Art Center.* Norman: University of Oklahoma Press, 1983.

Walker, James R. *Lakota Belief and Ritual.* Edited by Raymond J. DeMallie and Elaine A. Jahner. Lincoln: University of Nebraska Press, 1980. Reprint, Winnipeg, MB: Bison Books, 1991.

———. *Lakota Society.* Edited by Raymond J. DeMallie. Lincoln: University of Nebraska Press, 1982.

Wallace, Ernest. *Ranald S. Mackenzie on the Texas Frontier.* College Station: Texas A&M University Press, 1993.

Weltfish, Gene. *The Lost Universe: Pawnee Life and Culture.* Lincoln: University of Nebraska Press, 1977.

White, Richard. *"It's Your Misfortune and None of My Own": A History of the American West.* Norman: University of Oklahoma Press, 1991.

Wissler, Clark. *Societies and Ceremonial Associations of the Oglala Division of the Teton-Dakota.* Anthropological Papers of the American Museum of Natural History 11 (1912), pt. 1: 1–99. New York: Published by order of the Trustees [of the American Museum of Natural History].

Young, Gloria A., and Erik D. Gooding. "Celebrations and Giveaways." In *Handbook of North American Indians.* Vol. 13, pt. 2: 1011–25. Washington, D.C.: Smithsonian Institution Press, 2001.

Zontek, Ken. *Buffalo Nation: American Indian Efforts to Restore the Bison.* Lincoln: University of Nebraska Press, 2007.

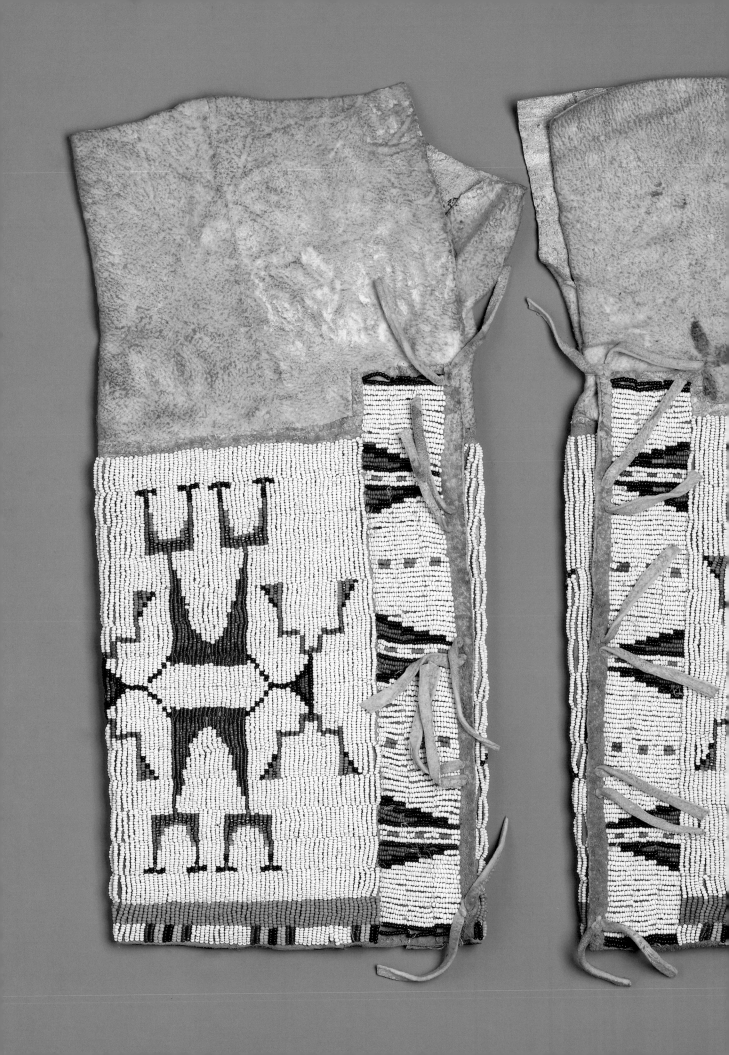

CONTRIBUTORS

HEYWOOD and MARY LOU BIG DAY (Crow) are tribal elders well versed in Crow oral histories and traditions. He teaches museum audiences about Crow traditions, history, and art. She is an award-winning doll maker who has participated in education programs at the Plains Indian Museum, Cody, Wyoming, and the Indian Arts and Crafts Board, Washington, D.C.

CHRISTINA E. BURKE is Curator of Native American and Non-Western Art at the Philbrook Museum of Art, Tulsa, Oklahoma. She was a contributor to *The Year the Stars Fell: Lakota Winter Counts at the Smithsonian* (2007).

TERI GREEVES (Kiowa) is an award-winning artist whose beadwork is represented in museum collections throughout the world, including those of the Brooklyn Museum; the British Museum, London; the Denver Art Museum; the Heard Museum, Phoenix; and the National Museum of the American Indian, Washington, D.C.

BARBARA A. HAIL is Curator Emerita, Haffenreffer Museum of Anthropology, Brown University, Providence, Rhode Island. She is the author of *Gifts of Pride and Love: Kiowa and Comanche Cradles* (2000) and *Hau, Kóla! The Plains Indian Collection of the Haffenreffer Museum of Anthropology* (1980).

EMMA I. HANSEN (Pawnee) is Senior Curator at the Plains Indian Museum, Buffalo Bill Historical Center, Cody, Wyoming. She is the author of *Memory and Vision: Arts, Cultures, and Lives of Plains Indian People* (2008).

MICHAEL P. JORDAN is Curatorial Assistant in the Ethnology Department at the Sam Noble Oklahoma Museum of Natural History, Norman. He is completing a Ph.D. in sociocultural anthropology at the University of Oklahoma, Norman, specializing in the Kiowa tribe.

SUSAN KENNEDY ZELLER, Ph.D., is Associate Curator of Native American Art at the Brooklyn Museum. She has taught at Columbia University, Long Island University, and the New School for Social Research. Her articles on Native American art and Aboriginal art of Australia have appeared in scholarly journals.

DIXON PALMER (Kiowa) is a Charter Member of the Kiowa Black Leggings Warrior Society. He served in the U.S. Army in World War II.

LYNDRETH PALMER (Kiowa) is Commander of the Kiowa Black Leggings Warrior Society. He served in the U.S. Navy in the Vietnam War.

HARVEY PRATT (Southern Cheyenne/Arapaho) is a peace chief in the Southern Cheyenne Chief's Lodge and a noted forensic artist, sculptor, and painter. He served in the U.S. Marines in the Vietnam War.

NANCY B. ROSOFF is Andrew W. Mellon Curator, Arts of the Americas, at the Brooklyn Museum. She has contributed to *Museums and Source Communities: A Routledge Reader* (2003) and *Native American Dance: Ceremonies and Social Traditions* (1992) and to numerous exhibition catalogues, including *Sacred Spain: Art and Belief in the Spanish World* (2009), *The Aztec Empire* (2004), and *Creation's Journey: Native American Identity and Belief* (1994).

BENTLY SPANG (Northern Cheyenne) is a multimedia artist, curator, and educator. His artwork, which addresses issues of his Northern Cheyenne identity, has been featured in solo and group exhibitions throughout North America and can be found in the permanent collections of the Heard Museum, Phoenix; the Montclair Art Museum, Montclair, New Jersey; and the National Museum of the American Indian, Washington, D.C., among others.

DENNIS SUN RHODES (Arapaho) is President and founder of AmerINDIAN Architecture, now called Great Horse Group. He has designed numerous architectural projects, including the award-winning Native American Center for the Living Arts (The Turtle) at Niagara Falls, New York, and the Lower Brule Administrative Building, Lower Brule Reservation, South Dakota.

DANIEL C. SWAN, Ph.D., is Associate Curator of Ethnology at the Sam Noble Oklahoma Museum of Natural History, Norman, and Associate Professor of Anthropology at the University of Oklahoma, Norman. His recent exhibitions and publications include *Art of the Osage* (2004), with Garrick Bailey, and *Peyote Religious Art: Symbols of Faith and Belief* (1999).

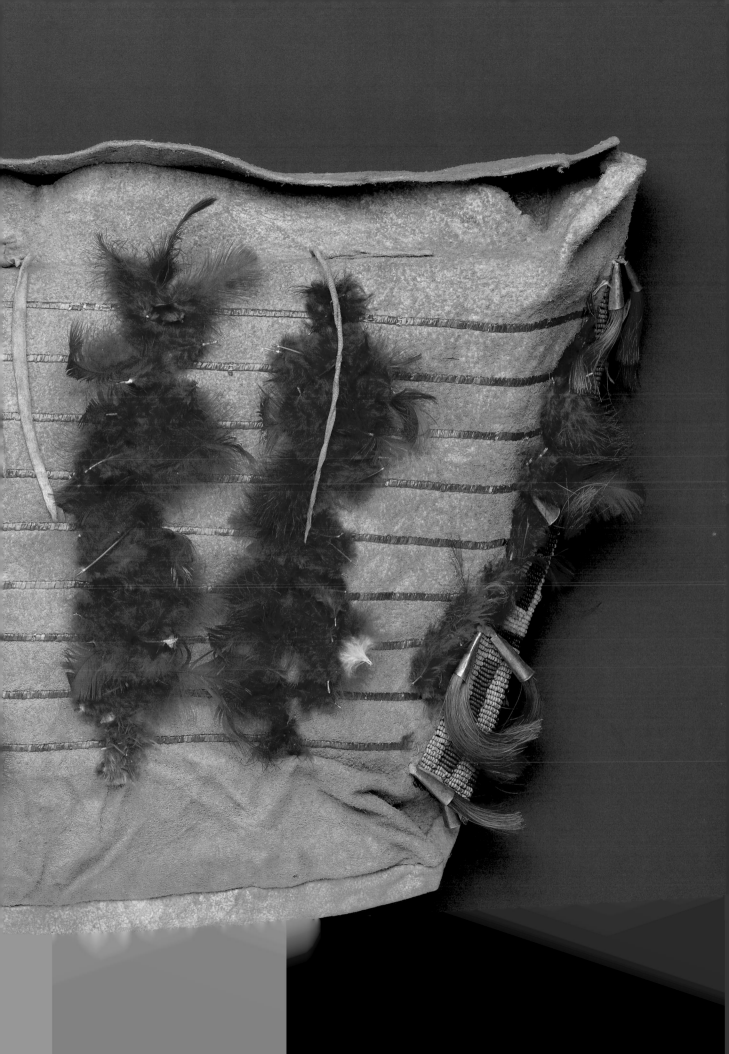

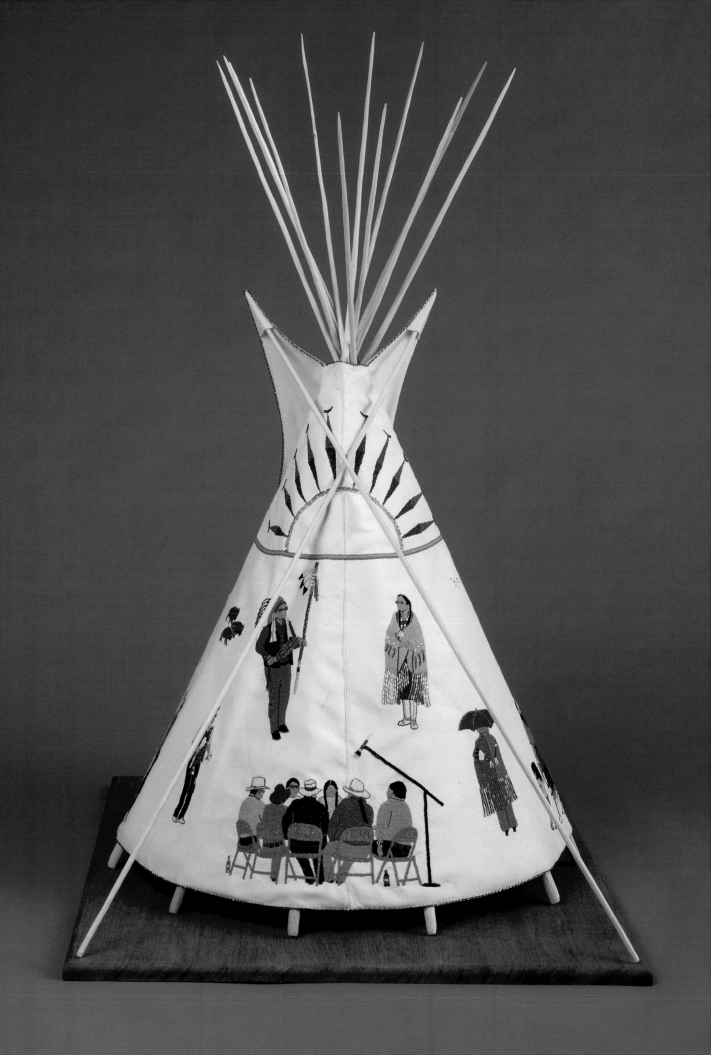

INDEX

Page numbers in italics refer to figures.

warfare, intertribal: depictions of, 83–84, 91, 126, 145, 146, 150–51, 163, 181; impact on tipi construction, 60; influence of horses on, 19; prevalence of, 5, 84; songs about, 84; and victory dances, 147, *150*

warrior sashes, Kiowa, 151–52, *153*

warrior societies: celebration of buffalo by, 17; among Kiowa, 151–63; purpose (function) of, 84, 145; use of tipis by, 10, 84, 151–63

warrior songs, 84, 166

warriors: as defenders of tipis, 145; training of, 84, 151, 191

Washington, George: Washington Peace Medallion (1789), 27, *28*

wealth, expressed through horse ownership, 19–20

weapons: ammunition for, 101; children's versions of, 183–85; depictions of, 83, 90–92; prevalence of, 5; storage of, 51; trade in, 27. *See also* hunting equipment; warfare, intertribal —types of. *See* axes; guns and ammunition; knives

White Buffalo Calf Woman (Lakota), 84

Whitebull, Imogene (Southern Cheyenne): beaded tipi cover by, 121, *124*

Wick, Elsie (Northern Cheyenne), 114

wicky ups (brush-lodges), 82. *See also* wigwams

Wigwam Motel, 109–12, *110, 112*

Wigwam Village, 109–12, *111*

Wigwam Village Inn, 109

wigwams, 109–10

willow saplings, 42, 125

willow-stick backrests, 47, *125*, 125–26

Winchester rifles, 91

Wind Cave National Park, South Dakota, *4*

Wind River [Indian] Reservation, Wyoming, 31, 57, 141; Nellie Three Bulls Sun Rhodes's cabin on, 58–60, *59*

winter counts (calendars): characteristics of, 78, 86, *86–87*; commissioning of, 96

Wolf Dance, depictions of, *30,* 31

women's societies, for beadwork and quillwork, 51, 120–25

women's sphere: in embellishment and decorative arts, 51, 119–38; tipi as, 40, 41–42, 43–45, 47–51, 61, 71, 74, 119–20, 181, 191; and victory dances, 147, *150. See also* gender roles

World War I, Native service in, 161, 167

World War II, Native service in, 123, 158, 161, 166–67

Wounded Knee, Massacre of (1890), 95, 202n.44

Wyoming: history of tipis in, 13; obsidian sources in, 26

Y

Yankton artists, works by: bow, bow case, and quiver (early 19th century), 51, *52*; pemmican bag (circa 1883), *26, 27*; side-fold dress (early 19th century), 131, *133*

Yanktonai artists, works by: moccasins (early 19th century), *16*; pemmican bag (circa 1883), *26, 27*; shirt for Chief's War Dress (early 19th century), 20, *116* (detail), 146, *146*; strap dress (early 19th century), 131, *134*; warrior leggings (early 19th century), 146, *148*; warrior shirt (early 19th century), 131, *135*

yapahe (Kiowa, male societies), meetings of, 151–57

Yellow Cloud Augusta, Todd (Oglala Lakota): baby bonnet (1993), 31, 173, *177*; bib (1994), 31, 173, *177*

Yellow Leggings (Issaatshíilish, Crow), 41

Yellow Tipi designs, 163

Yellowhair, Jeff (Kiowa), 161, *162*

Yuwipi ceremony, Sioux, 138

Z

zebat (Kiowa, arrow lance), 156

Zepkoyet (Big Bow, Kiowa): leggings of, 146; tipis of, 152, *154, 155,* 163